C++ in Embedded Systems

A practical transition from C to modern C++

Amar Mahmutbegović

C++ in Embedded Systems

Copyright © 2025 Packt Publishing

All rights reserved. No part of this book may be reproduced, stored in a retrieval system, or transmitted in any form or by any means, without the prior written permission of the publisher, except in the case of brief quotations embedded in critical articles or reviews.

The author acknowledges the use of cutting-edge AI, such as ChatGPT, with the sole aim of enhancing the language and clarity within the book, thereby ensuring a smooth reading experience for readers. It's important to note that the content itself has been crafted by the author and edited by a professional publishing team.

Every effort has been made in the preparation of this book to ensure the accuracy of the information presented. However, the information contained in this book is sold without warranty, either express or implied. Neither the author nor Packt Publishing or its dealers and distributors will be held liable for any damages caused or alleged to have been caused directly or indirectly by this book.

Packt Publishing has endeavored to provide trademark information about all of the companies and products mentioned in this book by the appropriate use of capitals. However, Packt Publishing cannot guarantee the accuracy of this information.

Portfolio Director: Rohit Rajkumar

Relationship Lead: Tanisha Mehrotra

Project Manager: Sandip Tadge

Content Engineer: Rashi Dubey

Technical Editor: Tejas Mhasvekar

Copy Editor: Safis Editing

Indexer: Pratik Shirodkar

Proofreader: Rashi Dubey

Production Designer: Shankar Kalbhor

Growth Leads: Namita Velgekar and Lee Booth

First published: July 2025

Production reference: 2021225

Published by Packt Publishing Ltd.
Grosvenor House
11 St Paul's Square
Birmingham
B3 1RB, UK.

ISBN 978-1-83588-114-9

www.packtpub.com

To my wife, Ferisa, and to my parents, Safet and Enisa, for their love and support.

– Amar

Foreword

In this book, C++ in Embedded Systems, Amar Mahmutbegović shows you how to apply modern C++ for embedded systems. These systems must often run in constrained environments, with limited CPU power, memory, and electrical power, and must satisfy strict requirements for timing and reliability. They may need to avoid programming practices such as recursion and dynamic memory management.

C has long been the language of choice for embedded systems. However, C++ offers more expressive abstractions and design paradigms, better type safety, and better resource and memory safety, while retaining the low-level hardware access of C. You may have been reluctant to use C++ because of past concerns about its suitability for embedded systems. The language and its compilers have evolved over the decades to eliminate those concerns. Better type- and memory-safety mean the compiler finds more errors at compile time without runtime overhead.

Amar takes you through the features of modern C++ (through C++23) that achieve these improvements. These include techniques such as static and dynamic binding, dynamic and compile-time polymorphism, templates and metaprogramming, resource management, and compile-time computation, as well as patterns and principles that support robust design. He provides simple, practical examples written from the perspective of an experienced embedded systems developer.

He shows you how to use tools such as Compiler Explorer and Renode to examine the generated machine code and simulate embedded targets to convince yourself that these methods deliver on their promises.

The methods you learn here will help you build more reliable, flexible, maintainable, reusable, adaptable, and efficient embedded systems.

Steve Branam

Senior Software Development Engineer, Amazon Robotics

Contributors

About the author

Amar Mahmutbegović is the co-founder and head of engineering at Semblie, where he leads the utilization of modern C++ for firmware development. His expertise extends to working on BLE consumer devices and medical devices, delivering sophisticated solutions for a wide range of clients, including start-ups. Amar's dedication to innovation helps bring electronic product ideas to the world. Amar actively shares C++ benefits in the embedded community via blogs and LinkedIn. He also mentors young engineers, enhancing their skills in modern development practices. His work aims to make embedded systems more accessible, maintainable, and scalable, bridging the gap between traditional methods and modern efficiencies for developers worldwide.

My deepest thanks go to my wife, friend, and the love of my life, Ferisa Živčić, for putting up with me over the past year. Writing a book while working a full-time job took up much of my free time and energy, and I'm endlessly grateful for her patience, understanding, and support.

I am grateful to have the best parents, Enisa and Safet. They taught me the importance of learning and hard work and guided me with strong moral values.

Big thanks to all my family, friends, and colleagues who supported me and helped in any way.

About the reviewers

Dirk Jan ten Kate is a senior embedded software engineer with over 15 years of experience in embedded systems, specializing in automotive and gas measuring industries. At his current employer, he developed a modular, hardware-independent firmware platform that forms the foundation for all new products. Dirk Jan is passionate about software quality, driving the adoption of test-driven development and continuous integration practices. His expertise spans system design, microcontroller development, RTOS, CAN, BLE, high-level communication protocols, low-level serial protocols, and programming in C and C++.

Rugved Hattekar is a skilled engineer with a strong background in embedded systems, robotics, and autonomous vehicle technology. He has developed software for safety-critical systems using C/C++, with a focus on hardware-software integration, sensor fusion, and real-time performance. At GPR, Inc., he contributed to vehicle localization and mapping systems using ground-penetrating radar. At Luminar Technologies, he works as a senior Lidar software developer specializing in embedded digital signal processing for Lidar sensors. Rugved brings deep technical insight into embedded C++ applications that drive advanced sensing and autonomous vehicle technologies.

Jacob Beningo helps embedded teams modernize their architecture, development processes, and skills to deliver high-quality, real-time systems. With two decades of experience and over 100 projects completed, he provides expert training, consulting, and coaching through Beningo Embedded Group and the Embedded Software Academy.

Table of Contents

Chapter 3: Embedded C++ Ecosystem   55

Chapter 4: Setting Up the Development Environment for a C++ Embedded Project   77

Part II: C++ Fundamentals 93

Chapter 5: Classes — Building Blocks of C++ Applications 95

Part III: C++ Advanced Concepts 153

Chapter 8: Building Generic and Reusable Code with Templates 155

Chapter 9: Improving Type-Safety with Strong Types 171

Chapter 10: Writing Expressive Code with Lambdas   199

Chapter 11: Compile-Time Computation   215

Part IV: Applying C++ to Solving Embedded Domain Problems   239

Chapter 12: Writing C++ HAL   241

Chapter 13: Working with C Libraries 259

Chapter 14: Enhancing Super-Loop with Sequencer 277

Chapter 17: Libraries and Frameworks 327

Preface

C++ is a general-purpose, multi-paradigm programming language, supporting procedural, object-oriented, and, to some extent, functional programming paradigms. It started out as C with classes, but over time it transformed into a modern language that enables writing highly expressive code without sacrificing performance. Despite this, C remains the dominant language in embedded development, primarily due to its simplicity and gentler learning curve.

However, the simplicity of C often makes writing complex systems overly verbose, increasing the cognitive burden on developers and making code more error-prone. This is where C++ excels. With features such as generic programming, runtime and compile-time polymorphism, compile-time computation, and enhanced type and memory safety, it is a superb choice for embedded system development.

Myths about C++, such as code bloat and runtime overhead, are still widespread. This book begins by debunking these misconceptions and guiding you through C++ fundamentals. It then shifts focus to more advanced modern C++ concepts, applying them to solve real-world problems in embedded development.

The goal of this book is to show you how modern C++ can be effectively used in embedded systems through carefully selected examples and by applying good software development practices.

Who this book is for

This book is for embedded developers who mainly use C in their daily jobs and would like to discover modern C++. Some familiarity with C++ is expected but not necessary, as the book also covers C++ basics.

What this book covers

Chapter 1, Debunking Common Myths About C++, explores widespread misconceptions about C++ and systematically debunks them. You will also gain insight into the history of C++ and the zero-overhead principle.

Chapter 2, Challenges in Embedded Systems with Limited Resources, examines the design challenges faced in resource-constrained embedded systems, with a focus on profiling techniques and memory management. It also shows how to avoid potentially problematic language features such as exceptions and RTTI.

Chapter 3, Embedded C++ Ecosystem, reviews the tools available for C++ development in the embedded domain, including toolchains, static analyzers, profiling tools, and testing frameworks.

Chapter 4, Setting Up the Development Environment for a C++ Embedded Project, walks you through setting up a modern development environment for C++ embedded projects, including using a simulator to test your code in a virtual setting.

Chapter 5, Classes – Building Blocks of C++ Applications, guides you through understanding classes in C++, including storage duration and initialization and inheritance and dynamic polymorphism.

Chapter 6, Beyond Classes – Fundamental C++ Concepts, covers fundamental C++ features such as namespaces and function overloading. It also discusses interoperability with C and introduces standard library containers and algorithms.

Chapter 7, Strengthening Firmware – Practical C++ Error Handling Methods, goes through various error handling techniques in C++, including error codes, asserts, and global handlers. It also explains the mechanics of exceptions and how they work.

Chapter 8, Building Generic and Reusable Code with Templates, goes through templates and concepts. It also provides an introduction to template metaprogramming and compile-time polymorphism.

Chapter 9, Improving Type-Safety with Strong Types, discusses implicit and explicit type conversions in C++ and introduces the concept of strong types. A practical example from an embedded library demonstrates how to improve type safety.

Chapter 10, Writing Expressive Code with Lambdas, introduces lambdas and shows you how to use them within a command design pattern to implement an expressive interrupt manager.

Chapter 11, Compile-Time Computation, explores C++'s compile-time computation capabilities and demonstrates how to use them to build a signal generator library that generates lookup tables at compile time.

Chapter 12, Writing C++ HAL, demonstrates the implementation of HAL in C++, using template-metaprogramming to ensure type-safety.

Chapter 13, Working with C Libraries, shows how to effectively use C libraries in C++ projects. It demonstrates the RAII principle in an example of using a filesystem C library.

Chapter 14, Enhancing Super-Loop with Sequencer, shows how to improve simple super-loop-based designs using a sequencer. It also introduces the **Embedded Template Library** (**ETL**) and its container class templates with fixed sizes known at compile time.

Chapter 15, Practical Patterns – Building a Temperature Publisher, guides you through the Observer design pattern and demonstrates how to apply it in systems such as thermostats and HVAC controllers.

Chapter 16, Designing Scalable Finite State Machines, explores different ways to implement finite state machines. It begins with a basic enum-switch approach, introduces the State design pattern, and then presents the Boost.SML library.

Chapter 17, Libraries and Frameworks, highlights parts of the C++ Standard Template Library that are useful for firmware development in constrained systems. It also features the CIB and Pigweed libraries.

Chapter 18, Cross-Platform Development, discusses the importance of good software design for achieving portability and testability in embedded software.

To get the most out of this book

Many examples in the book can be run in Compiler Explorer (`https://godbolt.org/`). Use it to observe the assembly output of the compiler. Experiment with the examples, tweak them, and compile them with different optimization levels and compiler flags to understand how those changes affect the compiler output.

Most of the examples can also be run in the Renode simulator. The book is accompanied by a Docker container, which includes the GCC toolchain and the Renode simulator, enabling you to run the code in an embedded target simulation.

Software/hardware covered in the book	Operating system requirements
Docker	Windows, macOS, or Linux

If you are using the digital version of this book, we advise you to type the code yourself or access the code from the book's GitHub repository (a link is available in the next section). Doing so will help you avoid any potential errors related to the copying and pasting of code.

Download the example code files

The code bundle for the book is hosted on GitHub at `https://github.com/PacktPublishing/Cpp-in-Embedded-Systems`. We also have other code bundles from our rich catalog of books and videos available at `https://github.com/PacktPublishing`. Check them out!

Download the color images

We also provide a PDF file that has color images of the screenshots/diagrams used in this book. You can download it here: `https://packt.link/gbp/9781835881149`.

Conventions used

There are a number of text conventions used throughout this book.

`CodeInText`: Indicates code words in text, database table names, folder names, filenames, file extensions, pathnames, dummy URLs, user input, and Twitter handles. For example: "The `PT100` class is also a `TemperatureSensor` class, and the `TemperatureController` class has a member (object) of `TemperatureSensor` and a `PidController` class."

A block of code is set as follows:

```
#define N 20
int buffer[N];

for(int i = 0; i < N; i ++) {
    printf("%d ", buffer[i]);
}
```

Any command-line input or output is written as follows:

```
The output of this simple program might be surprising:

resistance = 3.00
```

Bold: Indicates a new term, an important word, or words that you see on the screen. For instance, words in menus or dialog boxes appear in the text like this. For example: "Now, we need to add the Google Test library by clicking on the **Libraries** button in the execution pane."

Warnings or important notes appear like this.

Tips and tricks appear like this.

Get in touch

Feedback from our readers is always welcome.

General feedback: Email `feedback@packtpub.com` and mention the book's title in the subject of your message. If you have questions about any aspect of this book, please email us at `questions@packtpub.com`.

Errata: Although we have taken every care to ensure the accuracy of our content, mistakes do happen. If you have found a mistake in this book, we would be grateful if you reported this to us. Please visit `http://www.packtpub.com/submit-errata`, click **Submit Errata**, and fill in the form.

Piracy: If you come across any illegal copies of our works in any form on the internet, we would be grateful if you would provide us with the location address or website name. Please contact us at `copyright@packtpub.com` with a link to the material.

If you are interested in becoming an author: If there is a topic that you have expertise in and you are interested in either writing or contributing to a book, please visit `http://authors.packtpub.com/`.

Subscribe to Game Dev Assembly Newsletter!

We are excited to introduce Game Dev Assembly, our brand-new newsletter dedicated to everything game development. Whether you're a programmer, designer, artist, animator, or studio lead, you'll get exclusive insights, industry trends, and expert tips to help you build better games and grow your skills. Sign up today and become part of a growing community of creators, innovators, and game changers. `https://packt.link/gamedev-newsletter`

Scan the QR code to join instantly

Join our community on Discord

Join our community's Discord space for discussions with the authors and other readers:

`https://packt.link/embeddedsystems`

Free Benefits with Your Book

This book comes with free benefits to support your learning. Activate them now for instant access (see the "*How to Unlock*" section for instructions).

Here's a quick overview of what you can instantly unlock with your purchase:

PDF and ePub Copies

Next-Gen Web-Based Reader

 Access a DRM-free PDF copy of this book to read anywhere, on any device.

 Use a DRM-free ePub version with your favorite e-reader.

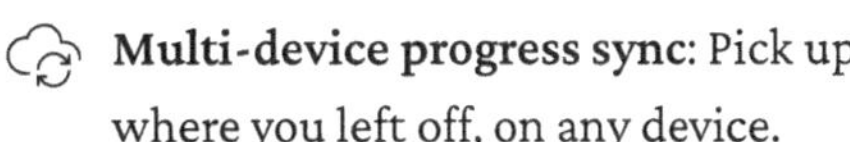 **Multi-device progress sync**: Pick up where you left off, on any device.

 **Highlighting and notetaking**: Capture ideas and turn reading into lasting knowledge.

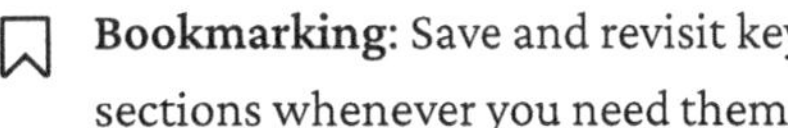 **Bookmarking**: Save and revisit key sections whenever you need them.

 **Dark mode**: Reduce eye strain by switching to dark or sepia themes.

How to Unlock

Scan the QR code (or go to packtpub.com/unlock). Search for this book by name, confirm the edition, and then follow the steps on the page.

Note: Keep your invoice handy. Purchases made directly from Packt don't require one.

Share your thoughts

Once you've read *C++ in Embedded Systems*, we'd love to hear your thoughts! Scan the QR code below to go straight to the Amazon review page for this book and share your feedback.

https://packt.link/r/1835881157

Your review is important to us and the tech community and will help us make sure we're delivering excellent quality content.

Part 1

Introduction to C++ in Embedded Development

The book begins by exploring common myths about C++ and debunking them. You will gain insight into the history of C++ and develop an understanding of the zero-overhead principle. In addition, you will examine design challenges in embedded systems and learn how to address them using C++. This part also covers the embedded C++ ecosystem and guides you through setting up the development environment for a C++ embedded project, including configuring the toolchain, build system, and simulator.

This part has the following chapters:

- *Chapter 1, Debunking Common Myths about C++*
- *Chapter 2, Challenges in Embedded Systems with Limited Resources*
- *Chapter 3, Embedded C++ Ecosystem*
- *Chapter 4, Setting Up the Development Environment for a C++ Embedded Project*

1

Debunking Common Myths about C++

Writing software for microcontrollers and embedded systems is challenging. In order to get the most out of resource-constrained systems, embedded developers need to have a good knowledge of platform architecture. They need to be aware of available resources, including processor capabilities, available memory, and peripherals. The need to have direct access to hardware through memory-mapped peripherals has made **C** the language of choice for embedded systems for half a century.

The goal of any programming language is to carry out the process of converting application-specific abstractions into code that can be transformed into machine code. For instance, **Common Business-Oriented Language (COBOL)** is used for banking applications, and **Fortran** is used for scientific research and heavy mathematic calculations. C is, on the other hand, a general-purpose programming language commonly used in **operating systems (OSs)** and embedded system applications.

C is a language with a simple and easy-to-learn syntax. Having a simple syntax means it is incapable of expressing complex ideas. C allows for complex operations but requires more explicit and detailed code to manage complexity, compared to higher-level languages that abstract these details away.

In the late 1970s, high-level languages couldn't meet the performance of C. This motivated Danish computer scientist Bjarne Stroustrup to start working on **C with Classes**, a predecessor to C++. Nowadays, C++ is a multiparadigm language designed with performance in mind. The origin of C++ is still a source of some myths, which often causes hesitation in adopting it for embedded systems programming. This chapter will introduce you to those myths and debunk them. The following topics will be covered in this chapter:

- A short history of C++
- C with Classes
- Bloat and runtime overhead

Free Benefits with Your Book

Your purchase includes a free PDF copy of this book along with other exclusive benefits. Check the *Free Benefits with Your Book* section in the Preface to unlock them instantly and maximize your learning experience.

Technical requirements

To get the most out of this chapter, I strongly recommend using Compiler Explorer (`https://godbolt.org/`) as you read through the examples. Select GCC as your compiler and target x86 architecture. This will allow you to see standard output (stdio) results and better observe the code's behavior. The examples from this chapter are available on GitHub (`https://github.com/PacktPublishing/Cpp-in-Embedded-Systems/tree/main/Chapter01`).

A short history of C++

In the mid-60s, the simulation programming language **SIMULA** introduced classes and objects to the world of software development. **Classes** are abstractions that allow us to represent real-world concepts in programming in a concise way, making the code more human-readable. In embedded development, **UART**, **SPI**, **TemperatureSensor**, **PidController**, and **TemperatureController** are some concepts that can be implemented as classes. SIMULA also introduced hierarchical relationships between classes. For example, `PT100` class is also a `TemperatureSensor` class, and `TemperatureController` class has a member instance (object) of `TemperatureSensor` and a `PidController`. This became known as **object-oriented programming (OOP)**.

In reflecting on the evolution of programming languages, Bjarne Stroustrup, the creator of C++, shared his approach to designing C++. Stroustrup aimed to bridge the gap between high-level abstractions and low-level efficiency.

He said the following:

> *My idea was very simple. To take ideas from SIMULA for general abstractions for the benefits of humans representing things, so humans could get it, with low-level stuff, which at that time the best language for that was C, which was done at Bell Labs by Dennis Ritchie. And take those two ideas and bring them together so that you could do high-level abstraction, but efficiently enough and close enough to hardware, for really demanding computing tasks*

Originally started as C with Classes by Bjarne Stroustrup, C++ transformed into a modern programming language that still provides direct access to hardware and memory-mapped peripherals. Using powerful abstractions makes writing expressive and highly modular code possible in C++. C++ is a general-purpose, multiparadigm language supporting procedural, object-oriented, and, to some extent, functional programming paradigms.

While C is still the language of choice for embedded development, accounting for up to 60% of embedded projects, the adoption of C++ has grown steadily. With an estimated usage of 20-30% in the embedded development field, C++ offers classes, improved type safety, and compile-time computation, among other features.

Despite the features that C++ offers, C is still dominant in embedded programming. There are many reasons for this, and this chapter will address some of them. C++ is a more complex language than C, making it harder for beginner developers. C is easier to learn and makes it possible to involve beginner developers in a project faster.

The simplicity of C is good as it allows beginner developers to start contributing to projects faster, but it also makes writing complex logic too verbose. This usually results in a larger code base due to a lack of expressiveness. This is where C++ steps in with higher abstractions, which, if embraced, make code easier to read and comprehend.

The other reasons why C++ is not more widely adopted are related to myths about C++. It is still believed that C++ is just "C with classes," that using C++ is absolutely unacceptable for safety-critical systems due to dynamic memory allocation in the standard library, or that it produces bloat code and adds space and time overhead. This chapter will address some of the most common myths about C++ in the context of embedded development. Let's debunk these myths and shine a new light on C++ in embedded systems!

C with Classes

Historically speaking, C++ started as C with Classes. The first C++ compiler, **Cfront**, converted C++ to C, but that was a long time ago. Over time, C and C++ evolved separately and are now defined by separate language standards. C has maintained its simplicity, while C++ has become a modern language that enables abstract solutions for problems without sacrificing performance levels. But C++ is still sometimes called C with Classes, which implies that there is no added value in C++ except the classes.

The C++11 standard was released in 2011, and it is the second major version of C++. It is packed with features that modernize the language, such as range-based loops, lambdas, and constexpr. Subsequent releases, C++14, C++17, C++20, and C++23, kept modernizing the language and introducing features that make C with Classes merely a distant predecessor of modern C++.

Modern C++

To demonstrate that C++ is not just C with Classes, let's explore a couple of short C code examples and their modern C++ equivalents. Let's start with a simple example of printing elements from an integer buffer:

```c
#define N 20
int buffer[N];

for(int i = 0; i < N; i ++) {
    printf("%d ", buffer[i]);
}
```

The preceding C code can be translated into the following C++ code:

```cpp
std::array<int, 20> buffer;

for(const auto& element : buffer) {
    printf("%d ", element);
}
```

The first thing we notice is that the C++ version is shorter. It has fewer words, and it's closer to English than the C code. It is easier to read. Now, if you come from a C background and have not been exposed to higher-level languages, the first version may look easier to read, but let's compare them. The first thing we notice is that the C code has defined the constant N, which determines the size of buffer. This constant is used to define buffer and as a boundary for the for loop.

Range-based loops, introduced in C++11, remove the cognitive burden of using the size of the container in the loop stop condition. The size information is already contained in the `std::array` container, which is utilized by the range-based loop to iterate through the array effortlessly. Also, there is no indexing of the buffer, as elements are accessed using constant reference, ensuring that the elements are not modified inside the loop.

Let's look at some simple C code that copies all elements from the `array_a` integer to `array_b` if smaller than 10:

```
int w_idx = 0;
for(int i = 0; i < sizeof(array_a)/sizeof(int); i++) {
    if(array_a[i] < 10) {
        array_b[w_idx++] = array_a[i];
    }
}
```

Here is the C++ code with the same functionality:

```
auto less_than_10 =  [](auto x) -> bool {
    return x < 10;
};


std::copy_if(std::begin(array_a), std::end(array_a), std::begin(array_b),
less_than_10);
```

Instead of manually iterating through `array_a` and copying elements to `array_b` only if they exceed 10, we can use the `copy_if` function from C++'s standard template library. The first two arguments for `std::copy_if` are iterators that define the range of elements to consider in `array_a`: the first iterator points to the beginning of the array, and the second iterator points to the position just beyond the last element. The third argument is the iterator pointing to the start of `array_b`, and the fourth is the `less_than_10` lambda expression.

A lambda expression is an anonymous function object that can be declared at a location where it's invoked or passed as an argument to a function. Please note that lambdas will be covered in more detail in *Chapter 10*. In the case of `std::copy_if`, the `less_than_10` lambda is used to determine whether elements from `array_a` are to be copied to `array_b`. We could also define a standalone `less_than_10` function that accepts an integer and returns a Boolean if it is larger than 10, but using a lambda, we can write this functionality close to the place where we pass it to an algorithm, which makes code more compact and expressive.

Generic types

Previous examples used the `std::array` standard library container. It is a class template that wraps a C-style array along with its size information. Please note that templates will be covered in more detail in *Chapter 8*. When you use `std::array` with a specific underlying type and size, the compiler defines a new type in the process of **instantiation**.

`std::array<int, 10>` creates a container type that has an underlying C-style array of integers with a size of 10. The `std::array<int, 20>` is a container type that has an underlying C-style array of integers with a size of 20. The `std::array<int, 10>` and `std::array<int, 20>` are different types. Both have the same underlying type, but a different size.

`std::array<float, 10>` would result in a third type, as it differs from `std::array<int, 10>` by the underlying type. Using different parameters yields different types. Template types are generic types that become concrete only upon instantiation.

To better understand generic types and appreciate them, let's examine the implementation of a ring buffer in C and compare it with a template-based solution in C++.

Ring buffer in C

A **ring** or **circular buffer** is a commonly used data structure in embedded programming. It is commonly implemented as a set of functions around an array with write and read indexes used to access elements of the array. The `count` variable is used for array space management. The interface consists of push and pop functions, which are explained here:

- A **push** function is used to store elements in a ring buffer. On every push, a data element is stored in the array, and the write index is incremented. If the write index becomes equal to the number of elements in the data array, it is reset to 0.
- A **pop** function is used to retrieve an element from a ring buffer. On every pop, if the underlying array is not empty, we return an element of the array indexed with the read index. We increment the read index.

On every push, we increment the `count` variable and decrement it on pop. If the count becomes equal to the size of the data array, we need to move the read index forward.

Let us define the implementation requirements of the ring buffer we want to implement in our C module:

- It should not use dynamic memory allocation
- When the buffer is full, we will overwrite the oldest element

- Provide push and pop functions for storing data in the buffer and retrieving it
- Integers will be stored in the ring buffer

Here is a simple solution for the preceding requirements in C:

```c
#include <stdio.h>

#define BUFFER_SIZE 5

typedef struct {
    int arr[BUFFER_SIZE]; // Array to store int values directly
    size_t write_idx;     // Index of the next element to write (push)
    size_t read_idx;      // Index of the next element to read (pop)
    size_t count;         // Number of elements in the buffer
} int_ring_buffer;

void int_ring_buffer_init(int_ring_buffer *rb) {
    rb->write_idx = 0;
    rb->read_idx = 0;
    rb->count = 0;
}

void int_ring_buffer_push(int_ring_buffer *rb, int value) {
    rb->arr[rb->write_idx] = value;
    rb->write_idx = (rb->write_idx + 1) % BUFFER_SIZE;
    if (rb->count < BUFFER_SIZE) {
        rb->count++;
    } else {
        // Buffer is full, move read_idx forward
        rb->read_idx = (rb->read_idx + 1) % BUFFER_SIZE;
    }
}

int int_ring_buffer_pop(int_ring_buffer *rb) {
    if (rb->count == 0) {
        return 0;
    }
    int value = rb->arr[rb->read_idx];
```

```
    rb->read_idx = (rb->read_idx + 1) % BUFFER_SIZE;
    rb->count--;
    return value;
}


int main() {
  int_ring_buffer rb;
  int_ring_buffer_init(&rb);

  for (int i = 0; i < 10; i++) {
    int_ring_buffer_push(&rb, i);
  }


  while (rb.count > 0) {
    int value = int_ring_buffer_pop(&rb);
    printf("%d\n", value);
  }
  return 0;
}
```

We are using a for loop to initialize the buffer. As the buffer size is 5, values from 5 to 9 will be stored in the buffer as the ring buffer overwrites the existing data. Now, what if we want to store floats in our ring buffer, chars, or a user-defined data structure? We could implement the same logic for different types and create a new set of data structures and functions called float_ring_buffer or char_ring_buffer. Can we make a solution that could store different data types and use the same functions?

We could use an unsigned char array as storage for different data types and use a void pointer to pass different data types to push and pop functions. The only thing that's missing is knowing the size of the data type, and we can address that by adding a size_t elem_size member to the ring_buffer structure:

```
#include <stdio.h>
#include <string.h>


#define BUFFER_SIZE 20 // Total bytes available in the buffer


typedef struct {
```

```c
  unsigned char data[BUFFER_SIZE]; // Array to store byte values
  size_t write_idx;               // Index of the next byte to write
  size_t read_idx;                // Index of the next byte to read
  size_t count;      // Number of bytes currently used in the buffer
  size_t elem_size; // Size of each element in bytes
} ring_buffer;

void ring_buffer_init(ring_buffer *rb, size_t elem_size) {
  rb->write_idx = 0;
  rb->read_idx = 0;
  rb->count = 0;
  rb->elem_size = elem_size;
}

void ring_buffer_push(ring_buffer *rb, void *value) {
  if (rb->count + rb->elem_size <= BUFFER_SIZE) {
    rb->count += rb->elem_size;
  } else {
    rb->read_idx = (rb->read_idx + rb->elem_size) % BUFFER_SIZE;
  }

  memcpy(&rb->data[rb->write_idx], value, rb->elem_size);
  rb->write_idx = (rb->write_idx + rb->elem_size) % BUFFER_SIZE;
}

int ring_buffer_pop(ring_buffer *rb, void *value) {
  if (rb->count < rb->elem_size) {
    // Not enough data to pop
    return 0;
  }

  memcpy(value, &rb->data[rb->read_idx], rb->elem_size);
  rb->read_idx = (rb->read_idx + rb->elem_size) % BUFFER_SIZE;
  rb->count -= rb->elem_size;
  return 1; // Success
}

int main() {
```

```c
  ring_buffer rb;
  ring_buffer_init(&rb, sizeof(int)); // Initialize buffer for int values

  for (int i = 0; i < 10; i++) {
    int val = i;
    ring_buffer_push(&rb, &val);
  }

  int pop_value;
  while (ring_buffer_pop(&rb, &pop_value)) {
    printf("%d\n", pop_value);
  }
  return 0;
}
```

This ring buffer solution can be used to store different data types. As we avoid using dynamic memory allocation and the data buffer size was determined at compile time, we are not flexible when it comes to defining the size of the memory needed for different instances of the ring buffer. Another problem we have is type safety. We can easily call `ring_buffer_push` with a pointer to a float and `ring_buffer_pop` with a pointer to an integer. The compiler can't address this concern, and the possibility of a catastrophe is real. Also, by using a void pointer, we added a layer of indirection as we have to rely on memory to retrieve data from the data buffer.

Can we address type-safety concerns and make it possible to define the size of the ring buffer in C? We can use the token-pasting (##) operator to create a set of functions for different types and sizes using macros. Let's quickly go through a simple example of using the ## operator before jumping into ring buffer implementation using this technique:

```c
#include <stdio.h>

// Macro to define a function for summing two numbers
#define DEFINE_SUM_FUNCTION(TYPE) \
TYPE sum_##TYPE(TYPE a, TYPE b) { \
    return a + b; \
}

// Define sum functions for int and float
DEFINE_SUM_FUNCTION(int)
```

```c
DEFINE_SUM_FUNCTION(float)

int main() {
    int result_int = sum_int(5, 3);
    printf("Sum of integers: %d\n", result_int);

    float result_float = sum_float(3.5f, 2.5f);
    printf("Sum of floats: %.2f\n", result_float);

    return 0;
}
```

`DEFINE_SUM_FUNCTION(int)` will create a `sum_int` function that accepts and returns integers. If we call the `DEFINE_SUM_FUNCTION` macro with `float`, it will result in creating `sum_float`. Now that we have a good understanding of the token-pasting operator, let's continue with ring buffer implementation:

```c
#include <stdio.h>
#include <string.h>

// Macro to declare ring buffer type and functions for a specific type and
size
#define DECLARE_RING_BUFFER(TYPE, SIZE) \
typedef struct { \
    TYPE data[SIZE]; \
    size_t write_idx; \
    size_t read_idx; \
    size_t count; \
} ring_buffer_##TYPE##_##SIZE; \
void ring_buffer_init_##TYPE##_##SIZE(ring_buffer_##TYPE##_##SIZE *rb) { \
    rb->write_idx = 0; \
    rb->read_idx = 0; \
    rb->count = 0; \
} \
void ring_buffer_push_##TYPE##_##SIZE(ring_buffer_##TYPE##_##SIZE *rb,
TYPE value) { \
    rb->data[rb->write_idx] = value; \
    rb->write_idx = (rb->write_idx + 1) % SIZE; \
```

```c
        if (rb->count < SIZE) { \
            rb->count++; \
        } else { \
            rb->read_idx = (rb->read_idx + 1) % SIZE; \
        } \
    } \
    int ring_buffer_pop_##TYPE##_##SIZE(ring_buffer_##TYPE##_##SIZE *rb, TYPE *value) { \
        if (rb->count == 0) { \
            return 0; /* Buffer is empty */ \
        } \
        *value = rb->data[rb->read_idx]; \
        rb->read_idx = (rb->read_idx + 1) % SIZE; \
        rb->count--; \
        return 1; /* Success */ \
    }


// Example usage with int type and size 5
DECLARE_RING_BUFFER(int, 5) // Declare the ring buffer type and functions
for integers

int main() {
    ring_buffer_int_5 rb;
    ring_buffer_init_int_5(&rb); // Initialize the ring buffer

    // Push values into the ring buffer
    for (int i = 0; i < 10; ++i) {
        ring_buffer_push_int_5(&rb, i);
    }

    // Pop values from the ring buffer and print them
    int value;
    while (ring_buffer_pop_int_5(&rb, &value)) {
        printf("%d\n", value);
    }

    return 0;
}
```

Now, this solution solves our problems of type safety and defining the size of a ring buffer, but it suffers from readability, both in implementation and when using it. We need to "call" `DECLARE_RING_BUFFER` outside of any function, as it is basically a macro that defines a set of functions. We also need to know what it does and the signature of functions it will generate. We can do this better with templates. Let's see what an implementation of a ring buffer looks like in C++.

Ring buffer in C++

Let's make a generic implementation of a ring buffer using templates. We can use a `std::array` class template as the underlying type and wrap our push-and-pop logic around it. The following is code that illustrates how the `ring_buffer` type could look in C++:

```cpp
#include <array>
#include <cstdio>

template <class T, std::size_t N> struct ring_buffer {
  std::array<T, N> arr;
  std::size_t write_idx = 0; // Index of the next element to write (push)
  std::size_t read_idx = 0;  // Index of the next element to read (pop)
  std::size_t count = 0;     // Number of elements in the buffer

  void push(T t) {
    arr.at(write_idx) = t;
    write_idx = (write_idx + 1) % N;
    if (count < N) {
      count++;
    } else {
      // buffer is full, move forward read_idx
      read_idx = (read_idx + 1) % N;
    }
  }

  T pop() {
    if (count == 0) {
      // Buffer is empty, return a default-constructed T.
      return T{};
    }
    T value = arr.at(read_idx);
```

```cpp
    read_idx = (read_idx + 1) % N;
    --count;
    return value;
  }


  bool is_empty() const { return count == 0; }
};

int main() {
  ring_buffer<int, 5> rb;

  for (int i = 0; i < 10; ++i) {
    rb.push(i);
  }

  while (!rb.is_empty()) {
    printf("%d\n", rb.pop());
  }

  return 0;
}
```

The ring buffer implementation in C++ using templates is more readable and easier to use than the token-pasting-based solution in C. The `ring_buffer` template class can be used to instantiate ring buffer types with integer, float, or any other underlying types with different sizes. The same push-and-pop logic can be applied to ring buffers with different underlying types. We can apply the **Don't Repeat Yourself** (**DRY**) principle to different types thanks to templates. **Templates** make generic types easy to implement, something that's quite challenging and verbose in C.

Templates are also used for **template metaprogramming** (**TMP**), a programming technique in which a compiler uses templates to generate temporary source code, which is merged by the compiler with the rest of the source code and then compiled. One of the most famous examples of TMP is calculating a **factorial at compile time**. TMP is an advanced technique that will be covered in *Chapter 8*. Modern C++ also features the `constexpr` specifier, a much more beginner-friendly technique for compile-time computation.

constexpr

C++11 introduced the `constexpr` specifier, which declares that it is possible to evaluate the value of the function or a variable at compile time. The specifier evolved over time, extending the functionality. A `constexpr` variable must be immediately initialized, and its type must be a `literal` type (int, float, etc.). This is how we declare a `constexpr` variable:

```cpp
constexpr double pi = 3.14159265359;
```

Using the `constexpr` specifier is the preferred way of declaring compile-time constants in C++ over using a C-style approach with macros. Let's analyze a simple example using C-style macros:

```cpp
#include <cstdio>

#define VOLTAGE 3300
#define CURRENT 1000

int main () {
    const float resistance = VOLTAGE / CURRENT;
    printf("resistance = %.2f\r\n", resistance);

    return 0;
}
```

The output of this simple program might be surprising:

```
resistance = 3.00
```

Both VOLTAGE and CURRENT are parsed as integer `literals`, and so is the result of the division. Floating-point `literals` are declared using the f suffix, which was omitted in this case. Using `constexpr` to define compile-time constants is safer, as it allows us to specify the type of a constant. This is how we would write the same example using `constexpr`:

```cpp
#include <cstdio>
constexpr float voltage = 3300;
constexpr float current = 1000;

int main () {
    const float resistance = voltage / current;
    printf("resistance = %.2f\r\n", resistance);
```

```
    return 0;
}
```

```
This would result in

resistance = 3.30
```

This simple example shows that `constexpr` compile-time constants are both safer and easier to read than traditional C-style macro constants. The other major usage of the `constexpr` specifier is to hint to the compiler that a function can be evaluated at compile time. Some of the requirements that a `constexpr` function must meet are as follows:

- The return type must be a `literal` type
- Each of the function parameters must be a `literal` type
- If the `constexpr` function is not a constructor, it needs to have precisely one `return` statement

Let us examine a simple example utilizing `constexpr` functions:

```cpp
int square(int a) {
    return a*a;
}

int main () {
    int ret = square(2);
    return ret;
}
```

To better understand what is going on under the hood, we will inspect the assembly output of the preceding code. Assembly is quite close to the machine code, or the instructions that will be executed on our target, thus inspecting it gives us an estimate of the work (number of instructions) performed by the processor. The assembly output of the compilation of the preceding program for the ARM architecture using an ARM GCC compiler and no optimization is shown in the following:

```
square(int):
        push    {r7}
        sub     sp, sp, #12
        add     r7, sp, #0
        str     r0, [r7, #4]
```

```
        ldr      r3, [r7, #4]
        mul      r3, r3, r3
        mov      r0, r3
        adds     r7, r7, #12
        mov      sp, r7
        ldr      r7, [sp], #4
        bx       lr
main:
        push     {r7, lr}
        sub      sp, sp, #8
        add      r7, sp, #0
        movs     r0, #2
        bl       square(int)
        str      r0, [r7, #4]
        ldr      r3, [r7, #4]
        mov      r0, r3
        adds     r7, r7, #8
        mov      sp, r7
        pop      {r7, pc}
```

The resulting assembly code is doing the following:

- Manipulating the stack pointer
- Calling the square function
- Storing value returned by r0 to address contained into r7 with offset 4
- Loading the value from address stored in r7 with offset 4 into r3
- Moving the value from r3 to r0, which is the ARM calling convention's designated register for storing return values

We can see that there are some unnecessary operations in the output binary, which both increase the binary size and affect the performance. This example is, both valid C and valid C++ code, and compiling it with both C and C++ compilers will yield the same assembly code.

If we use the constexpr specifier for the square function, we are instructing the compiler that it is possible to evaluate it at compile time:

```
constexpr int square(int a) {
    return a*a;
}
```

```cpp
int main() {
    constexpr int val = square(2);
    return ret;
}
```

This code results in a compile-time evaluation of the square(2) expression, making the val integer a constexpr variable, that is, a compile-time constant. The following is the resulting assembly code:

```
main:
        push    {r7}
        sub     sp, sp, #12
        add     r7, sp, #0
        movs    r3, #4
        str     r3, [r7, #4]
        movs    r3, #4
        mov     r0, r3
        adds    r7, r7, #12
        mov     sp, r7
        ldr     r7, [sp], #4
        bx      lr
```

As we can see, the program returns the value 4, which is the result of the square(2) compile-time computation. There is no square function in the generated assembly, just the result of the calculation that the compiler performed for us. This simple example demonstrates the power of compile-time computing. We can move heavy computation from runtime to compile time whenever we know all the computation parameters, which is often. This approach can be used to generate lookup tables or complex mathematical signals, which will be demonstrated in the following chapters of this book.

C++ has come a long way since C with Classes. The examples in this chapter show what C++ can offer over C – expressive, more readable, compact code; standard template library containers; algorithms; user-defined generic types; and compile-time computation, just to start with. I hope I managed to debunk the myth that C++ is just C with classes. The next common myth about C++ is that it makes bloated code and adds runtime overhead. Let's keep debunking the myths about C++!

Bloat and runtime overhead

The term **bloatware** describes unwanted software that is preinstalled with an OS on a device. Unwanted software in the world of programming describes code inserted in a binary by a framework, a library, or a language construct itself. Language constructs in C++ that are blamed for causing code bloat are constructors, destructors, and templates. We will analyze these misconceptions by examining assembly output generated from C++ code.

Constructors and destructors

The first thing that comes to mind to non-C++ developers when you mention C++ is that it is an object-oriented language and that you are bound to instantiate objects. Objects are instances of classes. They are variables that occupy memory. Special functions, called **constructors**, are used to construct or instantiate objects.

Constructors are used to initialize objects, including the initialization of class members, and destructors are used to clean up resources. They are tightly tied to an object's life cycle. An object is created using a constructor, and when the object variable goes out of scope, the **destructor** is called.

Constructors and destructors both increase the size of the binary and add runtime overhead, as their execution takes time. We will examine the impact of constructors and destructors on a simple example of a class with one private member, a constructor, a destructor, and a getter:

```cpp
class MyClass
{
    private:
        int num;
    public:
        MyClass(int t_num):num(t_num){}
        ~MyClass(){}

        int getNum() const {
            return num;
        }
};

int main () {
    MyClass obj(1);
    return obj.getNum();
}
```

MyClass is a very simple class that has one private member, which we set through the constructor. We can access it through a getter, and just for good measure, we declared a destructor, which is empty. The following is the assembly equivalent of the preceding code compiled with no optimization enabled:

```
MyClass::MyClass(int) [base object constructor]:
        push    {r7}
        sub     sp, sp, #12
        add     r7, sp, #0
        str     r0, [r7, #4]
        str     r1, [r7]
        ldr     r3, [r7, #4]
        ldr     r2, [r7]
        str     r2, [r3]
        ldr     r3, [r7, #4]
        mov     r0, r3
        adds    r7, r7, #12
        mov     sp, r7
        ldr     r7, [sp], #4
        bx      lr
MyClass::~MyClass() [base object destructor]:
        push    {r7}
        sub     sp, sp, #12
        add     r7, sp, #0
        str     r0, [r7, #4]
        ldr     r3, [r7, #4]
        mov     r0, r3
        adds    r7, r7, #12
        mov     sp, r7
        ldr     r7, [sp], #4
        bx      lr
MyClass::getNum() const:
        push    {r7}
        sub     sp, sp, #12
        add     r7, sp, #0
        str     r0, [r7, #4]
        ldr     r3, [r7, #4]
        ldr     r3, [r3]
```

```
            mov       r0, r3
            adds      r7, r7, #12
            mov       sp, r7
            ldr       r7, [sp], #4
            bx        lr
    main:
            push      {r4, r7, lr}
            sub       sp, sp, #12
            add       r7, sp, #0
            adds      r3, r7, #4
            movs      r1, #1
            mov       r0, r3
            bl        MyClass::MyClass(int) [complete object constructor]
            adds      r3, r7, #4
            mov       r0, r3
            bl        MyClass::getNum() const
            mov       r4, r0
            nop
            adds      r3, r7, #4
            mov       r0, r3
            bl        MyClass::~MyClass() [complete object destructor]
            mov       r3, r4
            mov       r0, r3
            adds      r7, r7, #12
            mov       sp, r7
            pop       {r4, r7, pc}
```

Don't worry about the assembly if you don't understand it. We can see there are some labels for functions and a whole lot of instructions. That's a lot of instructions for a simple abstraction of a class; this is the bloat code that we don't want in our binary. To be more precise, we have 59 lines of assembly code. If we were to enable optimization, the resulting assembly would be a couple of lines long, but let's keep analyzing this problem with no optimization involved. The first thing we are noticing is that the destructor doesn't do anything useful. If we remove it from the C++ code, the resulting assembly is 44 lines long:

```
MyClass::MyClass(int) [base object constructor]:
            push      {r7}
            sub       sp, sp, #12
```

```
        add     r7, sp, #0
        str     r0, [r7, #4]
        str     r1, [r7]
        ldr     r3, [r7, #4]
        ldr     r2, [r7]
        str     r2, [r3]
        ldr     r3, [r7, #4]
        mov     r0, r3
        adds    r7, r7, #12
        mov     sp, r7
        ldr     r7, [sp], #4
        bx      lr
MyClass::getNum() const:
        push    {r7}
        sub     sp, sp, #12
        add     r7, sp, #0
        str     r0, [r7, #4]
        ldr     r3, [r7, #4]
        ldr     r3, [r3]
        mov     r0, r3
        adds    r7, r7, #12
        mov     sp, r7
        ldr     r7, [sp], #4
        bx      lr
  main:
        push    {r7, lr}
        sub     sp, sp, #8
        add     r7, sp, #0
        adds    r3, r7, #4
        movs    r1, #1
        mov     r0, r3
        bl      MyClass::MyClass(int) [complete object constructor]
        adds    r3, r7, #4
        mov     r0, r3
        bl      MyClass::getNum() const
        mov     r3, r0
        nop
```

```
    mov       r0, r3
    adds      r7, r7, #8
    mov       sp, r7
    pop       {r7, pc}
```

As we can see, there is no call to the destructor, and there is no destructor code in the binary. The lesson is *you don't pay for what you don't use*. This is one of the design principles of C++. By deleting the destructor, there is no need for the compiler to generate any code for it and to call it when the object variable goes out of the scope.

The next thing we must realize is that C++ is not an OOP language. It is a multiparadigm language. It is procedural, object-oriented, generic, and even a little bit functional at the same time. If we want to have private members that can be set only through constructors, then we need to pay the price for that. Structs in C++ have public members by default, so let's change the `MyClass` class to a `MyClass` struct with no constructor:

```cpp
struct MyClass
{
    int num;
};

int main () {

    MyClass obj(1);

    return obj.num;
}
```

Setter and getter functions are common in the OOP paradigm, but C++ is not (just) an OOP language and we are not bound to using setters and getters. When we remove the `getNum` getter, we have a very basic example of a struct with just one member. The resulting assembly is only 14 lines long:

```
main:
    push      {r7}
    sub       sp, sp, #12
    add       r7, sp, #0
    movs      r3, #1
    str       r3, [r7, #4]
```

```
ldr     r3, [r7, #4]
mov     r0, r3
adds    r7, r7, #12
mov     sp, r7
ldr     r7, [sp], #4
bx      lr
```

As trivial as this example is, its purpose is to establish two ground truths:

- You don't pay for what you don't use
- Using C++ doesn't mean you are bound to an OOP paradigm

We need to pay the price in binary size if we want to use abstractions such as constructors and destructors. Using types (classes and structs) without instantiating objects in C++ offers significant benefits to your embedded software design beyond traditional object-oriented approaches. We'll explore this through detailed examples in the upcoming chapters.

In this and previous examples, we compiled C++ code with disabled optimizations, and we were able to see the resulting assembly code results in unnecessary operations that can be removed. Let's check the assembly code for the last example with the O3 optimization level enabled:

```
main:
        movs    r0, #1
        bx      lr
```

The preceding assembly is the output of the original example with the class, constructor, destructor, and getter function. The resulting program has just two instructions. The value of the num member of the obj variable is stored in the r0 register as the return value. Assembly code is stripped of all necessary instructions related to stack manipulation and usage of r3 to store a value in a stack pointer with an offset of 4, reload it to r3, and move it to r0. The resulting assembly is just a few lines of code.

Removing unnecessary instructions is a job for the optimization process. Yet, optimization is often avoided in embedded projects, as some claim that it breaks code. But is that true?

Optimization

Unoptimized code results in unnecessary instructions affecting binary size and performance. However, many embedded projects are still built with disabled optimization, as developers *do not trust the compiler* and are afraid it will *break the program*. There is some truth to this, but as it turns out, this happens when the program is not well formed. The program is not well formed if it contains undefined behavior.

One of the best-known examples of undefined behavior is signed **integer overflow**. The standard doesn't define what happens if you add 1 to the maximum value of the signed integer on your platform. The compiled program is not required to do anything meaningful. A program is not well formed. Let's examine the following code:

```cpp
#include <cstdio>
#include <limits>

int foo(int x) {
    int y = x + 1;
    return y > x;
}

int main() {

    if(foo(std::numeric_limits<int>::max())) {
        printf("X is larger than X + 1\r\n");
    }
    else {
        printf("X is NOT larger than X + 1. Oh nooo !\r\n");
    }
    return 0;
}
```

Compiling the code using GCC for both x86 and Arm Cortex-M4 will yield the same results. If the program is compiled without the optimization, the foo function returns 0, and you can see **X is NOT larger than X + 1. Oh nooo !** in the output. The compiler does the integer overflow, and if we pass the maximum integer value to foo, it will return 0. Keep in mind that the standard does not specify this, and this behavior depends on the compiler.

If we compile the program with optimization enabled, the output is **X is larger than X + 1,** which means that foo returns 1. Let's examine the assembly output of the program compiled with the optimization:

```
foo(int):
        movs    r0, #1
        bx      lr
.LC0:
        .ascii  "X is larger then X + 1\015\000"
```

```
main:
        push    {r3, lr}
        movw    r0, #:lower16:.LC0
        movt    r0, #:upper16:.LC0
        bl      puts
        movs    r0, #0
        pop     {r3, pc}
```

As we can see, foo doesn't perform any calculations. The compiler assumes that the program is well formed and that there is no undefined behavior. foo will always return 1. It is up to the developer to ensure that there is no undefined behavior in the program. This is exactly the reason why the myth that the optimization breaks the program is still alive. It is easier to blame the compiler for not handling the undefined behavior.

Of course, it is possible that there is a bug in a compiler that breaks the functionality of the program if the optimization is used, and the program works fine if it is disabled. This is very rare but not unheard of, and that's why there are verification techniques such as unit and integration testing that ensure the functionality of the code, whether it is built with or without the optimization enabled.

Optimization is reducing the binary size and improving performance by removing unnecessary instructions from the machine code. Undefined behavior is compiler-dependent and must be handled by the developer to ensure the program is well formed. Techniques such as unit and integration testing should be put in place to validate the functionality of the program, mitigating the risk of compiler malforming the program. The optimization process is essential for using abstractions in C++ code while keeping the binary footprint minimum and performance at a maximum. We will use the highest optimization level, O3, in the rest of the book.

The next suspect for code bloat that we will examine are templates. How do they cause the code bloat, and what value do they bring to our embedded code bases?

Templates

Instantiating **templates** with different parameters will result in the compiler generating distinct types, which effectively increases the binary size. This is to be expected. We have the exact same situation with the generic implementation of a ring buffer in C using the token-pasting operator and macros. An alternative is type erasure, which we used in C implementation using a void pointer. It suffers in flexibility if we impose the restriction of static data allocation and performance due to pointer indirection.

Using generic types is a choice of design. We can use them and pay the price in increased binary size, but that would also happen if we were to implement ring buffers for different data types separately (ring_buffer_int, ring_buffer_float, etc.). Maintaining a single templated type is much easier than fixing the same bug in a few different places in the code base. The usage of generic types doesn't result in a binary size any larger than the size of an equivalent implementation of individual types. Let's examine the impact of templates on binary size in relation to separate implementations using the ring_buffer example:

```
int main() {
#ifdef USE_TEMPLATES
  ring_buffer<int, 10> buffer1;
  ring_buffer<float, 10> buffer2;
#else
  ring_buffer_int buffer1;
  ring_buffer_float buffer2;
#endif
  for (int i = 0; i < 20; i++) {
    buffer1.push(i);
    buffer2.push(i + 0.2f);
  }

  for (int i = 0; i < 10; i++) {
    printf("%d, %.2f\r\n", buffer1.pop(), buffer2.pop());
  }

  return 0;
}
```

The program will use a generic ring_buffer type if built with USE_TEMPLATES defined, and it will use the ring_buffer_int and ring_buffer_float types otherwise. If we build this example with GCC with no optimization enabled, it will result in a slightly bigger binary size in the template version (24 bytes). This is due to larger symbols in the symbol table when using the templated version. If we strip the symbol table from the object files, they will result in the same size. Also, building two versions with 03 results in the same binary size.

Generic types do not increase the binary size more than if we wrote instantiated types by hand as separate types. Templates have an effect on the build time due to the instantiation of concrete types in different compilation units, and there are techniques to avoid this if needed. All functions related to the instantiated types with the same parameters will result in a single function in the binary, as the linker will remove duplicate symbols.

RTTI and exceptions

Runtime type information (RTTI) in C++ is a mechanism that allows the type of an object to be determined at runtime. Most compilers implement RTTI using the virtual tables. Each polymorphic class (a class with at least one virtual function) has a virtual table that, among other things, includes type information for runtime type identification. RTTI imposes both time and space costs. It increases binary size and affects the runtime performance if type identification is used. This is the reason why compilers have a way of disabling RTTI. Let's examine a simple example with a base and derived class:

```cpp
#include <cstdio>

struct Base {
    virtual void print () {
        printf("Base\r\n");
    }
};
struct Derived : public Base {
    void print () override {
        printf("Derived\r\n");
    }
};

void printer (Base &base) {
    base.print();
}

int main() {
    Base base;
    Derived derived;
    printer(base);
    printer(derived);
```

```
    return 0;
}
```

The output of the program is as follows:

```
Base
Derived
```

Classes with virtual functions have vtables that are used for dynamic dispatching. Dynamic dispatch is a process of selecting which implementation of a polymorphic function is used. The `printer` function accepts a reference to the `Base` class. Depending on the type of reference passed to `printer` (`Base` or `Derived`), the dynamic dispatching process will select the `print` method from either the `Base` or `Derived` class. Vtables are also used to store type information.

By using `dynamic_cast`, as a part of the RTTI mechanism, we can find the information about the type using a reference or pointer to the superclass. Let's modify the `printer` method from the previous example:

```cpp
void printer (Base &base) {
    base.print();
    if(Derived *derived = dynamic_cast<Derived*>(&base); derived!=nullptr)
    {
        printf("We found Base using RTTI!\r\n");
    }
}
```

The output is as follows:

```
Base
Derived
We found Base using RTTI!
```

As we already mentioned, RTTI can be disabled. In GCC, we can do this by passing the `-fno-rtti` flag to the compiler. If we try to compile the modified example using this flag, the compiler will raise `error: dynamic_cast' not permitted with '-fno-rtti'`. If we restore the `printer` method to the original implementation, remove the `if` statement, and build it with both RTTI enabled and then disabled, we can notice that the binary size is larger when RTTI is enabled. RTTI is useful in certain scenarios, but it adds a massive overhead to resource-constrained devices, so we will leave it disabled.

Another C++ feature that is often disabled in embedded projects in C++ is exceptions. **Exceptions are an error-handling mechanism based on a try-catch block.** Let's take a look at a simple example utilizing exceptions to understand them better:

```cpp
#include <cstdio>

struct A {
  A() { printf("A is created!\r\n"); }
  ~A() { printf("A is destroyed!\r\n"); }
};

struct B {
  B() { printf("B is created!\r\n"); }
  ~B() { printf("B is destroyed!\r\n"); }
};

void bar() {
    B b;
    throw 0;
}
void foo() {
  A a;
  bar();
  A a1;
}

int main() {
  try {
    foo();
  } catch (int &p) {
    printf("Catching an exception!\r\n");
  }
  return 0;
}
```

The output of the program is as follows:

```
A is created!
B is created!
B is destroyed!
A is destroyed!
Catching an exception!
```

In this simple example, `foo` is called in the `try` block. It creates a local object, a, and calls `bar`. The `bar` function creates a local object, b, and throws an exception. In the output, we see that A and B are created, then B gets destroyed, then A gets destroyed, and we finally see that the `catch` block gets executed. This is called **stack unwinding**, and for it to happen, standard implementations most commonly utilize unwind tables, which store information about catch handlers, destructors to be called, and so on. Unwind tables can grow large and become complex, which increases the memory footprint of the application and introduces non-determinism due to the mechanism used at runtime for exception handling. This is why exceptions are often disabled in embedded system projects.

Summary

C++ is guided by the **zero-overhead principle**. The only two language features that do not follow it are RTTI and exceptions, and that's why compilers support a switch for turning them off.

The zero-overhead principle is based on two statements that we established in this chapter:

- You don't pay for what you don't use
- What you do use is just as efficient as what you could reasonably write by hand

RTTI and exceptions are disabled in most embedded projects, so you don't pay for them. Using generic types and templates is a design choice and is no more expensive than writing individual types by hand (`ring_buffer_int`, `ring_buffer_float`, and so on), but it lets you reuse the code logic for different types, makes the code more readable and easier for maintenance.

Working on high-risk systems is not a reason to disable compiler optimization capabilities. Code functionality needs to be verified whether we are building a program with optimization disabled or enabled. The most common source of bugs when optimization is enabled is undefined behavior. Understanding the undefined behavior and preventing it is up to the developer.

Modern C++ is a language that has a lot to offer to the embedded world. The mission of this book is to help you discover C++ and what it can do for your embedded projects, so let's embark on the path of discovering C++ and utilizing it to solve problems in the embedded domain.

In the next chapter, we will go over challenges in embedded systems with limited resources and dynamic memory management in C++.

Join our community on Discord

Join our community's Discord space for discussions with the author and other readers:

`https://packt.link/embeddedsystems`

2
Challenges in Embedded Systems with Limited Resources

If you are reading this book, chances are you have a good grasp of embedded systems. There are many definitions of embedded systems, and while the following may not be the most common, it captures the essence shared by others. **Embedded systems** are specialized computing systems for specific use with a limited set of responsibilities, in contrast to general-purpose computing systems. Embedded systems can be embedded in a larger electronic or mechanical system, or act as a standalone device.

The line between embedded systems and general-purpose computing devices is sometimes blurred. We can all agree that the system that controls a toaster or a pump in an airplane is an embedded system. Cellphones and early smartphones were also considered embedded systems. Nowadays, smartphones are closer to the definition of a general-purpose computing device. In this book, we will focus on firmware development using modern C++ on small embedded systems or resource-constrained embedded systems.

Resource-constrained embedded systems are often employed in safety-critical applications. They have a responsibility to control a process in a timely manner and they cannot fail, as failure can mean the loss of human lives. In this chapter, we will cover limitations imposed by regulations on software development for safety-critical devices and implications for the usage of C++. We will learn how to mitigate these concerns.

In this chapter, we're going to cover the following main topics:

- Safety-critical and hard real-time embedded systems
- Dynamic memory management
- Disabling unwanted C++ features

Technical requirements

To get the most out of this chapter, I strongly recommend using Compiler Explorer (`https://godbolt.org/`) as you read through the examples. Select GCC as your compiler and target x86 architecture. This will allow you to see standard output (stdio) results and better observe the code's behavior. As we are using a lot of modern C++ features, make sure to select C++23 standard, by adding `-std=c++23` in compiler options box.

The examples from this chapter are available on GitHub (`https://github.com/PacktPublishing/Cpp-in-Embedded-Systems/tree/main/Chapter02`).

Safety-critical and hard real-time embedded systems

Safety-critical embedded systems are systems whose failure may result in damage to property or environment, injury to people, or even a loss of life. Failure of these systems is not acceptable. Brakes, steering systems, and airbags in cars are good examples of safety-critical systems. The correct functioning of these systems is essential for the safe operation of a vehicle.

Next, we will analyze the real-time requirements of an airbag control unit in a car.

Airbag control unit and real-time requirements

Safety-critical embedded systems often impose hard real-time requirements, meaning that any missed deadline results in system failure. An **Airbag Control Unit (ACU)** collects data from accelerometers and pressure sensors, runs an algorithm that processes the collected data, and detects side, front, and rear-end crashes. Upon the crash detection, the ACU controls the deployment of different restraint systems, including airbags and seat belt tensioners.

ACU implementations must be resilient to different scenarios, such as malfunctioning sensors and electronics. These are mitigated by redundant sensors, comparing data from sensors, comparing data against thresholds, and self-tests. Most importantly, ACUs need to meet timing requirements, as they have only a couple of milliseconds to collect data, make decisions, and initiate deployment of restraint systems.

The ACU fails if it doesn't detect a crash on time, but it also fails if it deploys restraint systems just a bit too late, as this can do more harm to a driver and passengers than if the ACU hadn't initiated a deployment at all. This is why an ACU must meet hard real-time requirements, and when it comes to firmware, this means all the worst-case execution times must be predictable.

The effect of delayed airbag deployment is the subject of many studies concerned with injuries caused to occupants. The following extract is part of the conclusion from the paper *Study regarding the influence of airbag deployment time on the occupant injury level during a frontal vehicle collision*, published at MATEC Web of Conferences 184(1):01007, by authors Alexandru Ionut Radu, Corneliu Cofaru, Bogdan Tolea, and Dragoș Sorin Dima, outlining results of simulations of delayed airbag deployment:

> *"It has been found that by increasing the delay of the airbag deployment time in the event of a frontal impact, the probability of injury to the occupant's head increases by up to 46%. Reducing the distance between the occupant's head and the dashboard / steering wheel when the airbag ignites would result in a force expansion of the gas that is transmitted to the occupant's head generating an extra acceleration and also throws back the occupant increasing the injury potential due to the impact between the head and headrest. Thus, an increase in injury probability of 8% was observed in the 0 ms delay of the airbag deployment, while a 100 ms delay resulted in a 54% increase in the head acceleration value. So, the role of the airbag is reversed, it no longer has the role of cushioning the collision, but to generate injuries."*

A graphic illustration of collision and delayed airbag deployment is shown in the following figure (source: `https://www.researchgate.net/publication/326715516_Study_regarding_the_influence_of_airbag_deployment_time_on_the_occupant_injury_level_during_a_frontal_vehicle_collision`):

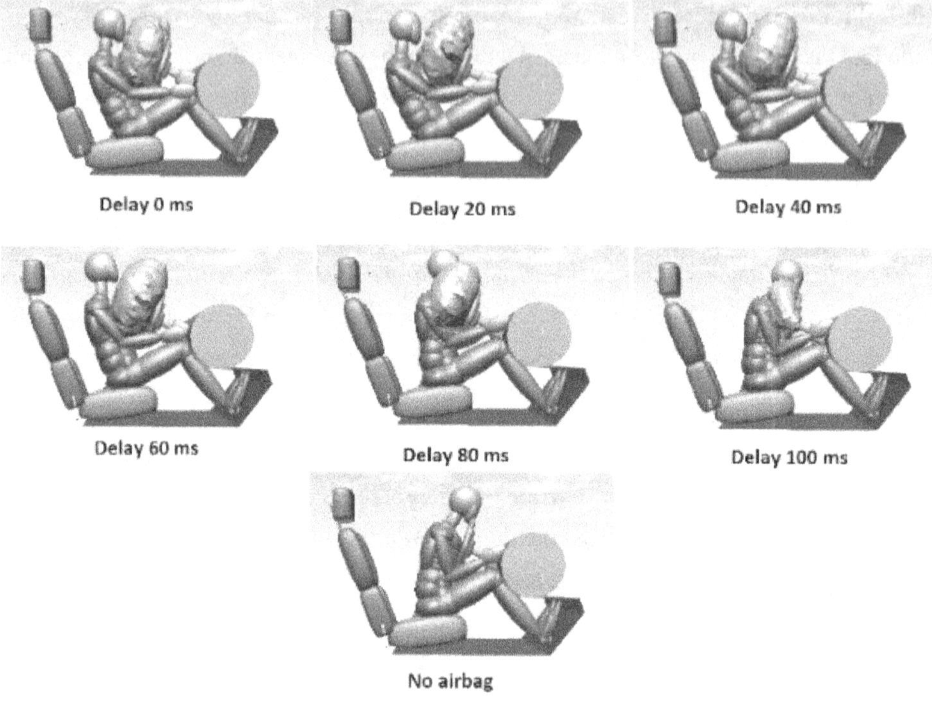

Figure 2.1 – Crash simulation with delayed restraint system deployment

Figure 2.1 effectively illustrates what happens if an ACU doesn't meet hard real-time requirements and produces delayed results. The figure is taken from the paper *Study regarding the influence of airbag deployment time on the occupant injury level during a frontal vehicle collision.*

There are multiple reasons why an ACU may fail and cause no or a delayed deployment:

- Sensor malfunctioning
- Electronics malfunctioning
- Crash detection algorithm failure
- Firmware failure to meet a deadline

Sensors and electronics malfunctioning are mitigated by redundancy, data sanity checks, cross-comparison, and startup and runtime self-tests. This puts additional stress on firmware and its correct functioning. A crash detection algorithm may fail due to a bad model that was built upon, or other factors that are out of firmware responsibilities. The firmware's job is to feed the algorithm with sensors' data on time, execute it in a timely manner within a set time window, and act based on the output of the algorithm.

Measuring firmware performance and non-determinism

How do we ensure that the firmware will run all functions within imposed real-time requirements? We measure it. We can measure different metrics, such as performance profiling, response to external events, and A-B timing. Performance profiling will tell us in which functions the program spends the most time. Response to external events will indicate how much time it takes for a system to respond to an external event, such as an interrupt or a message on a communication bus.

A-B timing and real-time execution

The most important metric when dealing with real-time requirements is **A-B timing**. We measure how long it takes for firmware to execute a program from point A to point B. A-B timing can measure a function's duration, but not necessarily. We can use it to measure different things. Going from A to B can take different times, based on the state of the system and inputs.

A simple way to make an A-B measurement is toggling a **General Purpose Input Output (GPIO)** and using an oscilloscope to measure the time between changes of a GPIO. It's a simple solution that works well but doesn't scale, as we would need a GPIO for every function we want to measure or we'd need to measure one function at a time. We could also use the internal timer of a **Microcontroller Unit (MCU)** to make precise measurements and output that information over a UART port. This would require us to utilize a general-purpose timer just for the sake of measuring. Most microcontrollers have specialized units for instrumentation and profiling.

Some ARM-based microcontrollers have a **Data Watchpoint and Trace (DWT)** unit. DWT is used for data tracing and system profiling, including the following:

- **Program Counter (PC)** sampling
- Cycle counting

DWT generates events and outputs them using an **Instrumentation Trace Macrocell (ITM)** unit. The ITM unit can also be used to output data generated from the firmware itself, in the `printf` style. ITM buffers data and sends it over to an ITM sink. **Single Wire Output (SWO)** can be used as an ITM sink.

We can utilize DWT and ITM for profiling as follows:

1. DWT can generate periodic sampling of the PC and use ITM to send them over SWO.
2. On a host machine, we capture and analyze the received data.
3. By using a linker map file for our firmware, we can generate the distribution of time spent in each of the functions in our program.

This can help us to see which function takes the most time. It's not particularly useful for A-B timing measurements, but it allows us to see where the program spends most of the time without any direct software instrumentation except setting up DWT and ITM units.

Sotware instrumentation with GCC

GNU Compiler Collection (GCC) supports software instrumentation by using the `-finstrument-functions` flag to instrument functions' entries and exists. This inserts entry and exit calls to each function with the following signature:

```cpp
__attribute__((no_instrument_function))
void __cyg_profile_func_enter(void *this_fn, void *call_site)
{
}

__attribute__((no_instrument_function))
void __cyg_profile_func_exit(void *this_fn, void *call_site)
{
}
```

We can utilize DWT and ITM in the `__cyg_profile_func_enter` and `__cyg_profile_func_exit` functions to send the clock cycle count and analyze it on the host machine to make A-B timing measurements. The following is an example of a simplified implementation of entry and exit functions:

```cpp
extern "C" {
__attribute__((no_instrument_function))
void __cyg_profile_func_enter(void *this_fn, void *call_site)
{
    printf("entry, %p, %d", this_fn, DWT_CYCCNT);
}
__attribute__((no_instrument_function))
void __cyg_profile_func_exit(void *this_fn, void *call_site)
{
    printf("exit, %p, %d", this_fn, DWT_CYCCNT);
}
}
```

The preceding implementation uses `extern "C"` as a linkage language specifier for `entry` and `exit` instrumentation functions as they are linked with C libraries by the compiler. The example also assumes that `printf` is redirected to use ITM as output and that the cycle counter register in DWT is started.

Another option is to use ITM's timestamping and send both timestamps and function addresses from entry and exit instrumentation functions. With the help of a linker map file, we can then reconstruct the sequence of function calls and returns. There are specialized formats for sending traces, such as **Common Trace Format (CTF)**, and desktop tools called **trace viewers** that can allow us to streamline software instrumentation. CTF is an open format used to serialize an event in a packet with one or more fields. Specialized tools, such as **barectf** (`https://barectf.org/docs/barectf/3.1/index.html`) are used to facilitate CTF packet generation.

Events are described using a **YAML Ain't Markup Language (YAML)** configuration file. A simple C library containing trace functions is generated by `barectf` using the configuration file. These functions are used in source code in places where we want to emit traces.

CTF traces can be sent over different transport layers such as ITM or serial. Traces can be analyzed using tools such as Babeltrace (`https://babeltrace.org`) and TraceCompass (`https://eclipse.dev/tracecompass`). There are other tools that facilitate trace generation, transfer, and viewing such as SEGGER SystemView. On the target side, a small software module provided by SEGGER is included to make calls to tracing functions. Traces are sent over SEGGER's **Real Time Transfer (RTT)** protocol using SWD and analyzed in SystemView.

We covered some basic approaches to A-B timing. There are more advanced techniques, and they often depend on the target capabilities, as there are some more advanced tracing units that can be utilized for A-B measurements.

Determinism vs. Non-Determinism in Firmware

If we measure the duration of a function using the A-B timing approach and have the same duration and function output for the same inputs, we say that the function is **deterministic**. If a function depends on a global state and the measured duration is different for the same inputs, we say it is **non-deterministic**.

Default dynamic memory allocators in C++ tend to be non-deterministic. The duration of allocation depends on the current global state of the allocator and the complexity of the allocating algorithm. We can measure duration for the same inputs with different global states, but it is hard to evaluate all possible global states and to guarantee the **Worst-Case Execution Time (WCET)** with default allocators.

The non-deterministic behavior of dynamic memory allocation is just one problem for safety-critical systems. The other problem is that it can fail. If there is no more available memory or if the memory is fragmented, then the allocation can fail. This is why many safety coding standards such as **Motor Industry Software Reliability Association (MISRA)** and **Automotive Open System Architecture (AUTOSAR)** discourage dynamic memory.

We will explore dynamic memory management implications and safety-critical concerns next.

Dynamic memory management

The C++ standard defines the following storage durations for objects:

- **Automatic storage duration**: Objects with automatic storage duration are automatically created and destroyed as the program enters and exits the block in which they are defined. These are typically local variables within functions, except those declared `static`, `extern`, or `thread_local`.

- **Static storage duration**: Objects with static storage duration are allocated when the program starts and deallocated when the program ends. All objects declared at the namespace scope (including the global namespace) have this static duration, plus those declared with `static` or `extern`.

- **Thread storage duration**: Introduced in C++11, objects with thread storage duration are created and destroyed with the thread in which they are defined, allowing each thread to have its own instance of a variable. They are declared with the `thread_local` specifier.

- **Dynamic storage duration**: Objects with dynamic storage duration are explicitly created and destroyed using dynamic memory allocation functions (`new` and `delete` in C++), giving the software developer control over the lifetime of these objects.

Dynamic storage gives great flexibility to a software developer, providing full control over an object's lifetime. With great power comes great responsibility. Objects are dynamically allocated using the `new` operator and freed using `delete`. Every object that is allocated dynamically must be freed exactly once and should never be accessed after it has been freed. This is a straightforward rule but failing to follow it causes a range of problems, such as the following:

- Memory leaks occur when dynamically allocated memory is not freed properly. Over time, this unused memory accumulates potentially exhausting system resources.

- Dangling pointers happen when a pointer still references a memory location that has been freed. Accessing such a pointer leads to undefined behavior.

- Double free errors occur when memory that has already been freed is deleted again, leading to undefined behavior.

Another problem with dynamic memory management is memory fragmentation.

Memory fragmentation

Memory fragmentation occurs when free memory is divided into small, non-contiguous blocks over time, making it difficult or impossible to allocate large blocks of memory even when there is enough free memory available in total. There are two main types:

- **External fragmentation**: This happens when there is enough total memory available to satisfy an allocation request but no single continuous block is large enough due to fragmentation. It's common in systems where memory allocation and deallocation occur frequently, and sizes vary significantly.

- **Internal fragmentation**: This occurs when allocated memory blocks are larger than the requested memory, leading to wasted space within allocated blocks. It happens when using allocators that have fixed-size memory blocks or memory pools and with allocators designed to give WCET.

Memory fragmentation leads to inefficient memory use, reducing the performance or preventing further allocations resulting in out-of-memory scenarios, even when it appears that sufficient memory is available. Let's visualize the memory region reserved for dynamic memory allocation in the following figure:

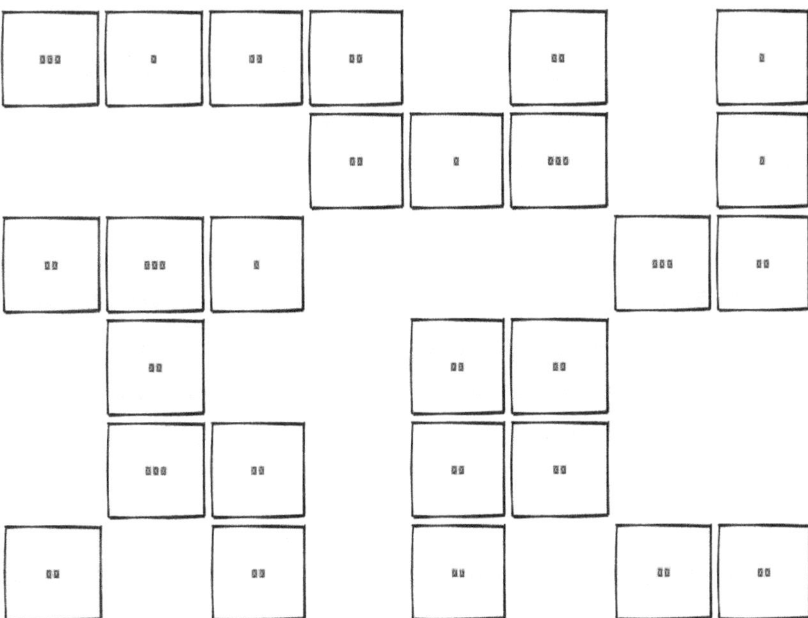

Figure 2.2 – Memory region used for dynamic allocation

In *Figure 2.2*, each block represents a memory unit allocated during the allocation process. Empty regions were not allocated, or they were freed using the `delete` operator. Even though there is plenty of memory available, if there were a request for the allocation of four memory units, the allocation would fail, as there are not four continuous memory blocks available due to memory fragmentation.

Non-deterministic behavior of default memory allocators and out-of-memory scenarios are major concerns for safety-critical systems. MISRA and AUTOSAR provide coding guidelines for the use of C++ in safety-critical systems.

MISRA is an organization that provides guidelines for the software developed for electronic components used in the automotive industry. It is a collaboration between vehicle manufacturers, component suppliers, and engineering consultancies. Standards produced by MISRA are also used in aerospace, defense, space, medical, and other industries.

AUTOSAR is a global development partnership by automotive manufacturers, suppliers, and other companies from the electronics, semiconductor, and software industries. AUTOSAR also produces guidelines for the use of C++ in critical and safety-related systems.

Safety-critical guidelines for dynamic memory management in C++

MISRA C++ 2008, which covers the C++03 standard, prohibits the usage of dynamic memory allocation, while AUTOSAR's *Guidelines for the use of the C++14 language in critical and safety-related systems* specifies, among others, the following rules:

- Rule A18-5-5 (required, toolchain, partially automated)

> *"Memory management functions shall ensure the following: (a) deterministic behavior resulting with the existence of worst-case execution time, (b) avoiding memory fragmentation, (c) avoid running out of memory, (d) avoiding mismatched allocations or deallocations, (e) no dependence on non-deterministic calls to kernel."*

- Rule A18-5-6 (required, verification / toolchain, non-automated)

> *"An analysis shall be performed to analyze the failure modes of dynamic memory management. In particular, the following failure modes shall be analyzed: (a) non-deterministic behavior resulting with nonexistence of worst-case execution time, (b) memory fragmentation, (c) running out of memory, (d) mismatched allocations and deallocations, (e) dependence on non-deterministic calls to kernel."*

Now, following these two rules to the letter is an extremely hard task. We can write a custom allocator that has deterministic WCET and minimizes fragmentation, but how do we write an allocator that avoids running out of memory? Or, in case it happens, how do we ensure the non-failure of the system? Every call to the allocator would need to verify the success of the operation and, in case of failure, somehow mitigate it. Or we would need to be able to estimate the amount of memory needed for an allocator accurately, so it doesn't run out of memory in runtime under any circumstances. This adds a whole new layer of complexity to our software design and adds more complexity than we would add value by allowing dynamic memory allocation.

An in-between approach to dynamic memory allocation policy is to allow it on startup, but not when the system is running. This is the policy used by **Joint Strike Fighter Air Vehicle C++ Coding Standards**. MISRA C++ 2023 also advises against the usage of dynamic memory allocation when the system is running, and as a mitigation policy, recommends using it at startup.

The C++ standard library uses dynamic memory allocation heavily. Exception handling mechanism implementations also often use dynamic allocation. Before dismissing the idea of using the standard library in embedded projects, let's discover the internal workings of the `std::vector` container and see what C++ offers to mitigate our concerns.

Dynamic memory management in the C++ standard library

We introduced `std::vector` as a container from the standard library that uses dynamic memory allocation. `vector` is a template class, and we can specify the underlying type. It stores the elements contiguously, and we can get direct access to the underlying contiguous storage using the `data` method.

The following code example demonstrates the usage of a vector:

```cpp
std::vector<std::uint8_t> vec;
constexpr std::size_t n_elem = 8;
for (std::uint8_t i = 0; i < n_elem; i++) {
  vec.push_back(i);
}
const auto print_array = [](uint8_t *arr, std::size_t n) {
  for (std::size_t i = 0; i < n; i++) {
    printf("%d ", arr[i]);
  }
  printf("\r\n");
};
print_array(vec.data(), n_elem);
```

We created a vector with the underlying uint8_t type and added values from 0 to 8 using the push_back method. The example also demonstrates access to a pointer to the underlying contiguous storage, which we provided as an argument to the print_array lambda.

The usual allocation strategy of vector is to allocate one element on the first insertion, then double it each time it reaches its capacity. Storing values for 0 to 8 would result in 4 allocation requests, as shown in the following figure:

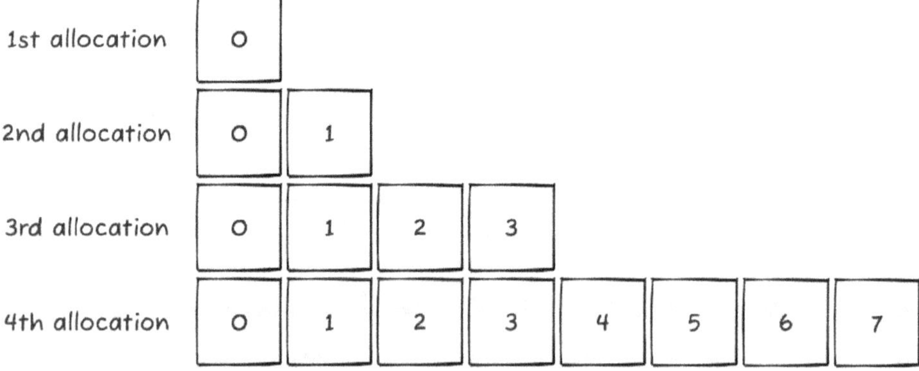

Figure 2.3 – Vector allocation requests

Figure 2.3 depicts the vector's allocation requests. In order to inspect vector implementation on any platform, we can overload the new and delete operators and monitor the allocation requests:

```
void *operator new(std::size_t count) {
  printf("%s, size = %ld\r\n", __PRETTY_FUNCTION__, count);
  return std::malloc(count);
}
void operator delete(void *ptr) noexcept {
  printf("%s\r\n", __PRETTY_FUNCTION__);
  std::free(ptr);
}
```

The new overloaded operator passes allocation calls to malloc, and it prints out the size requested by the caller. The delete overloaded operator just prints out the function signature so we can see when it is called. Some standard library implementations using GCC implement the new operator using malloc. Our vector allocation calls will result in the following output:

```
void* operator new(std::size_t), size = 1
void* operator new(std::size_t), size = 2
void operator delete(void*)
void* operator new(std::size_t), size = 4
void operator delete(void*)
void* operator new(std::size_t), size = 8
void operator delete(void*)
```

The preceding results are obtained using the GCC compiler, and they are the same both for x86_64 and Arm Cortex-M4 platforms. When the vector fills the available memory, it requests allocation of the doubled amount of currently used memory. It then copies data from the original storage to newly acquired memory. Afterward, it deletes previously used storage, as we can see from the preceding generated output.

Overloading the new and delete operators would allow us to change the allocation mechanism globally, in order to meet the safety-critical guidelines requesting for deterministic WTEC and avoiding out-of-memory scenarios, which is quite challenging.

The allocation requests from the vector can be optimized by using the reserve method if the number of elements is known beforehand:

```
vec.reserve(8);
```

Using the reserve method will make the vector request eight elements, and it will ask for more memory only if we go beyond eight elements. This makes it useful for projects that allow dynamic allocation at startup if we can guarantee that the number of elements at any point will stay within reserved memory. If we add a ninth element to the vector, it will make another allocation request, requesting the memory to fit 16 elements.

The C++ standard library also makes possible usage of local allocators for containers. Let's take a look at the vector's declaration:

```
template<
    class T,
    class Allocator = std::allocator<T>
> class vector;
```

We can see that the second template parameter is `Allocator`, and the default argument is `std::allocator`, which uses the `new` and `delete` operators. C++17 introduced `std::pmr::polymorphic_allocator`, an allocator that exhibits different allocation behavior depending upon the `std::pmr::memory_resource` type from which it is constructed.

There is a memory resource that can be constructed by providing it with an initial, statically allocated buffer, and it's called `std::pmr::monotonic_buffer_resource`. The monotonic buffer is built for performance, and it releases memory only when it is destroyed. Initializing it with a statically allocated buffer makes it suitable for embedded applications. Let's see how we can use it for a vector:

```
using namespace std;
using namespace std::pmr;
array<uint8_t, sizeof(uint8_t) * 8> buffer{0};
monotonic_buffer_resource mbr{buffer.data(), buffer.size()};
polymorphic_allocator<uint8_t> pa{&mbr};
std::pmr::vector<uint8_t> vec{pa};
```

In the preceding example, we do the following:

1. Create a `std::array` container, with an underlying type of `uint8_t`.

2. Construct a monotonic buffer and provide it with the array we just created as the initial buffer.

3. Use the monotonic buffer to create a polymorphic allocator, which we use to create a vector.

Please note that the vector is from the `std::pmr` namespace, and it's just a partial specialization of `std::vector`, as shown here:

```cpp
namespace pmr {
    template< class T >
    using vector = std::vector<T, std::pmr::polymorphic_allocator<T>>;
}
```

A vector created by utilizing a monotonic buffer will allocate memory in the space provided by the buffer. Let's examine the behavior of such a vector in the following example built from the previously explained code:

```cpp
#include <cstdio>
#include <cstdlib>

#include <array>
#include <memory_resource>
#include <vector>

#include <new>

void *operator new(std::size_t count, std::align_val_t al) {
  printf("%s, size = %ld\r\n", __PRETTY_FUNCTION__, count);
  return std::malloc(count);
}

int main() {
  using namespace std;
  using namespace std::pmr;

  constexpr size_t n_elem = 8;
  array<uint8_t, sizeof(uint8_t) * 8> buffer{0};
  monotonic_buffer_resource mbr{buffer.data(), buffer.size()};
  polymorphic_allocator<uint8_t> pa{&mbr};
  std::pmr::vector<uint8_t> vec{pa};
  //vec.reserve(n_elem);

  for (uint8_t i = 0; i < n_elem; i++) {
    vec.push_back(i);
```

```cpp
  }

  for (uint8_t data : buffer) {
    printf("%d ", data);
  }
  printf("\r\n");
  return 0;
}
```

The preceding program will provide the following output:

```
void* operator new(std::size_t, std::align_val_t), size = 64
0 0 1 0 1 2 3 0
```

We see that even though we used the monotonic buffer, the program called the new operator. You can notice that the call to the reserve method is commented. This will result in a vector-expanding strategy, as described previously. When the monotonic buffer initial memory is used, it will fall to the upstream memory resource pointer. The default upstream memory resource will use the new and delete operators.

If we print the buffer used as initial storage for monotonic_buffer_resource, we can see that the vector is allocating the first element and storing 0 to it, then it doubles it and stores 0 and 1, and then doubles it again, storing 0, 1, 2, and 3. When it tries to double it again, the monotonic buffer will not be able to meet the allocation request and will fall to using the default allocator, which relies on the new and delete operators. We can visualize this in the following figure:

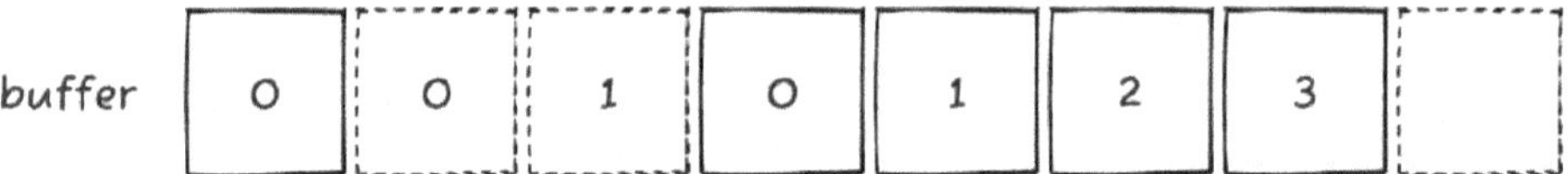

Figure 2.4 – State of the buffer used by the monotonic buffer resource

Figure 2.4 depicts the internal state of the used by the monotonic buffer resource. We can see that the monotonic buffer resource is not deallocating memory in any way. On an allocation buffer request, it returns a pointer to the last available element in the initial buffer if there is enough space in the buffer to fit the requested number of elements.

You will notice that the new operator used in this example has a different signature from the one previously used. Actually, the standard library defines different versions of new and matching delete operators, and it's hard to tell which version is used by a container from the standard library without inspection. This makes overloading them globally and replacing implementation with a custom one even more challenging, making a local allocator usually a better choice.

The polymorphic allocator utilizing a monotonic buffer initialized with a buffer on the stack may be a good option to mitigate some of the issues imposed by the dynamic memory management when working with containers from the standard C++ library. The approach we demonstrated on the vector can be used on other containers from standard libraries, such as list and map, but also other types from the library, such as basic_string.

Mitigating concerns of dynamic memory allocation is possible but it still poses some challenges. If you want to be absolutely sure that your C++ program is not calling a new operator, there are means to ensure it. Let us explore how we can disable unwanted C++ features.

Disabling unwanted C++ features

You may have noticed that we used printf from the C standard library for printing debug information on standard output instead of std::cout from the C++ standard library. The reason is twofold – the implementation of the std::cout global object from ostream has a large memory footprint and it uses dynamic memory allocation. C++ works well with the C standard library, and using printf is a good alternative for resource-constrained systems.

We already discussed the exception handling mechanism, which often relies on dynamic memory allocation. Disabling exceptions in C++ is as easy as passing the appropriate flag to the compiler. In the case of GCC, that flag is -fno-exceptions. The same goes for **Run-Time Type Information (RTTI)**. We can disable it with the -fno-rtti flag.

Disabling exceptions will result in calling std::terminate when an exception is thrown. We can replace the default terminate handler with our own implementation and handle it appropriately, as shown in the following example:

```cpp
#include <cstdio>
#include <cstdlib>
#include <exception>
#include <array>
int main() {
  constexpr auto my_terminate_handler = []() {
    printf("This is my_terminate_handler\r\n");
```

```cpp
    std::abort();
  };
  std::set_terminate(my_terminate_handler);
  std::array<int, 4> arr;
  for (int i = 0; i < 5; i++) {
   arr.at(i) = i;
  }
  return 0;
}
```

The preceding example demonstrates setting the terminate handler using `std::set_terminate` by our own implementation. This allows us to handle cases that shouldn't happen in runtime and try to recover from them or gracefully terminate them. Some features or behaviors in C++ can't be disabled by compiler flags, but there are other means to handle them,

As we saw previously, we can redefine global `new` and `delete` operators. We can also delete them, which will make the compilation fail if we use a software component that calls `new`, effectively allowing us to prevent any attempts of dynamic memory allocation if needed:

```cpp
#include <cstdio>
#include <vector>
#include <new>

void *operator new(std::size_t count) = delete;
void *operator new[](std::size_t count) = delete;
void *operator new(std::size_t count, std::align_val_t al) = delete;
void *operator new[](std::size_t count, std::align_val_t al) = delete;

void *operator new(std::size_t count, const std::nothrow_t &tag) = delete;
void *operator new[](std::size_t count, const std::nothrow_t &tag) =
delete;
void *operator new(std::size_t count, std::align_val_t al, const
std::nothrow_t &) = delete;
void *operator new[](std::size_t count, std::align_val_t al,const
std::nothrow_t &) = delete;

int main() {
  std::vector<int> vec;
  vec.push_back(123);
```

```cpp
    printf("vec[0] = %d\r\n", vec[0]);
    return 0;
}
```

The preceding example will fail with the following compiler message (among others):

```
/usr/include/c++/13/bits/new_allocator.h:143:59: error: use of deleted
function 'void* operator new(std::size_t, std::align_val_t)'
  143 |                return static_cast<_Tp*>(_GLIBCXX_OPERATOR_NEW (__n *
sizeof(_Tp),
```

By deleting new operators, we can make the compilation of a C++ program that is trying to use dynamic memory management fail. This is useful if we want to be sure our program is not using dynamic memory management.

Summary

C++ allows a great degree of flexibility. Resource-constrained embedded systems and safety-critical guidelines can impose some limitations on the usage of certain C++ features, such as exception handling, RTTI, and the usage of dynamic memory allocation by containers and other modules from the standard C++ library. C++ acknowledges those concerns and provides mechanisms for disabling unwanted features. In this chapter, we learned about different strategies for mitigating concerns of dynamic memory allocation by means of local allocators and overloading global new and delete operators.

The learning curve is steep but worth the effort, so let's continue our journey of discovering C++ in embedded systems.

In the next chapter, we will explore the C++ ecosystem for embedded development.

Get This Book's PDF Version and Exclusive Extras

Scan the QR code (or go to packtpub.com/unlock). Search for this book by name, confirm the edition, and then follow the steps on the page.

Note: Keep your invoice handy. Purchases made directly from Packt don't require an invoice.

3

Embedded C++ Ecosystem

At the heart of every embedded system sits a microcontroller. The transition from basic cores to more modern ones mirrors the evolution of technology. The microcontroller landscape is vast, ranging from cost-effective 8-bit cores and 16-bit cores to modern 32-bit Arm and RISC-V® based microcontrollers. This variety of architecture has impacted the development of tools and compilers. While some manufacturers have opted to focus on C support, many have recognized the importance of C++ and provided good support for C++ development within their toolchains.

As the embedded system is vast and it is impossible to cover all of the available architectures and vendors, we will focus on Arm® Cortex®-M as one of the dominant architectures for modern microcontrollers and **Systems on a Chip (SoCs)**. We will go through the available development environments and toolchains that provide support for development in C++ for the Arm Cortex-M. We will also go through tools such as static analyzers, learn how to profile an embedded target, and cover methodologies such as unit testing.

In this chapter, we're going to cover the following main topics:

- Compilers and development environments
- Static analyzers
- Unit testing
- Profiling

Technical requirements

To get the most out of this chapter, I strongly recommend using Compiler Explorer (`https://godbolt.org/`) as you read through the examples. Select GCC as your compiler and target x86 architecture. This will allow you to see standard output (stdio) results and better observe the code's behavior. As we are using a lot of modern C++ features, make sure to select C++23 standard, by adding `-std=c++23` in compiler options box.

The examples from this chapter are available on GitHub (`https://github.com/PacktPublishing/Cpp-in-Embedded-Systems/tree/main/Chapter03`).

Compilers and development environments

The adoption of C++ in embedded systems was influenced by compiler support. While most compilers supported C, the support for C++ was slower. Nowadays, there is a variety of compilers and toolchains available for C++ depending on the target architecture and functional safety requirements. Support for 32-bit architecture such as Arm Cortex-M is generally good, but the level of support depends on the toolchain vendor and functional safety requirements.

Many vendors offer functional safety versions of their tools that include certified compilers according to the safety standards for different industries. Functional safety standards are designed to ensure that software operates correctly and safely, even in the event of hardware failures or operational errors. IEC 61508 is the international umbrella safety standard for functional safety, and the following are safety standards for some industries:

- **ISO 26262**: Automotive safety standard
- **EN 50128**: European railways safety standard
- **IEC 62304**: International standard for medical software
- **IEC 60730-1**: Automatic electrical control for household appliances

Functional safety requirements are one of the first items on our checklist when selecting a compiler for a new project. If they call for qualified compilers, then we are limited to commercial versions of compilers that provide qualified compilers according to the exact standard in question.

While many vendors providing tools for embedded development provide functional safety versions of their tools and compilers, there are also free development environments and open source compilers for embedded system development that can be used in non-critical applications.

Development environments pack different tools to make the development process seamless and allow you to focus on the development. These tools can also be used individually and tailored according to individual or organizational preferences. Tools used for embedded development, either individually or integrated into a development environment, are listed as follows:

- **Code editor**: This can be as basic as a text editor or a more advanced tool such as Vim or Visual Studio Code supporting plugins for features such as syntax highlighting, autocompletion, code navigation across different source files, and refactoring.

- **Compiler and linker**: These are used to transform code into object files and link them to executable and binary files that can be flashed to a target. Some of the most popular C++ compilers are GCC, Clang, Arm Compiler for Embedded, and IAR C/C++ Compiler.

- **Debugger**: It is used to flash and debug a target. Parts of the debugging system are a debugger probe and software that communicates with a probe to debug the connected target.

- **Build system**: Tools such as GNU Make and Ninja are used to control the process of compiling and linking. CMake and Bazel are used for build automation and dependency management.

- **Static analysis tools**: These are used to analyze source code. Depending on capability, they can detect some forms of undefined behavior such as out-of-bound access, uninitialized variables, null pointer dereferences, and so on. Dedicated static analysis tools can check whether the code is MISRA or AUTOSAR-compliant.

- **Runtime profilers**: These are a combination of target capabilities, software instrumentation, and debugger probes used to measure function execution time and analyze the performance of your software.

Most embedded **integrated development environments (IDEs)** provide the following capabilities:

- Project creation and organization
- Build automation
- Debugging

Some development environments integrate more advanced features for code analysis, such as the following:

- Static analysis
- Profiling and performance analysis

We will cover some of the most used development environments and compilers in the industry on the next pages.

Arm Keil MDK and Arm Compiler for Embedded

Arm® Keil® MDK is a set of tools for embedded development on (mostly) Arm Cortex-M microcontrollers and it includes the following:

- Keil Studio, a set of extensions for VS Code
- Keil µVision, a legacy Windows®-based IDE
- Arm Compiler for Embedded, a C and C++ compiler
- Arm Virtual Hardware

Both **Keil Studio** and **Keil µVision** provide all the IDE features needed for embedded development, including project configuration for different targets, build, and debugging on target.

Keil µVision provides support for the integration of PC-Lint, a static C and C++ analyzer, while VS Code (Keil Studio) can be configured to use `clang-tidy` or `cppcheck`.

Keil µVision is packed with Keil Simulator, allowing running firmware on simulated targets on your PC, and it also has an integrated profiler as a part of the µVision debugger.

Arm Keil MDK comes with Arm Virtual Hardware Fixed Virtual Platforms, which is Arm's cloud platform that allows you to run binaries on simulated targets providing infrastructure for CI/CD in a simulated environment.

There is a basic version of Keil MDK available for non-commercial use (Community), and two commercial versions (Essential and Professional), depending on the features available. Only the Professional commercial version comes with functional safety support and extended maintenance. Next, we will cover Arm Compiler for Embedded, a C and C++ compiler that comes with MDK. It also includes linker and standard libraries.

Arm Compiler for Embedded is a C and C++ compiler provided by Arm. Arm also provides a **functional safety (FuSa)** version of the compiler that is certified according to IEC 61508, ISO 26262, EN 50128, and IEC 62304 safety standards.

The FuSa version is available only in the highest edition of MDK – Professional.

Arm Compiler for Embedded consists of the following toolchain components:

- `armclang`, a **low-level virtual machine (LLVM)**-based compiler
- `armlink`, a linker that combines objects and libraries to produce an executable
- Arm C libraries
- Arm C++ libraries based on the LLVM `libc++` project

Arm Compiler supports C++17 standard, while the latest version of Arm Compiler for Embedded FuSa 6.16 supports C++ 14. Even though we are in 2024 at the time of writing this book, the support for the latest version of the C++ standard is slow. After C++17, C++20 and C++23 were released.

Support of the latest C++ standard in commercial compilers is still rather slow, which makes the latest language features in these environments unavailable.

IAR C/C++ Compiler and IAR Embedded Workbench for Arm

IAR Embedded Workbench® is a development environment for Arm Cortex-M, Cortex-R, and Cortex-A cores (IAR stands for Ingenjörsfirma Anders Rundgren). It integrates the following tools:

- IDE, including a debugger and profiler
- IAR C/C++ Compiler
- IAR C-STAT®, a static analyzer
- IAR C-RUN®, a tool for runtime analysis

IAR Embedded Workbench is a well-rounded solution for the development of Arm Cortex-M cores. The IDE is packed with standard tools, such as a debugger, but also provides more advanced embedded tools, such as a profiler and running firmware in the simulator.

IAR offers C-STAT, a tool for static analysis that can run static analysis against safety coding standards such as MISRAC++2008.

IAR also provides C-RUN, a tool for runtime analysis that covers heap checks, bounds checking, buffer overrun, integer overflow, and other runtime checks by instrumenting your code.

IAR C/C++ Compiler supports C++17 from 9.30.1. The FuSa version of IAR Embedded Workbench for Arm, version 9.50.3 (February 2024), also provides C++17 support.

IAR C/C++ Compiler and Arm Compiler for Embedded are commercial options for embedded development. Besides the support you can expect from a commercial project, the strength of these tools is that they provide safety-qualified versions for safety-critical projects.

Some microcontroller vendors provide their own versions of development environments, usually based on Eclipse®, providing additional support for their own products.

Vendor-supported IDEs and GCC

Alternatives to commercial development environments are vendor-supported environments, which are based mostly on Eclipse and **GNU Compiler Collection (GCC)** tools and **GNU Project Debugger (GDB)** for debugging. Examples are STM32CubeIDE by ST® and MCUXpresso by NXP®.

These tools are packed with code configurator UIs that can generate C code used for GPIO configuration, clock setup, and peripheral drivers' initialization.

Some vendors, such as Nordic Semiconductor®, opted for VS Code as the basis of their IDE solution. They provide plugins for GPIO configuration and debugging. VS Code is a modern code editor that allows developers to use plugins such as IntelliSense for code completion, parameter information, syntax highlighting, and many others to enhance the development experience.

GCC

GCC is one of the most used C and C++ compilers in general. It is free software, and it is also the most popular compiler for non-critical applications that do not require a qualified compiler. However, even GCC can be qualified. The process of qualification includes compiling and running test programs and comparing outputs against expected results. All the issues that are found must be documented and a process must be put in place to mitigate them.

Besides the compiler, GCC also includes an assembler and linker, providing users with a so-called driver program (gcc for C and g++ for C++). When invoked, the driver program runs preprocessing, compilation, assembly, and linking. The following figure visualizes the GCC compilation process:

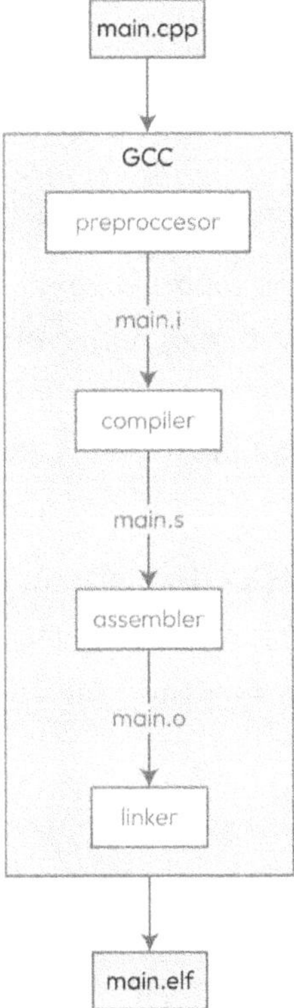

Figure 3.1 – GCC compilation process

In *Figure 3.1*, we see what happens when GCC is used to compile a single file, main.cpp:

1. GCC first runs the preprocessor, adding all header files specified with the #include directive and expanding macros in the translation unit.

2. The result from the preprocessor stage is run through the compiler, generating assembly.

3. The output of the assembly stage is an object file.

4. Finally, the linker links the object file with C and C++ standard libraries and generates an ELF file.

The GCC driver program can be supplied with additional arguments to provide outputs from intermediate phases. To redirect preprocessor output to standard output, one can use the -E flag:

```
arm-none-eabi-g++ -E main.cpp
```

The preceding command will result in a lengthy output if `main.cpp` includes the **C Standard Input and Output (cstdio)** library. You can write a simple `hello world` program and see it for yourself by running the preceding command, or you can use Compiler Explorer.

Compiler Explorer

Compiler Explorer (`https://github.com/compiler-explorer/compiler-explorer`) is an interactive online compiler that shows the assembly output of compiled C++, Rust, Go, and other code. You can try it online (`https://godbolt.org/`). It is a great tool that, by default, shows the assembly output and can be used to explore different language features with different compilers and compiler flags.

Let's use Compiler Explorer to explore the GCC compilation process. We will select **ARM GCC 11.2.1 (none)** as our compiler and provide it with an `-E` flag. **ARM GCC 11.2.1 (none)**, or **arm-none-eabi-gcc**, is the GCC used for Cortex-M architecture. In the following figure, we can see the preprocessor output in Compiler Explorer:

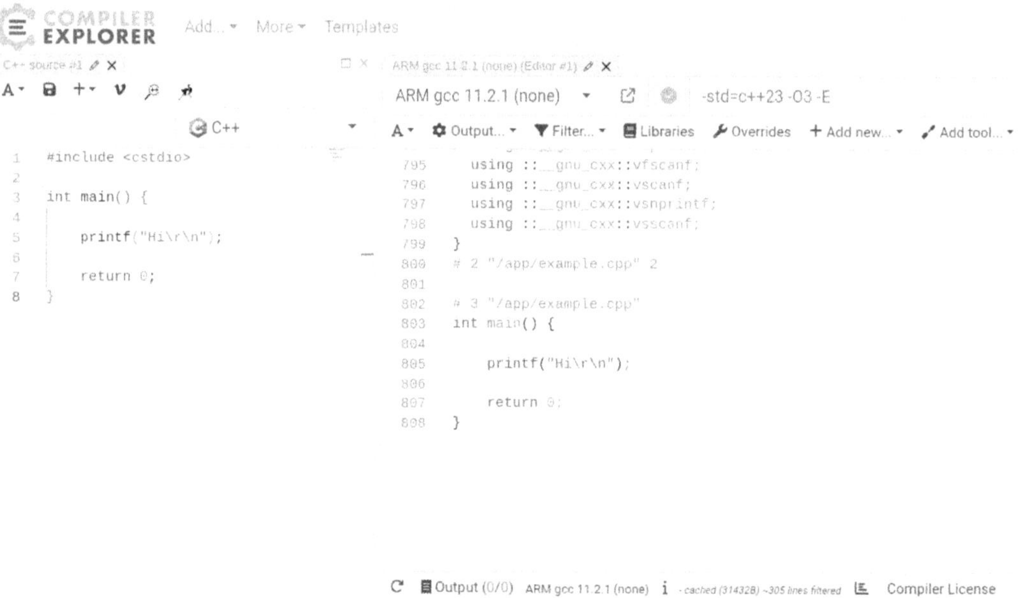

Figure 3.2 – Compiler Explorer: preprocessor output

In *Figure 3.2*, we can see that the preprocessor adds exactly 800 lines to our simple `hello world` example. The preprocessor goes through the `cstdio` file, resolves all preprocessor directives, and pastes the result in the translation unit, resulting in 808 lines of code.

The default view of Compiler Explorer is the assembly output, which we can get by simply removing the -E flag from the previous example, as shown in the following figure:

Figure 3.3 – Compiler Explorer: assembly output

In *Figure 3.3*, we can see the generated assembly output of GCC's compilation process. We can see that the optimization process replaced the printf function with puts. Also, we don't see the body of the puts function because this function is part of the C standard library that we link against. The next steps of the process are as follows:

1. The assembler will generate object code from the assembly code.

2. The linker will link the generated object code with the C standard library that contains the puts implementation (among other functions).

In this simple example, we went through GCC's compilation process, which will not result in the code that we can run on a microcontroller, as we also need to do the following steps:

1. Add clock and hardware peripheral initialization code.

2. Set compiler flags for the architecture and instruction set for our target.

3. Add a startup assembly script containing a reset handler and C and C++ runtime initialization.

4. Add a linker script defining different memory regions for a target, including RAM and Flash regions.

5. Add instructions for the linker to link against specific C and C++ standard libraries.

The output from the last stage of the GCC compilation process, the linking stage, is an **Executable and Linkable Format (ELF)** file. The ELF file is converted into binary or hex format using the objdump tool, as binary and hex formats are usually used by the flashing process to be loaded on the target.

From version 10, GCC has an integrated static analyzer, which can be enabled with the -fanalyzer compiler flag.

Static analyzers

Static analyzers are tools that go through source code and detect potential issues with the code such as undefined behavior, or they check whether the code is compliant with a safety standard such as MISRA® or AUTOSAR®. Not all static analyzers have the same capabilities, and only commercial versions support safety standards checks. Some of the issues that can be detected with static analyzers are as follows:

- Use of uninitialized data
- Out-of-bounds array access
- Null pointers dereference
- Division by zero
- Use after delete, double delete, and other memory management issues

We can enable GCC's static analyzer by providing the GCC driver program with the -fanalyzer flag. Let us take an example of a simple sum function that takes a std::array<int, 4> constant reference and returns the sum shown in the following example:

```cpp
#include <array>
int sum(const std::array<int, 4> &arr) {
    int ret;
    for(int elem: arr) {
        ret += elem;
    }
    return ret;
}
```

The issue with the preceding example is that we are not initializing the ret variable to zero. During the stack allocation of variables in the sum function, the value of the ret variable will be populated with anything on the allocated location, leading to undefined behavior. We can add the -fanalyzer flag in Compiler Explorer and open the compiler output, as shown in the following screenshot:

Figure 3.4 – Compiler Explorer: static analyzer, use of uninitialized value

In *Figure 3.4*, we can see compiler output in a new plane, which we enabled by clicking on **Output (0/42)**. We can see that the static analyzer recognized that we were using an uninitialized variable and issued the warning. GCC, like many other compilers, can issue compiler warnings, and can also detect different issues with code, including uninitialized variables. We can enable regular compiler warnings using flags such as -Wall, -Wextra, -Wpedantic, but in this case, they wouldn't catch uninitialized variables.

We can see this in the following screenshot:

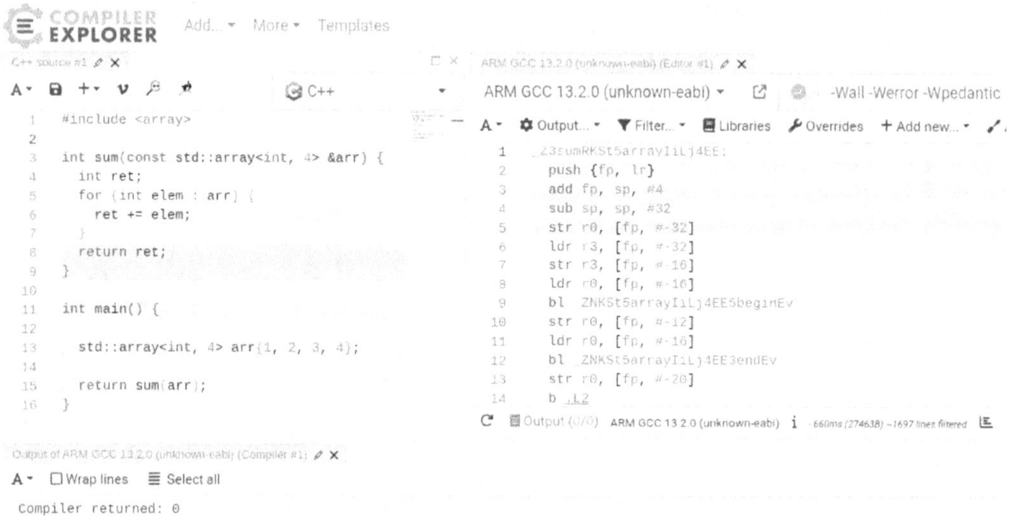

Figure 3.5 – Compiler Explorer: GCC warnings, uninitialized value

In *Figure 3.5*, we can see that GCC didn't issue a warning for uninitialized data using regular compiler warnings. Enabling a static analyzer using the -fanalyzer flag will help detect the issue, but also keep in mind that static analysis takes more time, which might be an issue with larger code bases. There is also a GCC flag, -Wuninitialized, which should generate a warning for uninitialized variables. In this particular example, it will generate a warning only if a program is compiled with an optimization flag different from 0 (e.g., -O2).

Different compilers have different capabilities, including detecting issues with code. If we were to compile this example using the clang compiler (switch the compiler to **armv7-a clang 11.0.1** in Compiler Explorer), we would see that the clang compiler would detect this uninitialized variable issue and emit a warning. Also, static analyzers have different capabilities, so it is a good practice to run your code through several static analyzers, as one may detect issues that the others can't, and vice versa.

Here is another example of a static analyzer in action, detecting out-of-bounds access:

Figure 3.6 – Compiler Explorer: static analyzer, out-of-bounds access

In *Figure 3.6*, we are trying to access the fifth element of an array that has four elements, which will result in undefined behavior. This was caught by the GCC's static analyzer, which issued a descriptive warning. In GCC, warnings can be treated as errors that will result in failed compilation and no ELF file generated. To treat warnings as errors, just add the -Werror compiler flag to the GCC driver program invocation.

There are other commonly used static analyzers, most notably clang-tidy and cppcheck. clang-tidy can be enabled in Compiler Explorer using the **Add tool** option. Both clang-tidy (https://clang.llvm.org/extra/clang-tidy/) and cppcheck (https://cppcheck.sourceforge.io/) are easy to install and use, and as previously stated, it is usually a good idea to use several static analyzers to catch different issues with the code.

Static analyzers are great for catching common programming errors and potential issues with your code or making sure that code is compliant according to a safety standard, but they don't guarantee that the code does what it is supposed to do. To validate the actual functionality of our firmware, we can run manual tests on a target or we can use unit testing to write test cases for individual pieces of our code.

Unit testing

Unit testing is the process of testing units of code by using a test framework that provides infrastructure for setting up tests, running them, and reporting them. So, what is a unit of code? It depends on what we want to test; it can be a function or a software module, or we can reason about unit testing as testing a unit of work. What does the firmware need to do if a user presses a button, or what does it need to do if we receive a specific packet over a **Bluetooth® Low Energy (BLE)** connection?

Depending on the granularity of unit testing, we can test different components of firmware on the individual level and their interaction to ensure proper functionality. Unit tests test the units of code or units of work in isolation from other software components. This forces us to focus on the functionality of said units during the development and split the responsibilities between components more easily, leading to more robust software.

Most of the C++ testing frameworks are not well suited for running on small, embedded targets due to the resulting binary size, most notably, due to the usage of ostream from the standard library. This leaves us with the option to run our unit tests on the host machine instead of the embedded target. This is not to say that unit tests can't be run on embedded targets. Running tests on a target takes more time, as all tests would need to be compiled for the target and flashed to it, and we'd need a report-catching mechanism on the host machine to read test results.

Running tests off the target on a host machine is a common practice. However, there are concerns about this approach, as tests are run on a different architecture where even data types can have different sizes. To address this, one can enforce the use of fixed-width data types (e.g., uint8_t or int32_t). Additionally, there may be differences between the compilers used for the host and target machines, so it is advisable to use the same versions of compilers. Running tests on a host machine is faster and easier, but the differences between architectures and setups can potentially have an impact on test results. There are manual target tests and system and integration tests that can discover potential issues with code functionality and serve as an additional layer of functionality validation.

There are different testing frameworks for C++, and some of the most used are as follows:

- Google Test
- Catch2
- Boost.Test
- CppUTest

We can easily try them in Compiler Explorer by adding the relevant libraries. The first thing to do is to add an **Execution Only** pane, as shown in the following figure:

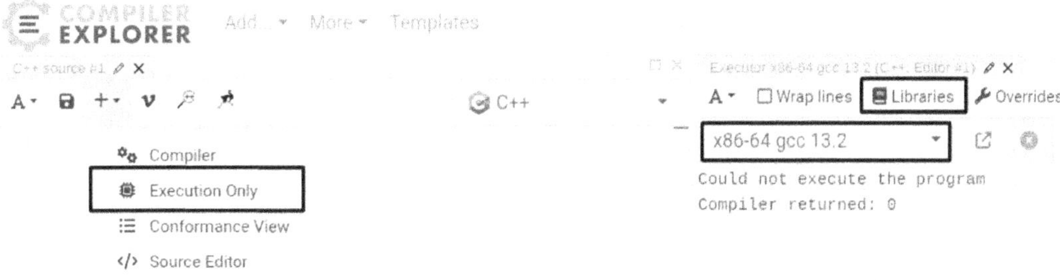

Figure 3.7 – Compiler Explorer: execution pane

In *Figure 3.7*, we added an execution pane and selected **x86-64 gcc 13.2** as the compiler. Now, we need to add the Google Test library by clicking on the **Libraries** button in the execution pane. It will open a new window in which we can search for a library and include it, as shown in the following figure:

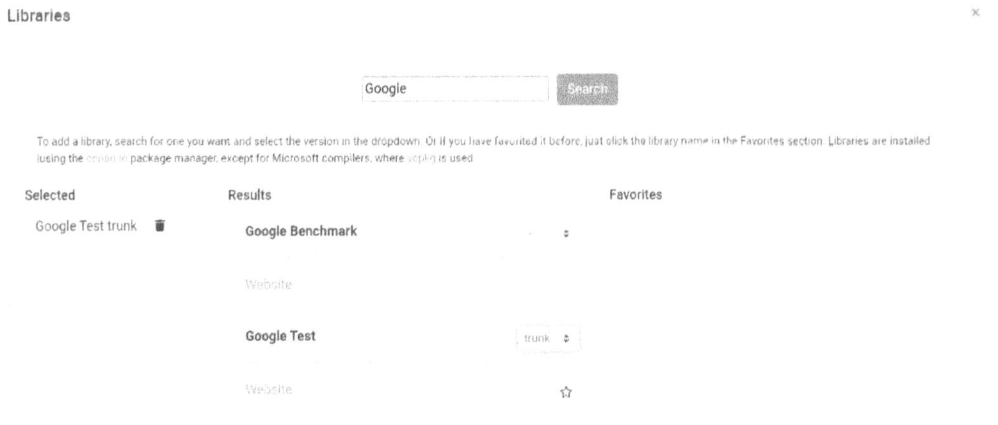

Figure 3.8 – Compiler Explorer: including a library

In *Figure 3.8*, we search for the Google Test library and we add it to the project by selecting the version in the drop-down menu. Let's see how we can test our generic ring buffer implementation from the first chapter using Google Test. The following is the code with ring buffer implementation and a couple of simple tests:

```cpp
#include <array>
#include <cstdio>

#include "gtest/gtest.h"

template <class T, std::size_t N> struct ring_buffer {
  std::array<T, N> arr;
  std::size_t write_idx = 0;
  std::size_t read_idx = 0;
  std::size_t count = 0;
  void push(T t) {
    arr.at(write_idx) = t;
    write_idx = (write_idx + 1) % N;
    if (count < N) {
      count++;
    } else {
      read_idx = (read_idx + 1) % N;
    }
  }
  T pop() {
    if (count == 0) {
      return T{};
    }
    T value = arr.at(read_idx);
    read_idx = (read_idx + 1) % N;
    --count;
    return value;
  }
  bool is_empty() const {
      return count == 0;
  }
  std::size_t get_count() const {
      return count;
```

```cpp
    }
};

TEST(RingBufferInt, PushPop) {
    ring_buffer<int, 2> rb;
    rb.push(1);
    rb.push(2);
    EXPECT_EQ(rb.pop(), 1);
    EXPECT_EQ(rb.pop(), 2);
}

TEST(RingBufferInt, GetCount) {
    ring_buffer<int, 20> rb;
    for(int i = 0; i < 50; i++) {
        rb.push(i);
    }
    EXPECT_EQ(rb.get_count(), 20);

    for(int i = 0; i < 10; i++) {
        rb.pop();
    }
    EXPECT_EQ(rb.get_count(), 10);
}

int main() {
  testing::InitGoogleTest();
  return RUN_ALL_TESTS();
}
```

In the preceding example, the ring buffer implementation is the same as in the first chapter with the addition of the get_count method, which returns the number of elements currently held by the buffer. We defined a test suite, RingBufferInt, using the TEST macro. We specified two tests named PushPop and GetCount.

In the PushPop test, we are testing the push and pop functionality of the ring buffer, making sure that pop will return pushed values in the correct order using the EXPECT_EQ macro.

In the GetCount test, we are checking whether the number of elements held by the buffer matches the intended functionality using the following scenario:

1. We first push 50 values to the buffer, which can hold a maximum of 20 values, making sure that get_count will return 20.

2. We then pop 10 values from the buffer and check whether the count will be equal to 10.

Running the preceding program will result in Google Test generating a report on standard output, as in the following figure:

```
35    };
36
37    TEST(RingBufferInt, PushPop) {
38        ring_buffer<int, 2> rb;
39        rb.push(1);
40        rb.push(2);
41        EXPECT_EQ(rb.pop(), 1);
42        EXPECT_EQ(rb.pop(), 2);
43    }
44
45    TEST(RingBufferInt, GetCount) {
46        ring_buffer<int, 20> rb;
47        for(int i = 0; i < 50; i++) {
48            rb.push(i);
49        }
50        EXPECT_EQ(rb.get_count(), 20);
51
52        for(int i = 0; i < 10; i++) {
53            rb.pop();
54        }
55        EXPECT_EQ(rb.get_count(), 10);
56    }
57
58    int main() {
59      testing::InitGoogleTest();
60      return RUN_ALL_TESTS();
61    }
```

```
Program returned: 0
Program stdout
[==========] Running 2 tests from 1 test suite.
[----------] Global test environment set-up.
[----------] 2 tests from RingBufferInt
[ RUN      ] RingBufferInt.PushPop
[       OK ] RingBufferInt.PushPop (0 ms)
[ RUN      ] RingBufferInt.GetCount
[       OK ] RingBufferInt.GetCount (0 ms)
[----------] 2 tests from RingBufferInt (0 ms total)

[----------] Global test environment tear-down
[==========] 2 tests from 1 test suite ran. (0 ms total)
[  PASSED  ] 2 tests.
```

Figure 3.9 – Compiler Explorer: Google Test execution

In *Figure 3.9*, we see the results of our tests in the execution pane. The TEST macro will ensure that tests are automatically registered in the framework so we don't need to add them manually. This allows us to focus on writing tests utilizing the infrastructure provided by the framework. Google Test offers a lot more, and this example is just a glimpse into its capabilities.

Writing unit tests makes us think about how our code interacts with other software modules in the system. By focusing on units of code, we can write code that is loosely coupled, making our software more flexible and robust. Unit tests are crucial for development techniques such as **Test-Driven Development (TDD)**, which requires us to write tests before we write the code. After we write a unit test, we write the actual code just to pass the test, and then we add more tests, refactor the implementation, and iterate on the process.

Unit tests are a powerful tool for validating the functionality of our code, whether we run them on the target or the host platform. Still, they don't tell us a lot about the performance of our firmware. For that, we need to run the production firmware on the target and measure the performance using profiler tools.

Profiling

Running code on the target and profiling is the best way to ensure the **Worst-Case Execution Time (WCET)** for critical functionality and make necessary optimizations if needed.

The challenge with profiling is that it is an intrusive operation, as the code source needs to be modified or instrumented to enable traces that can tell us more about what is happening internally on the target.

Profiling depends on target capabilities. Some cores have integrated units for tracing, as we saw in the previous chapter, providing profiling that is minimally invasive. Also, some targets have special interfaces that allow high-speed trace data transfer using advanced debugging and tracing probes connected to the host machine. We can see an example of profiling infrastructure used for some Cortex-M targets in the following figure:

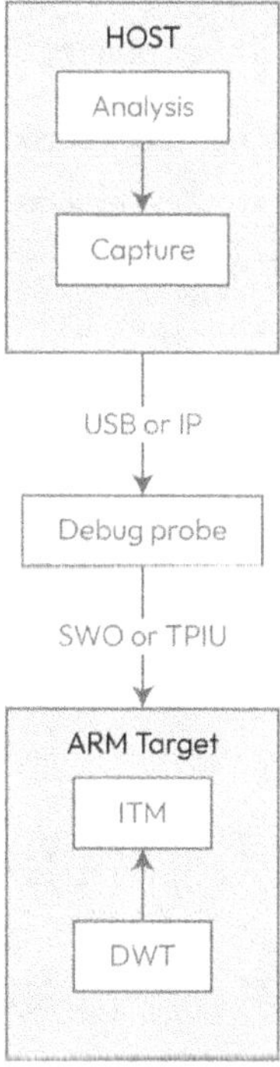

Figure 3.10 – Arm target connected to host machine over a debug probe

In *Figure 3.10*, we can see an Arm target connected over a debugging probe to a host machine. Profiling, or trace data flow, can be described through the next steps:

1. A **Program Counter (PC)** is sampled using DWT and generates an event.

2. ITM sends events generated by DWT and instrumented code over **Single Wire Output SWO** to a debugging probe.

3. The debugging probe transfers trace data to capturing software on the host machine over USB.

4. Capturing software is usually a part of a larger software package that can analyze and visualize captured received data.

In order to have precise information about function execution times, the source code needs to be instrumented by adding instructions that will generate trace data. We saw how this can be achieved in the previous chapter using GCC's compiler features for adding instructions to the entry and exit of every function. This data can be sent using ITM to profiler software running on the host machine. This approach has good accuracy, but by adding instructions to code, we are degrading performances for the sake of measurement.

PC sampling can be less intrusive than code instrumentation, but it is less accurate and can serve only to detect bottlenecks in the firmware without precise timing information.

Some Arm cores have an integrated **Embedded Trace Macrocell (ETM)**. ETM records instruction execution, generates trace data, and sends it to the connected probe. With the instruction trace data, a profiler can measure the execution time of functions accurately and create a call graph of each function call, the same as code instrumentation. ETM enables code profiling without the instrumentation cost.

Code instrumentation is still a very common approach as it depends less on the target's integrated tracing capabilities. SEGGER's SystemView is an example of a profiler for embedded targets. As we briefly discussed in the previous chapter, we need to use SEGGER's SystemView and RTT libraries on the target to enable trace generation. In the following, you can see data generated by SystemView:

Name	Type	Stack Information	Activations	Total Run Time	Time Interrupted	Min Run Time	Max Run Time
ETH_RX	⚡ #100		188	0. 006 848 994 s	0. 000 000 ms	0. 004 357 ms	0. 066 643 ms
ETH_TX	⚡ #99		171	0. 002 918 768 s	0. 000 000 ms	0. 004 393 ms	0. 057 750 ms
SysTick	⚡ #15		10 530	0. 051 237 833 s	0. 000 000 ms	0. 004 643 ms	0. 024 143 ms
Scheduler	↻		2 675	0. 022 078 815 s	0. 315 893 ms	0. 005 179 ms	0. 012 607 ms
IP_Task	@152	1280 @ 0x1FFF537C	1 279	0. 075 248 131 s	3. 413 690 ms	0. 012 179 ms	0. 424 429 ms
IP_WebServer	@151	3072 @ 0x1FFF0454	39	0. 003 670 036 s	0. 014 286 ms	0. 009 821 ms	0. 190 464 ms
Webserver Child	@150	2000 @ 0x1FFF5978	147	0. 028 838 440 s	2. 274 482 ms	0. 009 107 ms	1. 176 750 ms
Webserver Child	@150	2000 @ 0x1FFF6148	63	0. 013 861 399 s	0. 675 161 ms	0. 003 964 ms	1. 140 107 ms
Idle	⏻		1 147	10. 376 365 571 s	54. 282 976 ms	0. 003 429 ms	9. 890 607 ms

Figure 3.11 – SystemView

In *Figure 3.11*, we see the names of functions from instrumented firmware, including minimum and maximum running time. Profiling code can help with the optimization of time-critical sections of firmware, enabling us to ensure the system's timing requirements.

Summary

In this chapter, we discovered the available tools for C++ development in the *Embedded* domain. There is a variety of available development environments and compilers. While commercial solutions come with guaranteed support and have functional safety editions of their tools, free tools are also common and can even be qualified if needed.

Static analyzers can help in avoiding common programming issues and ensure safety guidelines compliances. By using unit tests, we can validate the functionality of our firmware, and profilers can help with detecting bottlenecks, measuring WCET, and ensuring timing requirements.

In the next chapter, we will create a development environment for C++ for embedded applications using selected free tools.

Join our community on Discord

Join our community's Discord space for discussions with the author and other readers:

https://packt.link/embeddedsystems

Setting Up the Development Environment for a C++ Embedded Project

In the previous chapter, we explored the embedded tools ecosystem and reviewed the most widely used tools in the industry. Now, we'll set requirements for a modern embedded development environment and each of its components. Then, we'll set up our development environment for running the examples that will be provided in the remainder of this book.

One of the major selling points of integrated environments is their ease of use. They provide you with everything you need through simple installation steps. Customized environments, on the other hand, require all components to be installed individually, including all the dependencies for each component. It's important to ensure reproducible builds and a reliable debugging environment, so containerizing customized environments is of great importance.

You'll be provided with a Docker container for the development environment that we'll be using in this book, but we'll analyze all of its components individually. Understanding the tools that we use in our daily work is necessary to comprehend and control the processes behind them.

In this chapter, we're going to cover the following main topics:

- Requirements for a modern software development environment
- Containerized development environment
- Containerized development environment and Visual Studio Code

Technical requirements

For this chapter, you will need to have Docker installed (`https://www.docker.com/`). Please follow the installation instructions provided for your specific operating system. This chapter will guide you through the basic steps for downloading and running a container with a preconfigured development environment. For more advanced Docker usage, please refer to the official Docker documentation available on their website.

The code from this chapter is available on GitHub (`https://github.com/PacktPublishing/Cpp-in-Embedded-Systems/tree/main/Chapter04`).

Requirements for a modern software development environment

Firmware development is no different than any other form of software development and the tools we use are crucial for effective work. To make this book and the examples accessible as much as possible, the first requirement we'll set is to use free tools. The **compiler** is the basis and the most important part of every development requirement, so let's define the requirements and choose a compiler for our needs.

Compiler

Since we're exploring modern C++, we'll require compiler support for the C++23 standard. The latest version of **ARM GNU Toolchain** (based on GCC) is 13.2; it supports C++23 and is free. It's also the most commonly used free compiler toolchain for ARM development, making it a perfect fit for our compiler.

ARM GNU Toolchain comes with C and C++ compilers, **GNU Debugger (GDB)**, which we'll use for debugging, and other useful tools, such as `objcopy`, `objdump`, `size`, and more, and can be downloaded from `https://developer.arm.com/downloads/-/arm-gnu-toolchain-downloads`. The architecture that we need for Arm Cortex-M is `arm-none-eabi`.

ARM GNU Toolchain for `arm-none-eabi` is available for all common host architectures:

- GNU/Linux x86_64 and AArch64 host architectures
- Windows x86 host architecture only (compatible with x86_64)
- macOS x86_64 and Apple silicon

Compiling a single file or few files is as simple as running a few commands in the terminal, but building even the simplest embedded projects involves the following steps:

1. Compile all C and C++ source files, the file that contains the main function, and at least several files from **Hardware Abstraction Layer (HAL)**. You'll learn more about HAL in *Chapter 12*.

2. Set up compiler include paths.

3. Set up compiler C and C++ flags.

4. Set up compiler define macros.

5. Compile the startup assembly script.

6. Set up linker options, including the linker script, static libraries, CPU architecture and instruction set, and standard library options.

Upon doing this, we must convert the ELF file into other formats that are commonly used by flashing programs, such as `bin` and `hex`.

Running all of these tasks manually in the terminal would be a tedious process, so the next requirement for our development environment is *build automation*. The first candidate for build automation is the **make** utility. It's a common tool that's used for automating huge amounts of software projects across different industries. It would be a good fit for the task, but it's an old tool with odd syntax. However, we can use **CMake**, a more flexible tool with more modern syntax that can generate Makefiles for us.

Build automation

CMake isn't an actual build automation tool, but it generates files for other automation tools, such as the make utility. It's cross-platform, free, and open source software for the build automation process, which involves testing, packaging, and installing software. It does so by using a compiler-independent method.

We'll use **CMake** to help us generate targets for the make utility that will do the following:

- Configure source files, including paths and linker settings to build ELF files
- Convert ELF files into hex and binary formats
- Start the simulator and load it with the generated ELF file

We'll use build automation not only to build the firmware but also to start the simulator that will run the firmware.

Simulator

To make this book accessible to a wide audience, we'll be using a **simulator** to run the examples that have been compiled for the ARM Cortex M target. **Renode** (`https://github.com/renode/renode`) is an open source simulating framework with good support for ARM targets.

Renode allows you to run simulations with multiple targets and simulate wireless and wired connections between them. We'll use it in a simple scenario that involves running simulations on a single target. Renode can also start a GDB server, allowing you to connect to it and debug the target.

We'll integrate simulation execution and debugging, as well as compiler and build automation, using the highly configurable **Visual Studio Code**.

Code editor

Visual Studio Code is a modern and flexible code editor. It provides us with all the extensions we need to integrate all our tools into a single environment. We'll install the following extensions in Visual Studio Code:

- **C/C++**: This extension provides syntax highlighting, code autocompletion, and code navigation
- **Cortex-Debug**: This extension allows debugging to be performed via GDB
- **CS 128 Clang-Tidy**: This extension integrates clang-tidy into Visual Studio Code
- **Dev Containers**: This extension attaches to running a container and uses it for development purposes

We'll base our development environment on a Docker container. Visual Studio Code will attach to that container and use it.

Containerized development environment

The Visual Studio Code Dev Containers extension allows Visual Studio Code to attach to a running Docker container and use all the tools inside it that have been installed. To use this feature, we need to build a container.

We'll use Docker to build a container with the following tools:

- ARM GNU Toolchain version 13.2
- CMake and the make utility
- Renode version 1.14

Make sure you've installed Docker on your host machine by following the instructions provided on the official website (`https://docs.docker.com`).

You can find the **Dockerfile** that will be used to build the container in this book's GitHub repository (`https://github.com/PacktPublishing/Cpp-in-Embedded-Systems`), in the `Chapter04` folder.

There's also an image that you can download from Docker Hub (`https://hub.docker.com/`). You can pull it using the following command:

```
$ docker pull mahmutbegovic/cpp_in_embedded_systems:latest
```

Make sure that the Docker daemon has been started by following the instructions for your platform; they're available on the official website. After downloading the image, start Docker using the following command:

```
$ docker run -d -it --name dev_env mahmutbegovic/cpp_in_embedded_systems
```

This will start the Docker container in detached and interactive mode. If you've already created A Docker container using the `docker run` command, you need to start it by running the following command:

```
$ docker start dev_env
```

To access the bash of the started container, we can use the following command:

```
$ docker exec -it dev_env /bin/bash
```

As shown in the following screenshot, we can run various commands to ensure the compiler, debugger, simulator, and other tools have been installed in the container:

```
constexpr@ec3be6044abb:/workspace$ arm-none-eabi-g++ --version
arm-none-eabi-g++ (Arm GNU Toolchain 13.2.rel1 (Build arm-13.7)) 13.2.1 20231009
Copyright (C) 2023 Free Software Foundation, Inc.
This is free software; see the source for copying conditions.  There is NO
warranty; not even for MERCHANTABILITY or FITNESS FOR A PARTICULAR PURPOSE.

constexpr@ec3be6044abb:/workspace$ arm-none-eabi-gdb --version
GNU gdb (Arm GNU Toolchain 13.2.rel1 (Build arm-13.7)) 13.2.90.20231008-git
Copyright (C) 2023 Free Software Foundation, Inc.
License GPLv3+: GNU GPL version 3 or later <http://gnu.org/licenses/gpl.html>
This is free software: you are free to change and redistribute it.
There is NO WARRANTY, to the extent permitted by law.
constexpr@ec3be6044abb:/workspace$ cmake --version
cmake version 3.16.3

CMake suite maintained and supported by Kitware (kitware.com/cmake).
constexpr@ec3be6044abb:/workspace$ make --version
GNU Make 4.2.1
Built for x86_64-pc-linux-gnu
Copyright (C) 1988-2016 Free Software Foundation, Inc.
License GPLv3+: GNU GPL version 3 or later <http://gnu.org/licenses/gpl.html>
This is free software: you are free to change and redistribute it.
There is NO WARRANTY, to the extent permitted by law.
constexpr@ec3be6044abb:/workspace$ renode --version
Renode v1.15.0.27975
  build: 9111b18e-202403181532
  build type: Release
  runtime: Mono 4.0.30319.42000
constexpr@ec3be6044abb:/workspace$ 
```

Figure 4.1 – Development environment container bash

Figure 4.1 shows the expected outputs from the commands we used to check the versions of the tools that we've installed.

We can use the running container as a self-contained environment. Let's start by cloning the project GitHub repository (`https://github.com/PacktPublishing/Cpp-in-Embedded-Systems`):

```
$ git clone https://github.com/PacktPublishing/Cpp-in-Embedded-Systems.git
```

Once you've done this, go to the `Chapter04/bare` folder. This folder contains the *Hello, World!* example firmware for STM32F072 that we'll run in Renode. The project is organized into the following folders:

- `app`: Contains the business layer code, including `main.cpp`

- `hal`: Contains the HAL C++ code

- `platform`: Contains platform-specific code, including the ST-provided HAL layer in C and the CMSIS, startup, and linker scripts
- `renode_scripts`: Contains Renode simulator scripts

In the project folder, you'll also see `CMakeLists.txt`, a CMake file that we'll use to specify how the firmware is built. Let's learn how to use CMake with the help of an example.

Building the Hello, World! program using CMake

We can use CMake to specify a toolchain, source files, compiler include paths, and compiler flags. The first thing we must do in a CMake file is specify the CMake version that's in use, as shown in the following line:

```
cmake_minimum_required(VERSION 3.13)
```

CMake is a powerful tool that allows us to write highly flexible build files. We can write toolchain details in separate files and include them in the main project file, which would allow us to reuse them for different architectures. However, in our example, we have the toolchain details in the main CMake file. The following lines specify various toolchain components:

```
set(CMAKE_C_COMPILER "arm-none-eabi-gcc")
set(CMAKE_CXX_COMPILER "arm-none-eabi-g++")
set(CMAKE_ASM_COMPILER "arm-none-eabi-gcc")
```

Using the `CMAKE_C_COMPILER`, `CMAKE_CXX_COMPILER`, and `CMAKE_ASM_COMPILER` CMake variables, we specify paths for the C, C++, and assembler compilers, respectively. We need to use all three since our project contains ST-provided HAL written in C, our C++ code, and an assembly startup script.

Now, we must specify various compiler options and preprocessor macros by running the following lines in our `CMakeLists.txt` file:

```
set(CDEFS "-DUSE_HAL_DRIVER -DSTM32F072xB")
set(MCU "-mcpu=cortex-m0 -mthumb")
set(COMMON_FLAGS "${MCU} ${CDEFS}  -fdata-sections -ffunction-sections
-Wno-address-of-packed-member -Wall -Wextra -Wno-unused-parameter")
set(CMAKE_C_FLAGS "${COMMON_FLAGS}")
set(CMAKE_CXX_FLAGS "${COMMON_FLAGS} -Wno-register -fno-exceptions -fno-
rtti -fno-threadsafe-statics")
```

Here, we set the `USE_HAL_DRIVER` and `STM32F072xB` compile-time macros, which are used by ST's HAL. Then, we set some compiler flags that are used for both C and C++ files:

- `-mcpu=cortex-m0` and `-mthumb`: Architecture-specific flags.
- `-fdata-sections`: This option tells the compiler to place data items in their own sections in the resulting objectfile. This can be useful for optimization purposes (removing unused sections).
- `-ffunction-sections`: Similar to `-fdata-sections`, but for functions. Each function gets its own section, allowing the linker to potentially discard unused functions.
- `-Wno-address-of-packed-member`: Suppresses warnings related to taking the address of a packed member of a structure.
- `-Wall`: Enables all the common warning messages recommended for normal operation.
- `-Wextra`: Enables extra warning flags that aren't enabled by `-Wall`.
- `-Wno-unused-parameter`: Disables warnings about unused parameters in functions.

Then, we set the C++-specific compiler flags:

- `-Wno-register`: Disables warnings about the use of the `register` keyword, which is deprecated in modern C++ but might be used in legacy code
- `-fno-exceptions`: Disables support for exceptions in C++
- `-fno-rtti`: Disables **Run-Time Type Information (RTTI)**
- `-fno-threadsafe-statics`: Prevents the compiler from using extra code to ensure that static local variables are initialized in a thread-safe way

The next part of our CMake file is project-specific: we must declare a new project, give it a name, enable the languages we want to use, and specify a CMake target, source files, and linker options.

This is our basic setup compiler setup for a C++ (mixed with C) project:

```
project(bare VERSION 1.0.6)
enable_language(C CXX ASM)

set(CMAKE_CXX_STANDARD 17)
set(CMAKE_CXX_STANDARD_REQUIRED True)

# global include directories
include_directories(
    ${CMAKE_SOURCE_DIR}/platform/inc
    ${CMAKE_SOURCE_DIR}/platform/CMSIS/Device/ST/STM32F0xx/Include
```

```
    ${CMAKE_SOURCE_DIR}/platform/CMSIS/Include
    ${CMAKE_SOURCE_DIR}/platform/STM32F0xx_HAL_Driver/Inc
    ${CMAKE_SOURCE_DIR}/app/inc
    ${CMAKE_SOURCE_DIR}/hal/uart/inc
    ${CMAKE_SOURCE_DIR}/hal/inc
    )
set(EXECUTABLE ${PROJECT_NAME}.elf)
add_executable(
    ${EXECUTABLE}
    platform/STM32F0xx_HAL_Driver/Src/stm32f0xx_hal.c
    platform/STM32F0xx_HAL_Driver/Src/stm32f0xx_hal_cortex.c
    platform/STM32F0xx_HAL_Driver/Src/stm32f0xx_hal_gpio.c
    platform/STM32F0xx_HAL_Driver/Src/stm32f0xx_hal_rcc.c
    platform/STM32F0xx_HAL_Driver/Src/stm32f0xx_hal_uart.c
    platform/STM32F0xx_HAL_Driver/Src/stm32f0xx_hal_uart_ex.c
    platform/startup_stm32f072xb.s
    platform/src/stm32f0xx_hal_msp.c
    platform/src/stm32f0xx_it.c
    platform/src/system_stm32f0xx.c
    app/src/main.cpp
    hal/uart/src/uart_stm32.cpp
    )
```

In the preceding CMake code, we have TARGET. This represents an entity that's being built by a CMake, be it the entire firmware (an executable file) or a static library. In our case, the target is the entire firmware, and the target name is created using the project name and .elf suffix, meaning CMake will create a bare.elf target for us.

The remaining step is to specify linker options using the following lines:

```
target_link_options(
    ${EXECUTABLE}
    PUBLIC
    -T${CMAKE_SOURCE_DIR}/platform/STM32F072C8Tx_FLASH.ld
    -mcpu=cortex-m0
    -mthumb
    -specs=nano.specs
    -Wl,--no-warn-rwx-segments
    -Wl,-Map=${PROJECT_NAME}.map,--cref
    -Wl,--gc-sections)
```

Here, we specify the linker script to be used – that is, STM32F072C8Tx_FLASH.ld – set a target CPU and instruction set, and specify the new-lib nano system library and map file to be created.

Now, let's build the firmware using CMake.

Building a firmware using CMake

Here, we'll create a build folder and configure the build in Debug mode using the following commands:

```
$ cd Cpp-in-Embedded-Systems/Chapter04/bare/
$ mkdir build && cd build
$ cmake .. -DCMAKE_BUILD_TYPE=Debug
```

If you list the files in the build folder using ls -1, you'll see that CMake generated Makefile, which is used to build the firmware. Let's run it to build the firmware:

```
$ make -j4
```

You should see the following output:

```
constexpr@ec3be6044abb:/workspace/Cpp-in-Embedded-Systems/Chapter04/bare/build$ make -j4
Scanning dependencies of target bare.elf
[ 15%] Building C object CMakeFiles/bare.elf.dir/platform/STM32F0xx_HAL_Driver/Src/stm32f0xx_hal_cortex.c.o
[ 15%] Building C object CMakeFiles/bare.elf.dir/platform/STM32F0xx_HAL_Driver/Src/stm32f0xx_hal_rcc.c.o
[ 23%] Building C object CMakeFiles/bare.elf.dir/platform/STM32F0xx_HAL_Driver/Src/stm32f0xx_hal_gpio.c.o
[ 30%] Building C object CMakeFiles/bare.elf.dir/platform/STM32F0xx_HAL_Driver/Src/stm32f0xx_hal.c.o
[ 38%] Building C object CMakeFiles/bare.elf.dir/platform/STM32F0xx_HAL_Driver/Src/stm32f0xx_hal_uart.c.o
[ 46%] Building C object CMakeFiles/bare.elf.dir/platform/STM32F0xx_HAL_Driver/Src/stm32f0xx_hal_uart_ex.c.o
[ 53%] Building ASM object CMakeFiles/bare.elf.dir/platform/startup_stm32f072xb.s.o
[ 69%] Building C object CMakeFiles/bare.elf.dir/platform/src/stm32f0xx_it.c.o
[ 69%] Building C object CMakeFiles/bare.elf.dir/platform/src/stm32f0xx_hal_msp.c.o
[ 76%] Building C object CMakeFiles/bare.elf.dir/platform/src/system_stm32f0xx.c.o
[ 84%] Building CXX object CMakeFiles/bare.elf.dir/app/src/main.cpp.o
[ 92%] Building CXX object CMakeFiles/bare.elf.dir/hal/uart/src/uart_stm32.cpp.o
[100%] Linking CXX executable bare.elf
   text    data     bss     dec     hex filename
   6336      20    1572    7928    1ef8 bare.elf
[100%] Built target bare.elf
```

Figure 4.2 – Building the firmware

Figure 4.2 shows the output of building the firmware. We can run the resulting ELF file, bare.elf, in Renode using the following command:

```
$ make run_in_renode
```

This will start the simulator using the `stm32f072.resc` Renode script from the `renode_scripts` folder. The script will create a new Renode machine using the STM32F072 target architecture and load it with the `bare.elf` file. We'll see the following as part of the terminal output:

```
constexpr@ec3be6044abb:/workspace/Cpp-in-Embedded-Systems/Chapter04/bare/build$ make run_in_renode
[100%] Built target bare.elf
11:04:33.7803 [INFO] Loaded monitor commands from: /opt/renode_1.15.0_portable/scripts/monitor.py
Renode, version 1.15.0.27975 (9111b18e-202403181532)

(monitor) i @/workspace/Cpp-in-Embedded-Systems/Chapter04/bare/renode_scripts/stm32f072.resc
11:04:34.1268 [INFO] Including script: /workspace/Cpp-in-Embedded-Systems/Chapter04/bare/renode_scripts/stm32f072.resc
11:04:34.1445 [INFO] System bus created.
Starting emulation...
11:04:35.7041 [INFO] cpu: Guessing VectorTableOffset value to be 0x8000000.
11:04:35.7169 [INFO] cpu: Setting initial values: PC = 0x9001379, SP = 0x20004000.
11:04:35.7125 [INFO] machine-0: Machine started.
(machine-0) start
Starting emulation...
11:04:35.8857 [INFO] usart2: [host: 0.3s (+0.3s)|virt: 0s (+0s)] Hello world !
(machine-0) 11:04:36.2208 [INFO] usart2: [host: 0.64s (+0.34s)|virt: 0.11s (+0.11s)] While loop 1000 ms ping ...
11:04:36.5125 [INFO] usart2: [host: 0.93s (+0.29s)|virt: 0.22s (+0.11s)] While loop 1000 ms ping ...
11:04:36.7494 [INFO] usart2: [host: 1.17s (+0.24s)|virt: 0.34s (+0.11s)] While loop 1000 ms ping ...
11:04:37.0430 [INFO] usart2: [host: 1.46s (+0.29s)|virt: 0.43s (+0.11s)] While loop 1000 ms ping ...
```

Figure 4.3 – Running firmware in Renode

Figure 4.3 shows the output of the simulation running in Renode in console mode with GUI disabled. To stop the simulation, type *q* and press *Enter*.

Keep in mind that if you stop or reset the Docker container, all the changes, including the cloned GitHub repository, will be lost. To prevent this from happening, you need to save them using the `docker commit` command.

At this point, we have a pretty development environment contained in a Docker container. However, to fully utilize it, we must connect it to Visual Studio Code.

Containerized development environment and Visual Studio Code

To start, install Visual Studio Code (`https://code.visualstudio.com/`). Once you've done this, go to **Extensions** and search for and install the following extensions:

- C/C++
- Cortex-Debug
- CS 128 Clang-Tidy
- Dev Containers

Once you've done this, open **View| Command Palette** (*Ctrl + Shift + P*), find **Dev Containers: Attach to Running Container,** and select dev_env. This should open a new Visual Studio Code window where the container's name is in the bottom left bar:

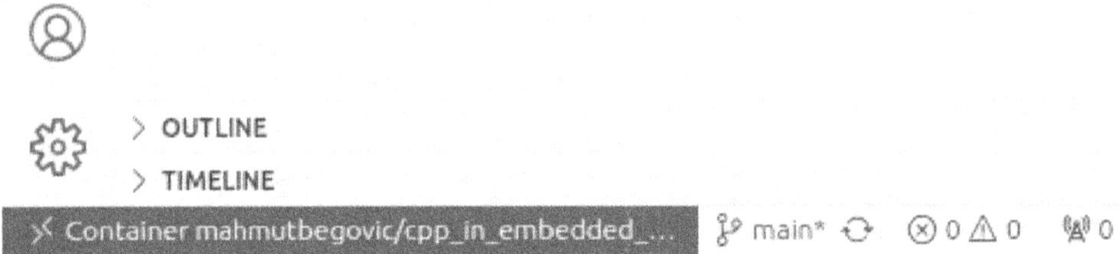

Figure 4.4 – Visual Studio Code attached to a running container

Figure 4.4 shows that Visual Studio Code was successfully attached to the running container. Now, let's open the project folder at /workspace/Cpp-in-Embedded-Systems/Chapter04/bare. Open main.cpp in the **EXPLORER** view and set a breakpoint on line 23, as shown in the following screenshot:

```cpp
#include <cstdint>

#include <hal.hpp>
#include <uart_stm32.hpp>
#include <stm32f072xb.h>

int main()
{
    hal::init();

    hal::uart_stm32 uart(USART2);
    uart.init();

    uart.puts("Hello world !\r\n");

    std::uint32_t time_prev = hal::time::get_ms();
    constexpr std::uint32_t c_1000_ms = 1000;
    while(true)
    {
        if(auto time_now = hal::time::get_ms();
            time_now - time_prev > c_1000_ms)
        {
            uart.puts("While loop 1000 ms ping ...\r\n");
            time_prev = time_now;
        }
    }
}
```

Figure 4.5 – Setting a breakpoint in Visual Studio Code

After setting a breakpoint, as shown in *Figure 4.5*, select **Run| Start Debugging** (*F5*). This will do the following:

- Configure the project in debug mode

- Start the simulator and load ELF

- Connect the GDB client to the GDB server running in the simulator

- Allow you to debug the target running in the simulator

If everything has been set up correctly, the program flow will stop on line 23, and you'll see the following output:

```
18        while(true)
19        {
20            if(auto time_now = hal::time::get_ms();
21                time_now - time_prev > c_1000_ms)
22            {
23                uart.puts("While loop 1000 ms ping ...\r\n");
24                time_prev = time_now;
25            }
26        }
27    }


PROBLEMS    OUTPUT    DEBUG CONSOLE    TERMINAL    ···          Filter (e.g. text, !exclude, \escape)

Reset_Handler () at /workspace/Cpp-in-Embedded-Systems/Chapter04/bare/platform/startup_stm32f072xb.s:52
52           ldr    r0, =_estack
Program stopped, probably due to a reset and/or halt issued by debugger
Starting emulation...

No such command or device: continue

Breakpoint 1, main () at /workspace/Cpp-in-Embedded-Systems/Chapter04/bare/app/src/main.cpp:23
23                    uart.puts("While loop 1000 ms ping ...\r\n");
```

Figure 4.6 – Visual Studio Code program flow

Figure 4.6 shows that the program flow stopped on line 23. We can switch to the **TERMINAL** view to see the output from Renode. Renode is in console mode, and it will also display **UART**. Let's switch to the **TERMINAL** view and hit **Continue** (*F5*). You should see the following output:

```
18        while(true)
19        {
20            if(auto time_now = hal::time::get_ms();
21               time_now - time_prev > c_1000_ms)
22            {
23                uart.puts("While loop 1000 ms ping ...\r\n");
24                time_prev = time_now;
25            }
26        }
```

PROBLEMS   OUTPUT   DEBUG CONSOLE   TERMINAL   PORTS ②   MEMORY   XRTOS

```
07:56:00.7048 [INFO] cpu: Guessing VectorTableOffset value to be 0x8000000.
07:56:00.7049 [INFO] cpu: Setting initial values: PC = 0x8001379, SP = 0x20004000.
07:56:00.7050 [INFO] machine-0: Machine resumed.
07:56:01.3680 [WARNING] sysbus: [cpu: 0x8000270] (tag: 'FLASH_INTERFACE') ReadDoubleWord from non existi
ng peripheral at 0x40022000, returning 0x00000000.
07:56:01.3682 [WARNING] sysbus: [cpu: 0x8000270] (tag: 'FLASH_INTERFACE') WriteDoubleWord to non existin
g peripheral at 0x40022000, value 0x10.
07:56:01.3902 [INFO] usart2: [host: 1.58s (+1.58s}|virt: 0s (+0s)] Hello world !
08:33:31.5077 [INFO] usart2: [host: 2.25ks (+2.25ks)|virt: 0.11s (+0.11s)] While loop 1000 ms ping ...
```

Figure 4.7 – Visual Studio Code Renode output

In *Figure 4.7*, we can see the Renode output in Visual Studio Code's **TERMINAL** view. To be able to debug assembly files, we need to do the following in Visual Studio Code:

1.   Go to **File|Preferences|Settings**.

2.   Search for Allow Breakpoints Everywhere and select the relevant checkbox.

Now, we can set a breakpoint in **platform/startup_stm32f072xb.s** on line 87, stop the debugging session, and run it again. The program flow should stop, as shown here:

```
87        bl SystemInit
88    /* Call static constructors */
89      bl __libc_init_array
90    /* Call the application's entry point.*/
91      bl main
92
93    LoopForever:
94        b LoopForever
95
96
97    .size Reset_Handler, .-Reset_Handler
98
99    /**
```

PROBLEMS   OUTPUT   DEBUG CONSOLE   TERMINAL   PORTS ②   MEMORY   XRTOS

```
Output radix now set to decimal 10, hex a, octal 12.
Input radix now set to decimal 10, hex a, octal 12.
Reset_Handler () at /workspace/Cpp-in-Embedded-Systems/Chapter04/bare/platform/startup_stm32f072xb.s:52
52          ldr    r0, =_estack
Program stopped, probably due to a reset and/or halt issued by debugger
Starting emulation...

No such command or device: continue

Breakpoint 2, Reset_Handler () at /workspace/Cpp-in-Embedded-Systems/Chapter04/bare/platform/startup_stm32
```

Figure 4.8 – Visual Studio Code assembly debugging

In *Figure 4.8*, we can see that the program flow executes the `SystemInit` function on line 87 of the assembly startup script, before the `main` function. If we use **Step Into** (*F11*), the program flow will enter the `SystemInit` function and Visual Studio Code will open `platform/src/system_stm32f0xx.c` file. If you keep moving using **Step Over** (*F10*), you'll eventually enter the main function. This shows us that `main` isn't the first function to be called.

Note that `Reset_Handler` from `startup_stm32f072xb.s` is the entry point of the firmware. This is defined in the linker script (`platform/STM32F072C8Tx_FLASH.ld`). It does the following:

- **Initializes the stack pointer**: It sets the initial stack pointer from the end of the stack (`_estack`).
- **Copies data**: It copies the initialization values from flash memory to SRAM for the data section, which ensures that initialized global/static variables are set up correctly.
- **Zeroes BSS**: It clears the BSS section by setting it to zero, which is required for uninitialized global/static variables.
- **Calls SystemInit**: The `SystemInit` function is used to set the default system clock (system clock source, PLL multiplier and divider factors, AHB/APBx prescalers, and flash settings).
- **Calls __libc_init_array**: The `__libc_init_array` function is used to initialize the static constructors in a C++ program or to run initialization functions in C programs.
- **Calls main**: This operation concludes the activities of the startup script and transfers program flow to the `main` function.

With our modern development environment now fully set up, we're ready to dive into learning C++ for embedded systems. The Renode simulator allows us to run, test, and debug our firmware efficiently, eliminating the need for physical hardware in the initial stages of development. This provides a flexible and efficient solution for embedded system learning and testing.

Summary

In this chapter, we defined the components of our development environment for C++ in embedded systems. We went through all of its components using a Docker container, which we connected to Visual Studio Code to enable a seamless development experience and debugging.

We also set up compiler flags using CMake, ran the firmware using the Renode simulator, and learned how to set up our C and C++ runtime environment by going through the relevant assembly startup script using a debugger.

In the next chapter, we'll use the development environment we created in this chapter to learn more about classes in C++.

Get This Book's PDF Version and Exclusive Extras

Scan the QR code (or go to packtpub.com/unlock). Search for this book by name, confirm the edition, and then follow the steps on the page.

Note: Keep your invoice handy. Purchases made directly from Packt don't require an invoice.

Part 2

C++ Fundamentals

After the introduction to C++ in embedded development, the book shifts focus to covering C++ fundamentals for newcomers and readers with limited prior experience. This part delves into core language features such as classes, including inheritance and runtime polymorphism, along with other fundamental concepts. It also explores the various error handling mechanisms available in C++, including the use of exceptions.

This part has the following chapters:

- *Chapter 5, Classes – Building Blocks of C++ Applications*
- *Chapter 6, Beyond Classes – Fundamental C++ Concepts*
- *Chapter 7, Strengthening Firmware – Practical C++ Error Handling Methods*

5

Classes – Building Blocks of C++ Applications

Classes in C++ are means of organizing code into logical units. They allow us to structure data and functions that perform operations on that data in blueprints. These blueprints can be used to build instances of the classes, known as **objects**. We can initialize objects with data, manipulate them by calling functions or methods on them, store them in containers, or pass their references to objects of other classes to make the interaction between different parts of a system.

Classes are the basic building blocks of C++ applications. They help us organize code in units with isolated responsibility reflecting dependencies and interactions with other parts of the system. They can be combined or extended, allowing us to reuse their functionality and add additional capabilities. We use them to make abstractions of different parts of an embedded system, including low-level components such as **Universal Asynchronous Receiver/Transmitter (UART)** drivers and libraries or business logic components such as a cellular modem library.

The goal of this chapter is to delve into C++ classes and learn how we can use them to write better code. In this chapter, we're going to cover the following main topics:

- Encapsulation
- Storage duration and initialization
- Inheritance and dynamic polymorphism

Technical requirements

To get the most out of this chapter, I strongly recommend using Compiler Explorer (`https://godbolt.org/`) as you read through the examples. Select GCC as your compiler and target x86 architecture. This will allow you to see standard output (stdio) results and better observe the code's behavior. As we are using a lot of modern C++ features make sure to select C++23 standard, by adding `-std=c++23` in compiler options box.

The examples from this chapter are available on GitHub (`https://github.com/PacktPublishing/Cpp-in-Embedded-Systems/tree/main/Chapter05`).

Encapsulation

Encapsulation is a programming concept that organizes code into units that contain both data and functions that operate on that data. It is not strictly related to **Object-Oriented Programming (OOP)** and is often used in other programming paradigms. Encapsulation allows us to decouple code into units with single responsibilities, making the code easier to reason about, improving readability, and facilitating maintenance.

In terms of OOP, encapsulation can also refer to hiding an object's members or restricting access to these members from the outside. In C++, this can be achieved using access specifiers. C++ has the following specifiers:

- Public
- Private
- Protected

Public and **private** are the most commonly used specifiers. They give us the ability to control the interface of the class, that is, to control which class members are available to the users of a class. The following example demonstrates how to define a class with public and private access sections, demonstrating the concept of encapsulation:

```cpp
#include <cstdint>

class uart {
public:
    uart(std::uint32_t baud = 9600): baudrate_(baud) {}
    void init() {
        write_brr(calculate_uartdiv());
    }
```

```cpp
private:
    std::uint32_t baudrate_;
    std::uint8_t calculate_uartdiv() {
        return baudrate_ / 32000;
    }
    void write_brr(std::uint8_t) {}
};

int main () {
    uart uart1(115200);
    uart1.init();
    return 0;
}
```

In this example, the uart class has public and private access sections. Let's go through the code step by step:

- The public section includes a constructor that initializes the baudrate_ private member variable

- We also have an init method in the public section, in which we write a value to a **Bit Rate Register (BRR)**, which is specific to the STM32 platform, using the write_brr private method

- The value written to the BRR register is calculated in the calculate_uartdiv private method

As we can see, methods with a public access specifier within the uart class can use private member variables and methods. However, if we tried to use write_brr on the uart1 object, as in uart1.write_brr(5), the compilation of the program would fail.

The private access specifier allows us to hide methods and data from the user of our class (in this case, the main function). This helps us define a clear interface for our classes in C++. By controlling which methods a user of the class can use, we are not only protecting the class but also the user from unwanted behavior.

This example serves the purpose of explaining access specifiers in C++, but let's also use it to explain the init method. Why do we need it if we have a constructor?

The purpose of init is to allow us to fully control the initialization of hardware. The object may also be constructed as a global or static variable. The initialization of static and global objects is done before reaching the main function and initializing hardware. That is why some kind of init method is common in classes in embedded projects. Using it, we can ensure that all hardware peripherals are initialized in the correct order.

The default access specifier for classes in C++ is private, so we could write the definition of the uart class from the previous example as follows:

```cpp
class uart {
    std::uint32_t baudrate_;
    std::uint8_t calculate_uartdiv();
    void write_brr(std::uint8_t);
public:
    uart(std::uint32_t baud = 9600);
    void init();
};
```

We chose to explicitly define the private access section. We put it after the public section, as publicly accessible members are the interface for our class, and when you read code and a class definition, the first thing you want to see is the interface. You want to see how to interact with the class and which methods are part of the public interface that you can use.

The only data member we have in this example is baudrate_. It is private, and the only option for a user of the uart class to set it up is through the constructor. It is a common practice for data members that we want to expose to the public to define setter and getter methods.

Setters and getters

In the uart class, we could define setters and getters for baudrate_ members as follows:

```cpp
std::uint32_t get_baudrate() const{
    return baudrate_;
}
void set_baudrate(baudrate) {
    baudrate_ = baudrate;
}
```

Now, this would allow us to set and get the baudrate value from the public interface, but these trivial setters and getters do not add any value to our interface. They are just exposing the baudrate_ member. It would be the same as if we put it under the public access specifier. Setters and getters should serve a clear purpose. For example, a setter can include validation logic, as follows:

```
void set_baudrate(baudrate) {
    if (baudrate <= c_max_baudrate) {
        baudrate_ = baudrate;
    } else {
        baudrate = c_max_baudrate;
    }
}
```

In the modified setter, we are making a sanity check of the value to be set and setting the private member only if it makes sense to do so, else setting it to the maximum baudrate (c_max_baudrate) supported in our system. This is just an example; it probably doesn't make sense to change the baudrate after the UART initialization.

Exposing data members through setters and getters in some sense breaks encapsulation. The idea of encapsulation is to hide the implementation details, and data members are implementation details. Therefore, setters and especially getters should be used sparingly and only when they serve a meaningful purpose.

We can use classes in C++ to encapsulate only functionality, without data, or data that is commonly shared with all users of a class. For that, we can use static methods.

Static methods

Static methods are C++ methods declared with static keywords, and they are accessible without object instantiation. In the uart class example, besides the constructor, we have the init method, which is part of the public interface. We use it by calling this method on an object we previously created using a single argument constructor by providing it with the baudrate. We could also design the uart class as a type that has all static methods and use it as follows:

```
#include <cstdint>

class uart {
public:
    static void init(std::uint32_t baudrate) {
        write_brr(calculate_uartdiv(baudrate));
```

```cpp
    }
private:
    static std::uint8_t calculate_uartdiv(std::uint32_t baudrate) {
        return baudrate / 32000;
    }
    static void write_brr(std::uint8_t) {}
};

int main () {
    uart::init(115200);
    return 0;
}
```

As you can see, we removed the single argument constructor and declared all methods as static. We also removed the baudrate_ private data member and passed it directly from the init method to the calculate_uartdiv method. We now have a type that we can use without object instantiation. We call the init method by using the class name followed by a double colon and the method name, as shown in the main function. It is worth noting that static methods can only use static data members and other static functions from a class as non-static members require the instantiation of an object.

We can group functions in C++ in a common *unit* by using namespaces. However, grouping them into a type is useful as we can pass types as template arguments. We will discuss namespaces and templates later in this book to better understand the benefits of this approach. Namespaces will be discussed in *Chapter 6* and templates in *Chapter 8*.

In C++, we can also use the struct keyword to define a type. The default access for struct members is public. Historically, structs were used for compatibility with C, so one could write a header file for a library that is used in both C and C++ programs. In this case, the struct we would share between C and C++ programs could only have common data types and couldn't have methods as members.

Structs

Structs are commonly used in C++ for types that only have data members that we want to make publicly available to users. They are mostly identical to classes, with a difference being in the default access level, which is public for structs.

Here is an example of a struct that only has data members:

```cpp
struct accelerometer_data {
    std::uint32_t x;
    std::uint32_t y;
    std::uint32_t z;
};
```

`accelerometer_data` could be produced by a `sensor` class, stored in a `ring_buffer` class, and consumed by a `sensor_fusion` class. The members of the `accelerometer_data` class are values from the x, y, and z axes, and they are publicly available to users of this class.

In this case, we use the `accelerometer_data` struct only as a data holder, and we implement the behavior related to this data in other places. This is just an example. Structuring data in simple structs versus using classes with data and complex behavior is a design choice and it depends on the exact application.

Structs are also used to group functions into types. They are usually all declared as static and made publicly available to users. Using a struct instead of a class is convenient in this use case as the default access specifier is public and it also reflects our intent as a struct is usually used when all members are made public.

Besides the public and private access specifiers, there is also the **protected specifier** in C++. The protected specifier is related to inheritance and will be explained later in this chapter.

Let us now move on to constructors and the initialization of variables and objects in C++. Object initialization is an important task and failing to do it properly can cause problems in programs. We will discuss different options for object initialization and analyze potential pitfalls and how to avoid them.

Storage duration and initialization

C++ objects with automatic storage duration are initialized upon declaration and destroyed when exiting the variable scope. Objects can also have a static storage duration. Data members of objects can also have static storage specifiers, and there are rules for the initialization of such members. We will first go through non-static member initialization.

Non-static member initialization

There are different ways to initialize non-static class members. The first thing that comes to mind when we discuss initialization and C++ is constructors. While constructors are powerful C++ features that allow us to have great control over the initialization, let us start with **default member initializers**.

Default member initializers

As of C++11, it is possible to set a default value for a member directly in a class definition, as follows:

```cpp
class my_class{
    int a = 4;
    int *ptr = nullptr;
}
```

This simple code snippet would fail to compile if we were to compile it with any pre-C++11 standard. The default member initializers allow us to set a default value for class members in a class definition, which improves readability and saves us from setting the same member variable if we have multiple constructors. This is particularly useful for setting default values for pointers.

If we didn't use the default initializer for ptr, it would be loaded with some random value from memory. Dereferencing such a pointer would result in reading from or writing to a random location, potentially leading to a serious fault. This hypothetical situation would be detected by a compiler or a static analyzer as they would report the usage of an uninitialized value, which is undefined behavior. Still, this shows the importance of initializing member variables with default values, and a default member initializer is an option for this task.

Constructors and member initializer lists

Constructors are nameless methods in class definition that can't be called explicitly. They are invoked upon the object initialization. A constructor that can be invoked with no arguments is called the default constructor. We already saw one in the uart class example:

```cpp
uart(std::uint32_t baud = 9600): baudrate_(baud) {
// empty constructor body
}
```

Even though this constructor has a parameter, we used the default argument that will be provided to the constructor if it is called with no arguments. If no argument is provided at the call site, the default value of 9600 will be used for the baud argument.

We use the following syntax when we want to use the default constructor:

```
uart uart1;
```

This is also called **default initialization**, and it is performed when the object is declared with no initializer. Please note that there are no parentheses as this would cause syntax ambiguity and would be interpreted by the compiler as a function declaration.

```
uart uart1();
```

The preceding line would be interpreted by the compiler as the declaration of a function named uart1 that returns the object of the uart class and accepts no arguments. This is the reason we are not using parentheses when using the default constructor.

As our uart class constructor can also accept an argument, we can use direct initialization syntax and provide the constructor with an argument, as follows:

```
uart uart1(115200);
```

This will call the uart class constructor and provide it with a value of 115200 for the baud argument. While we have explained nuances related to the syntax of the default constructor, we still need to explain the initialization of the baudrate_ member variable. In this case, we are using the member initializer list. It is specified after the colon character and before the opening brace of the compound statement as baudrate_(baud). In our case, we have only one item in the member initializer list; if there are more, they are delimited with a comma, as in the following example:

```
class sensor {
public:
    sensor(uart &u, std::uint32_t read_interval):
                uart_(u),
                read_interval_(read_interval) {}
private:
    uart &uart_;
    const std::uint32_t read_interval_;
};

int main() {
    uart uart1;
    sensor sensor1(uart1, 500);
    return 0;
}
```

In the preceding code, we are initializing a reference to uart and the read_interval_ unsigned integer in the member initializer list in the sensor constructor.

The important thing to notice is the reference to an object of the uart class. References in C++ are similar to pointers in C; that is, they point to an already-created object. However, they need to be initialized when declared and they can't be reassigned to point to another object. References and const-qualified members must be initialized using a member initializer list.

Constructors can have no or many parameters. If a constructor has one parameter and is declared without the **explicit specifier**, it is called a converting constructor.

Converting constructors and explicit specifiers

Converting constructors allow the compiler to make an implicit conversion from the type of its argument to the type of its class. To better understand this, let's take a look at the following example:

```cpp
#include <cstdio>
#include <student>

struct uart {
    uart(std::uint32_t baud = 9600): baudrate_(baud) {}
    std::uint32_t baudrate_;
};

void uart_consumer(uart u) {
    printf("Uart baudrate is %d\r\n", u.baudrate_);
}


int main() {
    uart uart1;
    uart_consumer(uart1);
    uart_consumer(115200);
    return 0;
}
```

The interesting part of this example is the call to the `uart_consumer` function with the `115200` argument. The `uart_consumer` function expects the object of the `uart` class as an argument, but due to rules of implicit conversion and the existing converting constructor, the compiler constructs an object of the `uart` class using `115200` as an argument, resulting in the following output of the program:

```
Uart baudrate is 9600
Uart baudrate is 115200
```

Implicit conversion can be unsafe, and it is often unwanted. To prevent it, we can declare a constructor using an explicit specifier, as follows:

```cpp
explicit uart(std::uint32_t baud = 9600): baudrate_(baud) {}
```

Compiling the preceding example with an explicit constructor will result in a compiler error:

```
<source>:19:19: error: could not convert '115200' from 'int' to 'uart'
   19 |        uart_consumer(115200);
```

By declaring a constructor as explicit, we can be sure that no user of our class will create a situation with potential implicit conversion, which may lead to unwanted behavior in our program. But what if we want to prevent calls to our constructor using the float type? It may not be a good example, but you can imagine a constructor expecting a `uint8_t` type and someone calling it with a `uint32_t` argument.

We can delete specific constructors, which will result in failed compilation. We can do it using the following syntax in the class declaration:

```cpp
uart(float) = delete;
```

Calling the constructor with a float type will result in the following compile error:

```
<source>:12:25: error: use of deleted function 'uart::uart(float)'
   12 |        uart uart1(100000.0f);
```

We can also use brace list initialization, which narrows down the conversion and prevents the float-to-integer conversion. We can use it as follows:

```cpp
uart uart1{100000.0f};
```

This call would result in the following compile error:

```
<source>:11:25: error: narrowing conversion of '1.0e+5f' from 'float' to
'uint8_t' {aka 'unsigned char'} [-Wnarrowing]
   11 |      uart uart1{100000.0f};
```

The list initialization limits the implicit conversion and helps with detecting problems at compile time.

Class data members can be declared using the `static` keyword, and there are special rules for initializing them.

Static member initialization

Static members are not tied to the objects of a class or struct. They are variables with static storage duration, and they can be accessed by any object of a class. Let's go through a simple example to better understand static members and how we initialize them:

```cpp
#include <cstdio>

struct object_counter {
    static int cnt;

    object_counter() {
        cnt++;
    }
    ~object_counter() {
        cnt--;
    }
};

int object_counter::cnt = 0;

int main() {
    {
        object_counter obj1;
        object_counter obj2;
        object_counter obj3;
        printf("Number of existing objects in this scope is: %d\r\n",
                                   object_counter::cnt);
    }
```

```
        printf("Number of existing objects in this scope is: %d\r\n",
                                    object_counter::cnt);
    return 0;
}
```

In this example, we have a simple object_counter struct. The struct has one static data member, the cnt integer. In the constructor, we are incrementing this counter variable, and in the destructor, we are decrementing it. In the main function, we are creating three object_counter objects in an unnamed scope.

When the program flow exits the unnamed scope, destructors will be called. We are printing the number of existing objects both inside the scope and after leaving it. Inside the unnamed scope, the cnt value should be equal to 3, as we created three objects, and when we exit it, and destructors decrement the cnt variable, it should be 0. The following is the output of the example:

```
Number of existing objects in this scope is: 3
Number of existing objects in this scope is: 0
```

The output shows that the behavior of the cnt static variable is as we predicted. In this case, we declared a static variable in the class declaration, but we defined it using the following line:

```
int object_counter::cnt = 0;
```

With the C++17 standard, it is possible to declare a static variable using an inline specifier inside the struct (or class) definition and provide it with the initializer, as follows:

```
struct object_counter {
    inline static int cnt = 0;
    ...
};
```

This makes the code more concise, easier to use as we don't need to define the variable outside the class definition, and easier to read.

We covered the basics of classes in C++, including access specifiers, initializing methods, and constructors. Now, we will see how we can reuse classes using inheritance and dynamic polymorphism.

Inheritance and dynamic polymorphism

In C++, we can expand the functionality of a class without modifying it with inheritance. Inheritance is an example of establishing a hierarchical relationship between classes; for example, ADXL345 is an accelerometer. Let us go through a trivial example that demonstrates inheritance in C++:

```cpp
#include <cstdio>

class A {
public:
    void method_1() {
        printf("Class A, method1\r\n");
    }

    void method_2() {
        printf("Class A, method2\r\n");
    }
protected:
    void method_protected() {
        printf("Class A, method_protected\r\n");
    }
};

class B : public A{
public:
    void method_1() {
        printf("Class B, method1\r\n");
    }

    void method_3() {
        printf("Class B, method3\r\n");
        A::method_2();
        A::method_protected();
    }
};

int main() {
```

```cpp
    B b;
    b.method_1();
    b.method_2();
    b.method_3();

    printf("-------------------\r\n");
    A &a = b;
    a.method_1();
    a.method_2();

    return 0;
}
```

In this example, `class B` inherits private and protected members from `class A`. `class A` is the base class, and `class B` is derived from it. The derived class has access to public and protected members of the base class. In the `main` function, we create an object of `class B`, and we call the `method_1`, `method_2`, and `method_3` methods. The output of this part of the code is shown here:

```
Class B, method1
Class A, method2
Class B, method3
Class A, method2
Class A, method_protected
```

In the first line of the `main` function, we see that the call to the `method_1` function on object b executes `method_1` defined in `class B` even though it is derived from `class A`, and `class A` has also defined `method_1`. This is called **static binding** as the decision to call `method_1` is defined in `class A` and is made by the compiler.

An object of the derived `class B` contains an object of the base `class A`. If we call `method_2` on object b, the compiler will find no definition in `class B`, but as class B inherits from class A, the compiler will call `method_2` on object a, which is a part of object b.

In `method_3`, we see that we can call methods of the base class from the derived class. We can also see that we can call protected methods of the base class. This is one of the use cases of private access specifiers; it allows access to derived classes.

We can assign the object of the derived class to a reference of the base class. We could also do the same for a pointer. Here is the result of calls of methods made on the reference:

```
Class A, method1
Class A, method2
```

Calling method_1 on a reference of the base class will result in a call to method_1 defined in class A. This is another instance of static binding in action. But what if we wanted that a call on a base class reference or pointer to result in executing a function on the derived class? And why would we want this? Let's first address the *how*. C++ provides a mechanism of dynamic binding through virtual functions.

Virtual functions

In our example, we assign a reference of type A& to an object of class B. If we want calls to method_1 on this reference (A& a) to execute the method_1 function defined in class B, we can declare method_1 as a virtual function in class A, as follows:

```cpp
class A {
public:
    virtual void method_1() {
        printf("Class A, method1\r\n");
    }
    ...
};
```

Now, the call to method_1 on the reference of class A, bound to the object of class B, will result in a call to method_1 defined in class B, as we can see in the output:

```
Class B, method1
Class A, method2
```

Here, we see the output of the method_1 call matches the definition of this method from class B. We say that class B is overriding method_1 from class A, and there is a special notion for this, as follows:

```cpp
class B: public A {
public:
    void method_1() override {
        printf("Class B, method1\r\n");
    }
```

```
    . . .
    };
```

The **override** keyword makes the compiler aware of our intention of overriding a virtual method from the base class. If the method we are overriding is not declared virtual, the compiler will raise an error.

Virtual functions in C++ are usually implemented using virtual tables. This is the work that a compiler does for us. It creates a virtual table that stores pointers for every virtual function, which points to the overridden implementation.

Virtual function implementation

Every class that overrides a virtual function has a virtual table. You can think of it as a hidden table of function pointers. Every object of a class has a pointer to this table. This pointer is used at runtime to access a table and find the correct function to be called on the object. Let us slightly modify our class A and class B to better understand this. The following is the code of the modified class A and class B:

```cpp
class A {
public:
    void method_1() virtual{
        printf("Class A, method1\r\n");
    }
    void method_2() virtual{
        printf("Class A, method2\r\n");
    }
};
class B : public A{
public:
    void method_2() override{
        printf("Class B, method2\r\n");
    }
};
```

We modified class A and class B so that class A has two virtual methods, method_1 and method_2. class B only overrides method_2. The compiler will generate a virtual table for class B and a pointer that every object of class B will hold. The virtual pointer points to the generated virtual table.

This can be visualized as follows:

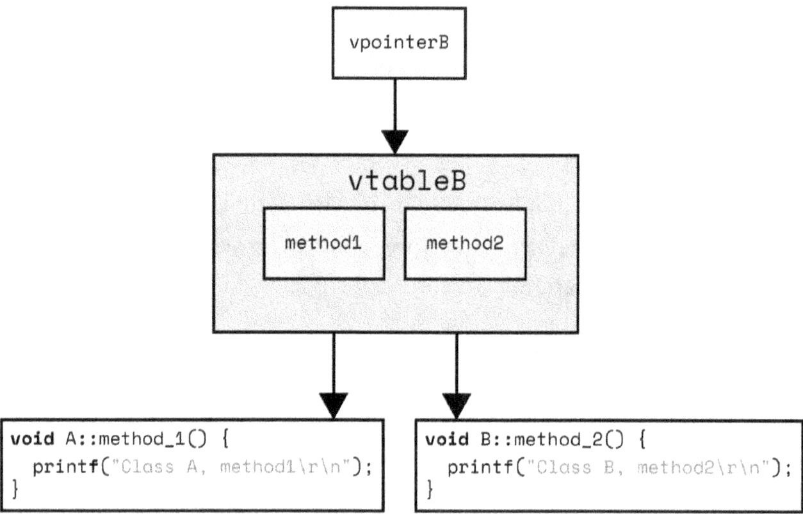

Figure 5.1 – Virtual table

Figure 5.1 depicts a possible implementation of virtual functions in C++ using virtual tables and virtual pointers. If we call method_2 on a reference to an object of class B, it will follow the virtual pointer to the virtual table and select the function pointer that points to the implementation of method_2 in class B, that is, the overridden virtual function. This mechanism happens at runtime. There is a layer of indirection to get to the overridden function, which results in space and time overhead.

In C++, we can define a virtual function to be a pure virtual function. If a class has a pure virtual function, it is called an **abstract class**, and it can't be instantiated. Derived classes must override pure virtual functions, or they are also abstract classes. Let's go through the following code example:

```
class A {
public:
    virtual void method_1() = 0;
};
class B : public A{
};
int main() {
    B b;
    return 0;
}
```

This program will fail to compile as `class B` didn't override the `method_1` virtual method from `class A`. Abstract classes shift the responsibility of the implementation of certain behaviors (methods) to derived classes. Classes that have all virtual methods are called interfaces.

Inheritance defines a hierarchical relationship between classes, and we can say that `class B` is `class A`, just as a cat is an animal. We can represent this relationship in a **Unified Modeling Language (UML)** diagram.

UML class diagrams

UML diagrams are used to describe software components. If they describe the relationship between classes, they are called UML class diagrams. One such diagram is shown in the following figure:

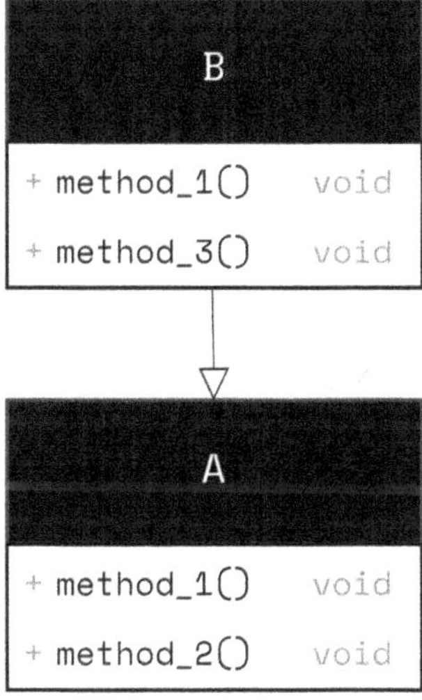

Figure 5.2 – UML diagram of class A and class B's relationship

Figure 5.2 depicts a UML class diagram visualizing the hierarchical relationship between A and B. The line connecting B and A with a hollow, unfilled triangular arrowhead pointing to A means B is A. This UML diagram also shows methods available in both classes.

UML diagrams are useful for describing design patterns, and we will use them in this book to help us visualize the relationship between software components in code examples.

We have learned what inheritance is and how we can use it with virtual functions to achieve dynamic binding. Let's get back to the question of why we need these mechanisms and how we can use them to create better software. The mechanisms we learned in this chapter provide the means for dynamic (runtime) polymorphism.

Dynamic polymorphism

Polymorphism is a mechanism that enables a single interface for different types. It can be static or dynamic. Dynamic polymorphism in C++ is achieved through inheritance and virtual functions. This type of polymorphism is also called **subtyping**, as it treats subtypes or derived classes through the interface based on the base class.

Polymorphism allows us to use a single interface for different implementations. Let us go through an example of the library for GSM modems. GSM modems usually communicate with the host microcontroller through the UART interface. A microcontroller may have multiple UART peripherals, such as UART and **Low-Power Universal Asynchronous Receiver/Transmitter (LPUART)** on STM32. We may also want to use the library on different microcontrollers.

We can define a common interface for different UART implementations on different platforms and use this interface in our GSM library. An implementation of UART will be provided by the platform on which we use the GSM library, and it will implement the common UART interface. We can use a UML class diagram to visualize our library design, as in the following figure:

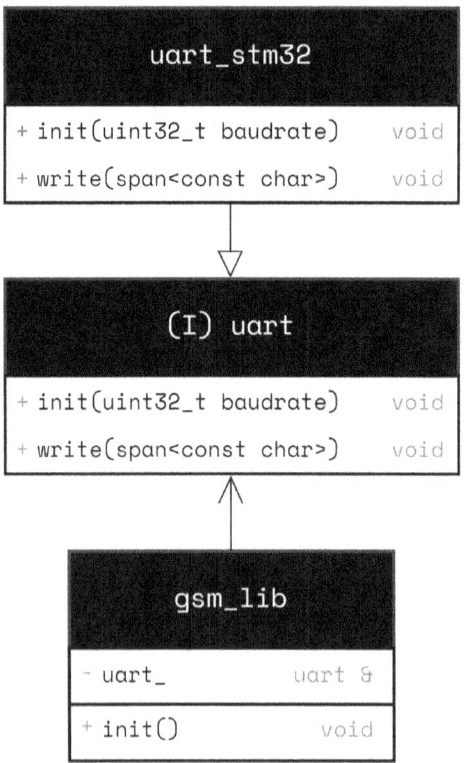

Figure 5.3 – UML diagram of GSM library and UART interface

In *Figure 5.3*, we see the relationship between the gsm_lib, uart, and uart_stm32 classes. GSM library functionality is implemented in the gsm_lib class, which uses the uart interface. The uart interface is implemented by the uart_stm32 class. The functionality of the GSM library is complex, but let's go through a very simplified code example just to demonstrate the relationship between these three classes and how they work together. The following is a simplified example:

```cpp
#include <span>
#include <cstdio>
#include <cstdint>
class uart {
public:
    virtual void init(std::uint32_t baudrate) = 0;
    virtual void write(std::span<const char> data) = 0;
};
class uart_stm32 : public uart{
public:
    void init(std::uint32_t baudrate = 9600) override {
        printf("uart_stm32::init: setting baudrate to %d\r\n", baudrate);
    }
    void write(std::span<const char> data) override {
        printf("uart_stm32::write: ");
        for(auto ch: data) {
            putc(ch, stdout);
        }
    }
};

class gsm_lib{
    public:
        gsm_lib(uart &u) : uart_(u) {}
        void init() {
            printf("gsm_lib::init: sending AT command\r\n");
            uart_.write("AT");
        }
    private:
        uart &uart_;
};
int main() {
    uart_stm32 uart_stm32_obj;
```

```cpp
    uart_stm32_obj.init(115200);

    gsm_lib gsm(uart_stm32_obj);
    gsm.init();
    return 0;
}
```

In this code example, we see that the uart class has two pure virtual functions, which makes it an interface class. This interface is inherited and implemented by the uart_stm32 class. In the main function, we create an object of the uart_stm32 class, whose reference is passed to the constructor of the gsm_lib class, where it is used to initialize a private member reference to the uart interface.

You can also run this program in a simulator environment, which we covered in the previous chapter. It is available in the Chapter05/gsm_lib folder.

The design of the GSM library using the UART interface allows us to have a flexible library that we can use on different platforms. This design also allows us to debug the communication between the library and GSM modem by providing it with a UART implementation that will serve as a tap, redirecting reads and writes and simultaneously logging them.

Summary

In this chapter, we covered the basics of classes in C++. We learned about member access specifiers, different ways of initializing objects, and inheritance. We also got to know virtual functions in more detail and learned how to use them for dynamic polymorphism.

In the next chapter, we will talk more about other basic concepts in C++, such as namespaces, function overloading, and the standard library.

Join our community on Discord

Join our community's Discord space for discussions with the author and other readers:

https://packt.link/embeddedsystems

6

Beyond Classes – Fundamental C++ Concepts

Historically, C++ started as C with classes, making classes one of the first concepts for developers with a C background to learn. In the previous chapter, we covered classes in detail, and before proceeding with more advanced concepts, we will cover other fundamental C++ concepts that make it so much more than C with classes.

Before we move on to more advanced topics, it's important to explore other fundamental concepts that make C++ distinct. In this chapter, we're going to cover the following main topics:

- Namespaces
- Function overloading
- Interoperability with C
- References
- Standard library containers and algorithms

Technical requirements

To get the most out of this chapter, I strongly recommend using Compiler Explorer (https://godbolt.org/) as you read through the examples. Select GCC as your compiler and target x86 architecture. This will allow you to see standard output (stdio) results and better observe the code's behavior. As we are using modern C++ features make sure to select C++23 standard, by adding `-std=c++23` in compiler options box.

Compiler Explorer makes it easy to try out the code, tweak it, and immediately see how it affects the output and generated assembly. The examples are available at GitHub (`https://github.com/PacktPublishing/Cpp-in-Embedded-Systems/tree/main/Chapter06`).

Namespaces

Namespaces in C++ are used as scope specifiers for accessing type names, functions, variables, and so on. They allow us to more easily differentiate types and function names in large code bases that use many software components and where there are often similar identifiers.

In C, we usually add a prefix to types and functions to make it easier to differentiate, for example:

```cpp
typedef struct hal_uart_stm32{
    UART_HandleTypeDef huart_;
    USART_TypeDef *instance_;
} hal_uart_stm32;
void hal_init();
uint32_t hal_get_ms();
```

In C++, we can use namespaces instead of C-style identifier prefixes to organize code in logical groups, as shown in the following example:

```cpp
namespace hal {
void init();

std::uint32_t tick_count;
std::uint32_t get_ms() {
    return tick_count;
}

class uart_stm32 {
private:
    UART_HandleTypeDef huart_;
    USART_TypeDef *instance_;
};
};
```

All members of the `hal` namespace are accessible unqualified from within the namespace. To access identifiers from the `hal` namespace, in code outside of it, we use the namespace as a qualifier followed by scope resolution operator (`::`), as shown in the following example:

```
hal::init();
std::uint32_t time_now = hal::get_ms();
```

In this example, beside the `hal` namespace, we also see the `std` namespace, which we used in previous examples. C++ standard library types and functions are declared in the `std` namespace.

We can use the `using` directive to access an identifier without qualifiers, as shown in the following example:

```
using std::array;
array<int, 4> arr;
```

The `using` directive can also be used for the entire namespace, as shown in the following example:

```
using namespace std;
array<int, 4> arr;
vector<int> vec;
```

It is recommended to use `using` directive sparingly, especially with `std`, using it for a limited scope, or even better, to bring in individual identifiers only.

The same namespace can be used across different header files to declare identifiers. For example, `std::vector` is declared in `vector.h`, and `std::array` is declared in `array.h` header files. This allows us to organize code from different headers that logically belong to the same group in a namespace.

Functions and types that are not declared within an explicit namespace are part of a global namespace. It is a good practice to organize all code in namespaces. The only function that can't be declared within a namespace and must be in a global namespace is `main`. To access the identifier from the global namespace, we use the scope resolution operator, as shown in the following example:

```
const int ret_val = 0;
int main() {
    return ::ret_val;
}
```

The line `return  ::ret_val;` uses the scope resolution operator, `::`, without specifying a namespace. This means it refers to the global namespace. So, `::ret_val` accesses the `ret_val` variable defined outside of any function or class—that is, at the global scope.

Unnamed namespaces

A namespace can be declared without the name qualifier. This allows us to declare functions and types that are local to the translation unit they are declared in. In the following example, we can see an example of an unnamed namespace:

```
namespace {
constexpr std::size_t c_max_retries;
std::size_t counter;
};
```

In the code, we have an unnamed namespace with a few variables declared in it. They have **internal linkage**, meaning they cannot be accessed by code from other translation units. We can achieve the same effect both in C and C++ by using the `static` storage specifier.

Nested namespaces

Namespaces can also be nested. We can have a namespace within a namespace, as shown in the following example:

```
namespace sensors {
namespace environmental {
class temperature {
};
class humidity {
};
};
namespace indoor_air_quality{
class c02{
};
class pm2_5{
};
};
};
```

In this example, we have organized sensors in namespaces. We have a top-level namespace, `sensors`, which has two namespaces: `environmental` and `indoor_air_quality`. C++17 standard allows us to write namespaces, as shown in the following example:

```cpp
namespace sensors::environmental {
class temperature {
};
class humidity {
};
};
```

Namespaces are a good way to make the code more readable, as they allow us to keep identifiers short, without C-style prefixes.

Function overloading

In the previous chapter, when we discussed inheritance, we mentioned **static binding**. We saw that we can have the same function names for functions that belong to different classes. However, we can also have the same function names for different function parameters, as shown in the following example:

```cpp
#include <cstdio>

void print(int a) {
    printf("Int %d\r\n", a);
}
void print(float a) {
    printf("Float %2.f\r\n", a);
}

int main() {
    print(2);
    print(2.f);
    return 0;
}
```

In this example, we have two `print` functions. One of them has an `int` as a parameter and the second one has a `float`. On the call site, the compiler will pick a `print` function based on the arguments passed to the function call.

Functions with the same names within the same scope are called **overloaded functions**. Instead of having two different names, such as `print_int` and `print_float`, we can use the same name for both these functions and let the compiler decide which function to call.

To distinguish between the two overloaded `print` functions – one accepting an `int` parameter and the other a `float` – the compiler employs a technique called **name mangling**. Name mangling modifies function names by encoding additional information, such as parameter types, into them. This ensures that each overloaded function has a unique symbol in the compiled code. If we examine the assembly output of the previous example, we can observe these mangled names:

```
_Z5printi:
            mov       r1, r0
            ldr       r0, .L2
            b         printf
_Z5printf:
            vcvt.f64.f32     d16, s0
            ldr       r0, .L5
            vmov      r2, r3, d16
            b         printf
```

We see that the compiler assigned _Z5printi and _Z5printf labels to `print` functions with `int` and `float` parameters respectively. This allows it to dispatch function calls according to argument matching.

Overloaded functions can have a different number of arguments. Return types cannot be used for function overloading. Two functions with the same name and same arguments cannot have different return types. The following code would result in a compile error:

```
int print(int a);
void print(int a);
```

This code would be treated by the compiler as a function redeclaration and would result in an error.

Function overloading is a basic but powerful feature of C++ that provides a mechanism for compile-time or static polymorphism.

Interoperability with C

Code examples from previous chapters that you were able to run in a Renode simulator are using both C++ and C code. We used vendor provided HAL library and **Common Microcontroller Software Interface Standard** (**CMSIS**) by Arm, both written in C and contained in the platform folder.

If you take a look at the CMakeLists.txt file and the add_executable function in it, you will see listed C files from the platform folder and just a few C++ files. Building a project will provide the following console output:

```
[  7%] Building C object CMakeFiles/bare.elf.dir/platform/STM32F0xx_HAL_
Driver/Src/stm32f0xx_hal.c.o
[ 15%] Building C object CMakeFiles/bare.elf.dir/platform/STM32F0xx_HAL_
Driver/Src/stm32f0xx_hal_cortex.c.o
[ 23%] Building C object CMakeFiles/bare.elf.dir/platform/STM32F0xx_HAL_
Driver/Src/stm32f0xx_hal_gpio.c.o
[ 30%] Building C object CMakeFiles/bare.elf.dir/platform/STM32F0xx_HAL_
Driver/Src/stm32f0xx_hal_rcc.c.o
[ 38%] Building C object CMakeFiles/bare.elf.dir/platform/STM32F0xx_HAL_
Driver/Src/stm32f0xx_hal_uart.c.o
[ 46%] Building C object CMakeFiles/bare.elf.dir/platform/STM32F0xx_HAL_
Driver/Src/stm32f0xx_hal_uart_ex.c.o
[ 53%] Building ASM object CMakeFiles/bare.elf.dir/platform/startup_
stm32f072xb.s.o
[ 61%] Building C object CMakeFiles/bare.elf.dir/platform/src/stm32f0xx_
hal_msp.c.o
[ 69%] Building C object CMakeFiles/bare.elf.dir/platform/src/stm32f0xx_
it.c.o
[ 76%] Building C object CMakeFiles/bare.elf.dir/platform/src/system_
stm32f0xx.c.o
[ 84%] Building CXX object CMakeFiles/bare.elf.dir/app/src/main.cpp.o
[ 92%] Building CXX object CMakeFiles/bare.elf.dir/hal/uart/src/uart_
stm32.cpp.o
[100%] Linking CXX executable bare.elf
```

Every C and C++ file is treated as a translation unit and built separately by C and C++ compilers respectively. After compilation, both C and C++ object files are linked into a single ELF file.

External and Language Linkage in C++

Variables and functions that can be referred to from other translation units have **external linkage**. This allows them to be linked with code in other files provided that the compiler has access to declarations. They also have a property called **language linkage**. This property allows linking C++ with C code. C language linkage in C++ is declared using the following syntax:

```
extern "C" {
void c_func();
}
```

Declaration with C language linkage will be linked according to C language linkage conventions, preventing name mangling (among other things) to ensure proper linking with code compiled within a C translation unit.

C standard library in C++

C++ wraps the C standard library and provides header files with the same name as the C language version but with a c prefix and no extension. For example, the C++ equivalent for the C language header file `<stdlib.h>` is `<cstdlib>`.

In GCC, implementation C++ wrappers include C standard library headers; for example, `<cstdio>` includes `<stdio.h>`. If you dive into `<stdio.h>`, you can see that it guards function declarations with `__BEGIN_DECLS` and `__END_DECLS` macros. Here's the definition of these macros:

```
/* C++ needs to know that types and declarations are C, not C++.  */
#ifdef      __cplusplus
# define __BEGIN_DECLS      extern "C" {
# define __END_DECLS        }
#else
# define __BEGIN_DECLS
# define __END_DECLS
#endif
```

Here, we can see that standard C library headers take care of C++ compatibility by adding a language linkage specifier if a C++ compiler is used. This practice is also used in many HAL implementations provided by microcontroller vendors. If you open any C header file in `platform/ STM32F0xx_HAL_Driver/Inc`, you will see that declarations are guarded with a C language linkage specifier when they are accessed by the C++ compiler, as shown here:

```
#ifdef __cplusplus
extern "C" {
```

```
#endif
// Declarations
#ifdef __cplusplus
}
#endif
```

C libraries are often used by C++ programs, especially in the embedded domain, so it is always a good idea to guard them with a language linkage specifier. If we are using a C library in a C++ program in which headers are not guarded internally, we can guard the headers at the `include` site, as shown here:

```
extern "C" {
#include "c_library.h"
}
```

The language linkage specifier for C language ensures proper linking of C++ code that is using C code, which is often a case in embedded projects.

References

In the previous chapter, we briefly mentioned references without explaining them in detail. References are object aliases; that is, they refer to objects and as such they must be immediately initialized. They are not objects, so there are no pointers to references or arrays of references.

There are two different types of references in C++: **lvalue** and **rvalue** references.

Value categories

C++ expressions have either lvalue or rvalue value categories. There is a more detailed division of value categories, but we will stay with this simple one which has a historical origin.

Lvalues usually appear on the left side of the assignment expression, but this is not always the case. Lvalues have an address that the program can access. Here are some examples of lvalues:

```
void bar();
int a = 42; // a is lvalue
int b = a; // a can also appear on the right side
int * p = &a; // pointer p is lvalue
void(*bar_ptr)() = bar; // func pointer bar_ptr is lvalue
```

Rvalues usually appear on the right side of the assignment expression. Examples are literals, function calls that do not return references, and built-in operator calls. We can think of them as temporary values. Some rvalues are shown in the following example:

```cpp
int a = 42; // 42 is rvalue
int b = a + 16; // a + 16 is rvalue
std::size_t size = sizeof(int); // sizeof(int) is rvalue
```

Here is another, full example to help you better understand rvalues:

```cpp
#include <cstdio>

struct my_struct {
    int a_;
    my_struct() : a_(0) {}
    my_struct(int a) : a_(a) {}
};

int main() {
    printf("a_ = %d\r\n", my_struct().a_);
    printf("a_ = %d\r\n", (my_struct()=my_struct(16)).a_);
    return 0;
}
```

In the preceding example, we can see the `my_struct()` rvalue expression on the left side of the assignment operator. The output of the example is as follows:

```
a_ = 0
a_ = 16
```

In the first `printf` call, we make a call to the constructor of `my_struct`, which returns a temporary object, and we access the a_ member. In the next line, we have the following expression: `my_struct()=my_struct(16)`. On the left side of this expression, we have a call to the default constructor, which returns a temporary object. Then we assign the result of the call to a constructor that accepts `int` to a temporary object on the left side, which will copy one temporary object to the other one.

Lvalue references

Lvalue references are used as aliases for existing objects. They can also be const-qualified. We declare them by adding & to type names. The following code demonstrates the usage of lvalue references:

```cpp
#include <cstdio>

int main() {
    int a = 42;
    int& a_ref = a;
    const int& a_const_ref = a;

    printf("a = %d\r\n", a);

    a_ref = 16;
    printf("a = %d\r\n", a);

    // a_const_ref = 16; compiler error
    return 0;
}
```

As shown in the example, we can manipulate the object using the reference. In the case of a constant reference, any attempts to change the value will result in a compiler error.

Rvalue references

Rvalue references are used to extend the lifetime of temporary rvalues. We declare them using && next to the type name. Here are example usages of rvalue references:

```cpp
int&& a = 42;
int b = 0;
// int&& b_ref = b; compiler error
int&& b_ref = b + 10; // ok, b + 10 is rvalue
```

Rvalue references cannot be bound to lvalues. Attempting to do so will result in a compiler error. Rvalue references are important for resource management, and they are used in move semantics, which allow resources to be moved from one object to another.

If we take a look at the documentation for the push_back method of std::vector, we will see two declarations:

```cpp
void push_back( const T& value );
void push_back( T&& value );
```

The first declaration is used to initialize a new vector member by copying value. The second declaration with rvalue reference will move value, meaning that a new vector member will take ownership of dynamically allocated resources from the value object. Let's take a look at the following example to understand the basics of move semantics:

```cpp
#include <string>
#include <vector>
#include <cstdio>

int main()
{
    std::string str = "Hello world, this is move semantics demo!!!";
    printf("str.data address is %p\r\n", (void*)str.data());

    std::vector<std::string> v;

    v.push_back(str);
    printf("str after copy is <%s>\r\n", str.data());

    v.push_back(std::move(str));
    //v.push_back(static_cast<std::string&&>(str));
    printf("str after move is <%s>\r\n", str.data());

    for(const auto & s:v) {
        printf("s is <%s>\r\n", s.data());
        printf("s.data address is %p\r\n", (void*)s.data());
    }
    return 0;
}
```

In this example, we have two calls to the push_back method of std::vector<std::string>. The first call, v.push_back(str);, performs a copy of str into the vector. After this operation, the original str remains unchanged, which is confirmed by the output:

```
str.data address is 0x84c2b0
str after copy is <Hello world, this is move semantics demo!!!>
```

The second call, v.push_back(std::move(str));, uses std::move to cast str to an rvalue reference. This signals to the compiler that the resources of str can be moved rather than copied. As a result, the internal data of str is transferred to the new string in the vector, and str is left in a valid but unspecified state, often becoming empty:

```
str after move is <>
s is <Hello world, this is move semantics demo!!!>
s.data address is 0x84d330
s is <Hello world, this is move semantics demo!!!>
s.data address is 0x84c2b0
```

In the preceding output, we are also printing addresses of the string's underlying character arrays using s.data() and str.data().Here's what's happening:

- The original str has its data at address 0x84c2b0

- After copying str into the vector, the first element, v[0], has its own copy of the data at a different address (0x84d330), confirming that a deep copy was made

After the move, the second element, v[1], in the vector now points to the original data address, 0x84c2b0. This indicates that the internal data of str was moved into v[1] without copying. This is just a glimpse into move semantics; there is much more to it, but as it is used mostly for managing dynamically allocated resources, we will not cover it in more detail.

Standard library containers and algorithms

We have already discussed some of the containers from the C++ library, such as std::vector and std::array, in previous chapters. As std::vector relies on dynamic memory allocation, std::array is usually the container of choice in embedded applications.

Array

Arrays from the standard library allocate a contiguous block of memory on the stack. We can consider an array as a simple wrapper of a C-style array that contains the size of the array inside the type. It is a templated type that is instantiated with an underlying data type and size.

We can access members of the array using a method that will throw an exception if indexed with an out-of-bounds index. This makes it a safer option than a C-style array as it allows us to catch out-of-bounds access runtime errors and handle them. If exceptions are disabled, we can set a global terminate handler with our functionality. We had the opportunity to see this in *Chapter 2* of this book when we were discussing exceptions.

We can use std:array to create a vector-like container that we can use with container adaptors such as std::stack or a std::priority queue. We will call our new type fixed_vector. It will inherit from std::array and implement the push_back, pop_back, empty, and end methods. Here is an implementation of our new type using an array from the standard library:

```cpp
template <typename T, size_t S> class fixed_vector : public std::array<T, S>
{
  public:
    void push_back(const T &el) {
        if(cnt_ < S) {
            this->at(cnt_) = el;
            ++cnt_;
        }
    }

    T &back() {
        return this->at(cnt_-1);
    }

    void pop_back() {
        if(cnt_) {
            --cnt_;
        }
    }

    auto end() {
        return std::array<T, S>::begin() + cnt_;
    }

    bool empty() const {
        return cnt_ == 0;
    }
```

```cpp
private:
    size_t cnt_ = 0;
};
```

Our new type, `fixed_vector`, exploits the underlying `std::array` and implements the `push_back` function to add elements at the end of the array. If we want to add more elements than is possible, it will fail silently. This behavior can be adjusted as per the application's requirements. It also implements the back method, which returns an lvalue reference to the last element, and `pop_back`, which decrements the private member, `cnt_`, used to keep track of the number of elements stored in the container.

We can use our new container type, `fixed_vector`, as an underlying container type for container adaptors such as stacks and priority queues.

Container adaptors

Stack is a simple **Last In-First Out (LIFO)** container adaptor, and the priority queue will sort the elements when inserting them. We can see how to use them with `fixed_vector` in the following example:

```cpp
int main() {
    std::priority_queue<int, fixed_vector<int, 10>> pq;

    pq.push(10);
    pq.push(4);
    pq.push(8);
    pq.push(1);
    pq.push(2);

    printf("Popping elements from priority queue: ");
    while(!pq.empty()) {
        printf("%d ", pq.top());
        pq.pop();
    }

    std::stack<int, fixed_vector<int, 10>> st;

    st.push(10);
```

```cpp
    st.push(4);
    st.push(8);
    st.push(1);
    st.push(2);

    printf("\r\nPopping elements from stack (LIFO): ");
    while(!st.empty()) {
        printf("%d ", st.top());
        st.pop();
    }

    return 0;
}
```

In this example, we are using `fixed_vector` to instantiate `std::stack` and `std::priority_queue` templated types. If we run this program, we will get the following output:

```
Popping elements from priority queue: 10 8 4 2 1
Popping elements from stack (LIFO): 2 1 8 4 10
```

As you can see from the output, elements in the priority queue are sorted, and those in the stack are popped by the LIFO principle.

The standard library provides a variety of containers, and we have just scratched the surface of the possibilities that it provides. It also provides algorithms that operate on containers.

Algorithms

C++ standard library offers a huge set of templated algorithm functions contained in the `algorithm` header that play well with different container types. We will go through some of them now.

std::copy and std::copy_if

`std::copy` and `std::copy_if` are used to copy elements from one container to another. `std::copy_if` also accepts a predicate function that controls whether a member is copied or not, as shown in the following example:

```cpp
#include <cstdio>
#include <vector>
#include <array>
#include <algorithm>
#include <numeric>
```

```cpp
void print_container(const auto& container) {
    for(auto& elem: container) {
        printf("%d ", elem);
    }
    printf("\r\n");
}


int main() {
    std::array<int, 10> src{0};
    std::array<int, 10> dst{0};

    std::iota(src.begin(), src.end(), 0);
    std::copy_if(src.begin(), src.end(), dst.begin(),[]
        (int x) {return x > 3;});

    print_container(src);
    print_container(dst);
    return 0;
}
```

In this example, we use `std::iota` from the numeric header to initialize the `src` array with incrementing values, starting with 0. Then, we copy all elements from the `src` array to the `dst` array that are larger than 3 using `std::copy_if`.

std::sort

`std::sort` is used to sort elements in a container. In the following example, we will generate elements randomly and sort them:

```cpp
int main() {

    std::array<int, 10> src{0};

    std::random_device rd;
    std::mt19937 gen(rd());
    std::uniform_int_distribution<> distrib(1, 6);

    auto rand = [&](int x) -> int {
        return distrib(gen);
    };
    std::transform(src.begin(), src.end(), src.begin(), rand);
```

```cpp
    print_container(src);

    std::sort(src.begin(), src.end());
    print_container(src);

    return 0;
}
```

In this example, we populate the `src` array using `std::transform`, which applies a rand lambda to every member of the `src` array. We used types from the `random` header to generate random numbers between 1 and 6. After we populate the array with random numbers, we sort it using `std::sort`. A possible output of this program is shown here:

```
6 6 1 1 6 5 4 4 1 1
1 1 1 1 4 4 5 6 6 6
```

We first see values in the array before sorting and then applying `std::sort`. We could have populated the initial array in a `for` loop, but we used the opportunity to demonstrate `std:transform` here.

These were some of the algorithms from the C++ standard library; there are many more that can be used to effectively solve common tasks in containers.

Summary

In this chapter, we covered C++ fundamentals such as namespaces, function overloading, references, and standard library containers and algorithms. We also learned how C interoperability is implemented and used in C++ programs.

In the next chapter, we will learn about error-handling mechanisms in C++.

Get This Book's PDF Version and Exclusive Extras

Scan the QR code (or go to `packtpub.com/unlock`). Search for this book by name, confirm the edition, and then follow the steps on the page.

Note: Keep your invoice handy. Purchases made directly from Packt don't require an invoice.

7

Strengthening Firmware – Practical C++ Error Handling Methods

To ensure the proper functioning of firmware, we must handle errors from vendor-specific code, libraries that we are using in a project, and our own code. Error codes are standard error-handling mechanisms in C, and they are also used in C++. However, C++ provides us with other tools, most notably exceptions that are often avoided in embedded projects due to the large binary footprint and non-determinism. Still, we will discuss exceptions in C++ in this chapter to show their benefits in the error-handling process.

Besides exceptions, C++ offers more options for error handling that will also be discussed in this chapter. The goal of this chapter is to understand potential issues with error codes and see how to mitigate them in C++.

In this chapter, we're going to cover the following main topics:

- Error codes and asserts
- Exceptions
- `std:: optional` and `std::expected`

Technical requirements

To get the most out of this chapter, I strongly recommend using Compiler Explorer (`https://godbolt.org/`) as you read through the examples. Select GCC as your compiler and target x86 architecture. This will allow you to see standard output (stdio) results and better observe the code's behavior. As we are using modern C++ features make sure to select C++23 standard, by adding `-std=c++23` in compiler options box.

Compiler Explorer makes it easy to try out the code, tweak it, and immediately see how it affects the output and generated assembly. The examples are available at GitHub (`https://github.com/PacktPublishing/Cpp-in-Embedded-Systems/tree/main/Chapter07`).

Error codes and asserts

Error codes are a common way of reporting and handling errors in C. They are also still used in C++. A function that fails reports an error through enumerated codes that are checked by a caller and handled appropriately. Let us analyze how error codes work from both the caller and the callee perspective.

A function that returns an error must have a list of errors that are exposed to callers. This list is maintained through a software life cycle, and it can be subject to changes. Enumerated error codes can be added, removed, or modified. A caller must be aware of the error codes that the callee is returning, and it needs to handle them. Or, if it doesn't know how to handle an error, it should propagate it further within a call stack.

Let's observe a simple example of a function that returns an error and analyze the implications this has for the code using this function:

```cpp
enum class error {
    Ok,
    Error1,
    Error2,
    Unknown
};
error h() {
    return error::Error1;
}
error g() {
    auto err = h();
    if(err!=error::Ok) {
```

```cpp
    if(err == error::Error1) {
        // handle error directly
    }
    else if(err == error::Error2) {
        // propagate this error
        return err;
    }
    else {
        // unknown error
        return error::Unknown;
    }
    }
    return error::Ok;
}
void f() {
    auto err = g();
    if(err==error::Ok) {
        printf("Succes\r\n");
    }
    else {
        // handle errors
    }
}
```

In the preceding example, the h function returns an error of enum class error. The g function calls the h function and executes the following steps:

1. Checks if h returned an error that is different from error::Ok. This indicates that the h function didn't perform its task and there is an error that should be handled.

2. If h returned an error, checks whether it is error::Error1. In this case, g knows how to handle this error and it handles it.

3. If h returned error::Error2, g is not capable of handling it, and it forwards it up the call stack.

4. Returns error::Ok to indicate up the call stack that everything went fine.

Function g is called by f, and f also needs to be aware of errors defined in enum class error. It should handle them or pass them up the stack.

Error codes rely on design contracts. The caller must check if the callee returned an error, and if it did, it needs to handle it or pass it up the call stack. Now, we can identify several potential problems with this simple approach:

- We cannot enforce error handling by a caller. It can just discard the return value.

- The caller can forget to handle some of the error cases.

- The caller can forget to pass the error up the call stack.

These are serious design flaws that put an extra burden on code development. There is no escape hatch in case we forget to handle an error somewhere. The program stays in an unknown state and this potentially leads to unwanted behavior.

We can address the first concern using the `nodiscard` attribute. It can be used with a function declaration or enumeration declaration. In our case, we can use it with an `enum class error` declaration as follows:

```cpp
enum class [[nodiscard]] error {
    Ok,
    Error1,
    Error2,
    Unknown
};
```

When a function returning the `enum class` error is called, and the return value is discarded, the compiler is encouraged to raise a warning. If we call the g or h function from our example, GCC will raise a warning similar to this one:

```
<source>:48:6: warning: ignoring returned value of type 'error', declared
with attribute 'nodiscard' [-Wunused-result]
```

If we set up the compiler to treat all warnings as errors, this would break the compilation process and force us to use the return value in code. Even though the `nodiscard` attribute is useful and should be used for similar use cases, it is not a complete solution to our problem. It will enforce usage of the return value, but the caller may still fail to check the error code for all possible cases and address it properly.

Almost every application has some types of errors that are unrecoverable and the only thing it makes sense to do is to log them, display them to a user (if possible), and terminate the program, as there is no sense in proceeding with such a program state. For these types of errors, we can use a global error handler, as they are too important to be left open in the wild and potentially not handled by a caller.

Global error handlers

Global error handlers can be implemented as free functions. They are used system-wide to address errors that are unrecoverable and when it is necessary to stop the execution of firmware due to the severity of an error.

Let's take a look at an example of firmware using an accelerometer. If there are any issues in I^2C communication with the accelerometer, it doesn't make sense to proceed further with code execution – the firmware will display a message to the user and terminate:

```cpp
#include <cstdio>
#include <cstdint>
#include <cstdlib>

int i2c_read(uint8_t *data, size_t len) {
    return 0;
}

namespace error {
    struct i2c_failed{};
    struct spi_failed{};

    void handler(i2c_failed err) {
        printf("I2C error!\r\n");
        exit(1);
    }
    void handler(spi_failed err) {
        printf("SPI error!\r\n");
        exit(1);
    }
};

class accelerometer {
public:
    struct data {
        int16_t x;
        int16_t y;
        int16_t z;
```

```cpp
    };
    data get_data() {
        uint8_t buff[6];
        if(i2c_read(buff, 6) != 6) {
            error::handler(error::i2c_failed{});
        }
        return data{};
    }
};


int main () {
    accelerometer accel;
    auto data = accel.get_data();
    return 0;
}
```

In the preceding example, we have an `accelerometer` class with the `get_data` method, which uses the `i2c_read` function from the vendor-specific HAL in C (let us pretend this is the case).

The `i2c_read` function returns the number of read bytes. In our example, the return value is stubbed to 0 so we can simulate the erroneous behavior of the accelerometer (or the I^2C bus). In case `i2c_read` returns a number different from the requested number of bytes, get_data will call `error::handler`.

We implemented an error handler using a tag-dispatching mechanism. We are overloading the `error::handler` function with so-called tags, or empty types. In our example, we have two tags, `i2c_failed` and `spi_failed`, and two overloaded error handlers. Tag dispatching has a couple of advantages over defining error codes with enum:

- We need to overload error handlers for every tag that is used in code. Error handlers are implemented individually for every error type. This adds to the readability of code.

- In case we make a call to an error handler that is not overloaded, the compilation will fail, forcing us to implement it.

In our example, the error handler will print a message using the `printf` function and make a call to the `exit` function, effectively terminating the program. In real-world situations, how we handle errors depends on the application. For example, for a medical device, if critical operations become unsafe after an error, we would first attempt to recover from the error.

If recovery failed, the system would enter a critical error state, alert medical personnel, and gracefully terminate the treatment operation.

An error on the I^{2}C bus or, more generally, failed communication with external devices must be handled appropriately through robust error-handling mechanisms.

On the other hand, there are conditions that indicate programming mistakes – situations that should never occur if the code is correct. These include violations of preconditions, such as input parameters being out of expected boundaries due to logic errors in the code. Proceeding under such circumstances could lead to undefined behavior or system instability. To detect these programming errors during development, we use asserts.

Asserts

Asserts are primarily used during development to detect programming mistakes by verifying that certain conditions hold true at specific points in the code. They help identify logical errors and incorrect assumptions by halting execution when an unexpected condition occurs. A macro assert is defined in `<cassert>` in the standard library. It is used to check a logical expression, and in case the logical expression is false, it prints diagnostic information and calls `std::abort`, effectively terminating the program.

To better understand asserts, and how to use them, let us take a look at the following code example:

```cpp
#include <cassert>
#include <cstdint>
enum class option : std::uint8_t {
    Option1 = 0,
    Option2,
    Option3,
    Last
};
option uint8_to_option(uint8_t num) {
    assert(num < static_cast<uint8_t>(option::Last));
    return static_cast<option>(num);
}
int main() {
    const option opt = uint8_to_option(3);
    return 0;
}
```

In the preceding example, we have defined the `option` enum class with `uint8_t` as an underlying type. We will use it to allow users to select an option over a network interface and we want to make sure that the conversion from `uint8_t` to the `option` enum is always correct. The `uint8_to_option` function will assert if the received `uint8_t` argument is not smaller than `option::Last`.

In the example, we called `uint8_to_option` with argument 3, which is not smaller than `option::Last`, meaning that the assert macro will print the following diagnostic information and make a call to `std::abort` to terminate the program:

```
assertion "num < static_cast<uint8_t>(option::Last)" failed: file "/home/
amar/projects/Cpp-in-Embedded Systems/Chapter07/error_handling/app/src/
main.cpp", line 21, function: option uint8_to_option(uint8_t)
```

Now, this is quite a lengthy debug statement. Let's take a look at the `assert` macro definition:

```cpp
#define assert(expr)                                \
    (static_cast <bool> (expr)                      \
     ? void (0)                                     \
     : __assert_fail (#expr,                        \
                        __ASSERT_FILE,              \
                        __ASSERT_LINE,              \
                        __ASSERT_FUNCTION))
```

We see that the expression is cast to a `bool` type and that the ternary operator does nothing if the expression is true, or it makes a call to the `__assert_fail` function if the expression is false. The `assert` macro passes the expression as a string literal, the filename as a string literal, the line number, and also a function name as a string literal. All these string literals must be stored in the binary, taking up precious memory.

Asserts can be disabled by defining the `NDEBUG` macro before including `<cassert>` as in the following lines:

```cpp
#define NDEBUG
#include <cassert>
```

We can also define `NDEBUG` using the build system. The `assert` macro will do nothing if `NDEBUG` is defined before `<cassert>` is included. This option is left to be used in case we want to disable asserts, as they are most commonly used in debug builds, and disabled in production builds. They should be disabled before the safety-critical software validation.

The `assert` macro, as implemented in the standard library, is not suitable for embedded systems as it includes the filename, function name, and `assert` expression as string literals, which end up stored in the flash of the embedded target. Moreover, asserts are mostly intended to be used during debugging, and they are often disabled in production builds. Still, there is a benefit of asserts enabled in production builds, as they can provide valuable insights for postmortem debugging if they are implemented to log data when the expression is evaluated as `false`.

We will examine an alternative approach to logging information using asserts. As we have already concluded, the default assert macro implementation is not well suited for embedded targets, even though it contains useful information for debugging: filename, function name, and line number. Instead of a lengthy string describing an exact location of the assert macro line in our code, we can simply log a program counter and use the map file and `addr2line` tool to convert the address to the exact line. We can see a simple macro definition and a helper function to implement this in the following code:

```cpp
void log_pc_and_halt(std::uint32_t pc) {
    printf("Assert at 0x%08lX\r\n", pc);
    while(true) {}
}
#define light_assert(expr)          \
        (static_cast<bool> (expr)   \
        ? void (0)                  \
        : log_pc_and_halt(hal::get_pc())    \
        )
```

We have defined a macro named `light_assert` that, instead of `__assert_failed`, calling `log_pc_and_halt`. It is passing the return value from `hal::get_pc` as an argument to `log_pc_and_halt`. To see this code in action, you can take a look at the example in the `Chapter07/error_handling` project.

The project for this chapter is configured so that you can configure it to use different main C++ files and configure which one is going to be used with CMake. Let us start our Docker container using the following commands:

```bash
$ docker start dev_env
$ docker exec -it dev_env /bin/bash
```

This should get us in the Docker terminal. Run `ls -l` to make sure that the `Cpp-in-Embedded-Systems` repo is cloned. If not, clone it using the following command:

```
$ git clone https://github.com/PacktPublishing/Cpp-in-Embedded-Systems.git
```

Start Visual Studio Code, attach it to the running container, and open `Chapter07/error_handling` project as described in *Chapter 4* and run the following commands in the Visual Studio Code terminal, or run them directly in the container terminal:

```
$ cd Chapter07/error_handling
$ cmake -B build -DCMAKE_BUILD_TYPE=Debug -DMAIN_CPP_FILE_NAME=main_
assert.cpp
$ cmake --build build --target run_in_renode
```

The preceding commands will build the firmware using the `app/src/main_assert.cpp` file and run it in Renode simulator. You should see similar output to this in the terminal:

```
14:11:06.6293 [INFO] usart2: [host: 0.31s (+0.31s)|virt: 0s (+0s)] Assert
example
14:11:06.6455 [INFO] usart2: [host: 0.32s (+15.87ms)|virt: 0.11ms
(+0.11ms)] Assert at 0x08000F74
```

As we can see, the assert evaluated expression to false and printed out the `0x08000F74` program counter value. We can convert this value to the line from a source file using the following command:

```
$ arm-none-eabi-addr2line --exe bare.elf 0x08000F74
```

This will result in the following output:

```
/workspace/Cpp-in-Embedded-Systems/Chapter07/error_handling/app/src/main_
assert.cpp:30 (discriminator 1)
```

As you can see, we are able to get the exact line of the source of the assert using this approach and by logging just 4 bytes of data (address). In this implementation, `log_pc_and_halt` just print the address. In production implementations, we can store the address in non-volatile memory and use it for postmortem debugging.

The `hal::get_pc()` function is declared with an `inline` specifier. We use `inline` as a hint to the compiler to insert instructions from a function directly to a call site, that is, not to make a function call. The compiler doesn't necessarily need to comply with our intentions, and that can be observed by building this example using the `O0` optimization level.

Exercise for you!

As an exercise, edit `CMAKE_C_FLAGS_DEBUG` and `CMAKE_CXX_FLAGS_DEBUG` in `CMakeLists.txt`, and instead of `Og`, use `O0`. Build and run the program and run the `addr2line` utility on the output. To mitigate this concern, you can define a macro to be used instead of the `hal::get_pc()` function.

We use asserts to catch programming errors – situations that should never occur if the code is correct. They are often employed to validate internal assumptions and invariants within critical functions. The primary purpose of asserts is for debugging; they help developers find and fix bugs during the development phase. However, as we've seen, customized asserts can also provide valuable insights into production builds for postmortem analysis. While asserts are useful for detecting programming mistakes during development, they are not a substitute for proper error handling in production code. Error codes can be cumbersome because they require manual propagation of errors up the call stack. C++ offers exceptions as a solution to these problems, providing a structured way to handle errors without cluttering the code with error-checking logic.

Next, we will go over C++ exceptions to better understand the benefits they offer from the error-handling aspect.

Exceptions

Exceptions in C++ are error-handling mechanisms that are based on the principle of throwing and catching objects of an arbitrary type. All exceptions that are thrown from the standard library derive from the `std::exception` class defined in the `<exception>` header. We put code that may throw an exception in the `try` block, and we define the type of exception we want to catch in the `catch` clause, as shown in the following example:

```cpp
std::array<int, 4> arr;
try {
  arr.at(5) = 6;
}
catch(std::out_of_range &e) {
  printf("Array out of range!\r\n");
}
```

In the preceding example, we have defined `std::array arr`, an array of integers with four members. In the `try` block, we are trying to access an element with index 5, which is clearly out of the defined range, and the at method will throw the `std::out_of_range` exception. In order to run this example, go to the `Chapter07/error_handling` folder, make sure that the `build` folder is deleted, and run the following commands:

```
$ mkdir build && cd build
$ cmake .. -DCMAKE_BUILD_TYPE=Debug -DMAIN_CPP_FILE_NAME=main_exceptions.
cpp
$ make -j4
$ make run_in_renode
```

You should see `Array out of range!` printed in the terminal.

Now, while building the example, you may have noticed that the size of the binary is a whooping 88 KB. What happened?

In order to enable exceptions, besides using the `-fexceptions` compiler flag, we also had to disable the nano specs that we used in previous examples. Nano specs define the usage of the C standard `newlib-nano` library and size-optimized `libstdc++` and `libsupc++` libraries. These are built without exception support and if we use them, any attempt at throwing exceptions will result in `std::abort` being called instead. By disabling nano specs, we are using an unoptimized C++ standard library, which results in the 88 KB binary size. A size-optimized standard C++ library can be built from sources with enabled exceptions, which would help reduce the binary footprint.

If an exception is not caught, `std::terminate_handler` will be called. We can replace the default handler using the `std::set_terminate` function as in the following example:

```cpp
std::set_terminate([]() {
    printf("My terminate handler!\r\n");
    while(true){}
});
```

In the preceding example, we provided a lambda as a terminate handler. As an exercise, try to access the array from the previous example with an index that is out of range, but out of a `try` block. This should trigger the terminate handler and make a call to the lambda we passed to the `std::set_terminate` function.

Exceptions are propagated up the call stack. Let us go through the following example to demonstrate exception propagation:

```cpp
template <class T, std::size_t N> struct ring_buffer {
  std::array<T, N> arr;
  std::size_t write_idx = 0;

  void push(T t) {
    arr.at(write_idx++) = t;
  }
};
int main()
{
    ring_buffer<int, 4> rb;
    try {
      for(int i = 0; i < 6; i++) {
        rb.push(i);
      }
    }
    catch(std::out_of_range &e) {
      printf("Ring buffer out of range!\r\n");
    }
    return 0;
}
```

The preceding example is based on a ring buffer from previous chapters that uses `std::array` as an underlying container. In the `push` method, it doesn't check the write index, meaning that the array's at method will throw an exception if we call the `push` method more than N times. An exception is thrown in the `push` method, where there is no `try-catch` block, and it gets caught only in the `main` function in the `catch` block.

You can run the preceding example in the Renode simulator using the following instructions. Start Visual Studio Code, attach it to the running container, open `Chapter07/error_handling` project as described in *Chapter 4*, and run the following commands in the Visual Studio Code terminal, or run them directly in the container terminal:

```
$ cd Chapter07/error_handling
$ cmake -B build -DCMAKE_BUILD_TYPE=Debug -DMAIN_CPP_FILE_NAME=main_
exceptions.cpp
$ cmake --build build --target run_in_renode
```

Exception propagation is useful for the type of errors that we don't want to propagate between the software layers manually using error codes. However, the problem with exceptions is that they are not visible from function declarations as is the case with error codes. We need to rely on good documentation to know which function throws an error and where those errors are handled.

There is a saying that exceptions are used for exceptional errors that are very rare. But what are exceptional errors? That depends on the library, application, and use case. It is hard to generalize. A failed read to the accelerometer may be a recoverable error that is solved by resetting it. We can throw an exception on a failed I^{2}C bus communication, and the upper layer that catches this error may decide to try resetting the accelerometer.

Failing to control boost voltage regulator output by DAC may also be recoverable, but we may want to terminate the program as we are implementing a medical device and that may be the best action possible to prevent any damage to a user. In this case, we want to react as fast as possible and exception propagation and stack unwinding are probably not desirable so we will rely on a global handler or asserts instead.

Exceptions come with a price, both in flash and RAM memory consumption, and the execution time can't always be guaranteed, which is a problem if we are working with hard real-time systems. But they also solve the problem of error propagation and enforce error handling. If there is not a `catch` clause for a specific type, `std::terminate_handler` will be called, and the program will not continue with the execution.

Error codes and exceptions can co-exist, and they often do. Embedded C++ projects often use C libraries, or legacy C++ code, which often uses error codes. We can benefit from exceptions by using them for very rare errors, adding additional robustness to our firmware. Still, the decision of whether to use them is influenced by available memory resources and the type of project we are working on.

Next, we will cover the C++ `std::optional` and `std::expected` template classes, which are used as return types from functions.

std:: optional and std::expected

C++17 introduced `std::optional`, a template class that either has a value or has nothing. This is useful for situations where a function may or may not return a value. To better understand it, let's go through the following example:

```cpp
#include <cstdio>
#include <optional>
struct sensor {
    struct data {
        int x;
        int y;
    };
    static inline bool ret_val = true;
    static std::optional<data> get_data() {
        ret_val = !ret_val;
        if(ret_val) {
            return data{4, 5};
        }
        else {
            return std::nullopt;
        }
    }
};

int main()
{
    const auto get_data_from_main = [] () {
        auto result = sensor::get_data();
        if(result) {
            printf("x = %d, y = %d\r\n", (*result).x, (*result).y);
        }
        else {
            printf("No data!\r\n");
        }
    };

    get_data_from_main();
```

```
    get_data_from_main();

    return 0;
}
```

In the preceding example, we have a `sensor` struct with the get_data method, which returns a value if some conditions are met. Otherwise, it doesn't return it. The sensor is not in an erroneous state, it just doesn't have data ready yet. For this, we are using `std::optional<data>` to declare that the sensor may or may not return the data struct. We used the `ret_val` bool to simulate data being ready at every second call of the get_data function.

In the main, we created the `get_data_from_main` lambda, which makes a call to the sensor's get_data. The `std::optional<data>` return value is converted to a bool in the `if` statement. If it is converted to `true`, it means it holds data, else it holds nothing. We access the data type by dereferencing the `result` object.

C++ 23 introduced `std::expected<T, E>`, a template class that either holds an expected object of class `T` or an unexpected object of class `E`. To understand this better, let us go through the following example:

```
#include <cstdio>
#include <expected>
struct ble_light_bulb {
    enum class error {
        disconnected,
        timeout
    };
    struct config {
        int r;
        int g;
        int b;
    };
    bool ret_val;
    std::expected<config, error> get_config() {
        ret_val = !ret_val;
        if(ret_val) {
            return config {10, 20, 30};
        }
        else {
```

```cpp
                return std::unexpected(error::timeout);
            }
        }
    };
    int main()
    {
        ble_light_bulb bulb;
        const auto get_config_from_main = [&bulb]() {
            auto result = bulb.get_config();
            if(result.has_value()) {
                auto conf = result.value();
                printf("Config r %d, g %d, b %d\r\n", conf.r, conf.g, conf.b);
            } else {
                auto err = result.error();
                using bulb_error = ble_light_bulb::error;
                if(err == bulb_error::disconnected) {
                    printf("The bulb is disconnected!\r\n");
                }
                else if(err == bulb_error::timeout) {
                    printf("Timeout!\r\n");
                }
            }
        };
        get_config_from_main();
        get_config_from_main();
        return 0;
    }
```

In the preceding example, we have a `ble_light_bulb` struct, a BLE (Bluetooth Low Energy) light bulb, with the `get_config` method, which reads some config data over the BLE connection from the bulb. This method returns `config`, or an error. In main, we defined the `get_config_from_main` lambda, which calls `get_config` on the `ble_light_bulb` object. We use the `has_value` method on the expected returned object to check if it holds an expected value. We use `value` methods to access the expected value or the `error` method to access the `error` object.

You can run the preceding example in the Renode simulator using the following instructions. Start Visual Studio Code, attach it to the running container, open `Chapter07/error_handling` project as described in *Chapter 4*, and run the following commands in the Visual Studio Code terminal, or run them directly in the container terminal:

```
$ cd Chapter07/error_handling
$ cmake -B build -DCMAKE_BUILD_TYPE=Debug -DMAIN_CPP_FILE_NAME=main_
expected.cpp
$ cmake --build build --target run_in_renode
```

Summary

In this chapter, we analyzed different error-handling strategies in C++. We went through error codes, global handlers, asserts, exceptions, `std::optional`, and `std::expected`. We learned the pros and cons of each and in which situations it makes sense to apply them.

In the next chapter, we will cover templates in more detail.

Join our community on Discord

Join our community's Discord space for discussions with the author and other readers:

`https://packt.link/embeddedsystems`

Part 3

C++ Advanced Concepts

Building on the fundamentals, this part introduces more advanced concepts such as templates, including static polymorphism and compile-time computation. It also guides you through increasing type safety in C++ and writing expressive code using lambdas. These advanced techniques are taught through practical examples.

This part has the following chapters:

- *Chapter 8, Building Generic and Reusable Code with Templates*
- *Chapter 9, Improving Type-Safety with Strong Types*
- *Chapter 10, Writing Expressive Code with Lambdas*
- *Chapter 11, Compile-Time Computation*

8

Building Generic and Reusable Code with Templates

We have used class templates in previous examples in this book without explaining them in detail. You should by now have a basic understanding of templates in C++ and know how to use template container classes from the standard library to specialize containers with different underlying types. We have also covered the `std::optional` and `std::expected` template classes, which we can use to handle different return types from functions.

As you have already seen, templates are used heavily in the C++ standard library. They allow us to implement the same functionality for different types, making our code reusable and generic, which is one of the strengths of C++. Templates are an extremely complex topic; entire books have been written on templates and metaprogramming in C++. This chapter will help you understand templates in C++ in more detail.

In this chapter, we're going to cover the following main topics:

- Template basics
- Metaprogramming
- Concepts
- Compile-time polymorphism

Technical requirements

To get the most out of this chapter, I strongly recommend using Compiler Explorer (https://godbolt.org/) as you read through the examples. Select GCC as your compiler for x86 architecture. This will allow you to see standard output and better observe the code's behavior. As we are using modern C++, make sure to select C++23 standard, by adding -std=c++23 in the compiler options box.

Compiler Explorer makes it easy to try the code, tweak it, and immediately see how it affects the output and generated assembly code. The examples from this chapter are available on GitHub (https://github.com/PacktPublishing/Cpp-in-Embedded-Systems/tree/main/Chapter08).

Template basics

One definition of the word "template" is "a gauge, pattern, or mold (such as a thin plate or board) used as a guide to the form of a piece being made. " This definition can be applied to templates in C++.

In C++, templates serve as patterns or molds for functions and classes, allowing the creation of actual functions and classes. From this perspective, templates are not real functions or types themselves; rather, they act as guides for generating concrete functions and types. To better understand this definition, let us take a look at the following code sample:

```cpp
#include <cstdio>

template<typename T>
T add(T a, T b) {
    return a + b;
}

int main() {
    int result_int = add(1, 4);
    float result_float = add(1.11f, 1.91f);
    printf("result_int = %d\r\n", result_int);
    printf("result_float = %.2f\r\n", result_float);
    return 0;
}
```

In this example, we have a template function, add, with the template type parameter T. In the main function, we see two calls to the add function:

- The first one has integers as arguments and a return value stored in result_int
- The second one has float arguments and a return value stored in the result_float float variable

Now, we previously said that template types and functions are not actual types and functions, so how can we make a call to the template function if it's not a real function?

Making a call to the template function

In this example, when the compiler sees a call to add a template function, it deduces the template argument and replaces the template parameter, in this case, type T, with type int in the first call and float in the second call to add. After argument deduction, the template is instantiated; that is, the compiler creates two instances of the add function: one with integers as arguments and one with floats. We can see this in the assembly output of the preceding example shown here:

```
_Z3addIiET_S0_S0_:
        push    rbp
        mov     rbp, rsp
        mov     DWORD PTR [rbp-4], edi
        mov     DWORD PTR [rbp-8], esi
        mov     edx, DWORD PTR [rbp-4]
        mov     eax, DWORD PTR [rbp-8]
        add     eax, edx
        pop     rbp
        ret
_Z3addIfET_S0_S0_:
        push    rbp
        mov     rbp, rsp
        movss   DWORD PTR s[rbp-4], xmm0
        movss   DWORD PTR [rbp-8], xmm1
        movss   xmm0, DWORD PTR [rbp-4]
        addss   xmm0, DWORD PTR [rbp-8]
        pop     rbp
        ret
```

In the preceding assembly output, we see there are two instances of the add function: `_Z3addIiET_`
`S0_S0_`, accepting integers, and `_Z3addIfET_S0_S0_`, accepting floats. The compiler instantiated
these two functions from the add template function, after it deduced template arguments on the
call site of this function. This is the basic working principle of templates in C++.

In the example of the add template function, the compiler will instantiate a new function for
every type for which there is a defined operator+. So, what would happen if we tried to call the
add template function on a type for which there is no defined operator+? Let's take a look at the
following example:

```cpp
struct point {
    int x;
    int y;
};

int main() {
    point a{1, 2};
    point b{2, 1};
    auto c = add(a, b);
    return 0;
}
```

In the preceding example, we defined a point struct, for which there is no defined operator+,
and we made a call to the add template function. This will result in a compiler error similar to
the one shown here:

```
<source>: In instantiation of 'T add(T, T) [with T = point]':
<source>:25:17:    required from here
    25 |      auto c = add(a, b);
       |               ~~~^~~~~~
<source>:6:13: error: no match for 'operator+' (operand types are 'point'
and 'point')
     6 |     return a + b;
       |            ~~^~~
```

So, what happened? When the compiler tried to instantiate a function using the add template with point as type T, the compilation failed due to no match for 'operator+' (operand types are 'point' and 'point'). We can solve this by defining operator+ for the point struct as follows:

```
struct point {
    int x;
    int y;
    point operator+(const point& other) const {
        return point{x + other.x, y + other.y};
    }
    void print() {
        printf("x = %d, y = %d\r\n", x, y);
    }
};
```

In the preceding implementation, we defined operator+ for the point struct, and we also defined the print function, which will help us to print the point. After this change, we can compile the example successfully.

What if we wanted, for some reason, that add function when used with type point behaves differently than just applying the operator+? Let's say we want to increment both x and y by 1 after summation. We can use template specialization for this.

Template specialization

Template specialization allows us to provide the compiler with the implementation of a template function for a specific type, as in the following example of specializing the add function for type point:

```
template<>
point add<point>(point a, point b) {
    return point{a.x+b.x+1, a.y+b.y+1};
}
```

In this case, when the add function is called with arguments of type point, the compiler skips the generic template instantiation and uses this specialized version instead. This allows us to customize the behavior of the function specifically for point objects, adding an extra 1 to each coordinate when two point instances are added together. Let us take a look at the full main function now:

```
int main() {
    point a{1, 2};
```

```cpp
    point b{2, 1};
    auto c = add(a, b);
    c.print();
    static_assert(std::is_same_v<decltype(c), point>);
    return 0;
}
```

If we run the example with template specialization from the previous step, we will get the following output:

```
x = 4, y = 4
```

The compiler used function specialization for the point type. Template specialization makes templates a flexible tool, allowing us to provide compilers with custom implementations when needed.

In the preceding example, we can see that for variable c, we used auto as a type specifier. The auto keyword was introduced in C++11, and when used, the compiler deduces the actual type of a variable from the initialization expression. In order to confirm that the deduced type of variable c is point, we used static_assert, which performs compile-time assertion checking.

As the argument of static_assert, we use a type trait from the metaprogramming library, std::is_same_v, which checks whether two types are identical and evaluates to true if they are. We determine the type of c using the decltype specifier, which retrieves the type of an expression at compile time. This allows us to verify that the type deduced for c is indeed point. If this assertion fails, the compiler will generate an error.

Template metaprogramming

Template metaprogramming involves using templates to write code that generates different functions, types, and constants at compile time based on the types used in the template arguments. Template metaprogramming is an advanced technique heavily utilized in modern C++ libraries. It may be overwhelming, so it is perfectly fine if it appears to be hard to understand. Take this as merely an introduction and an exploration of this interesting topic.

Let us go back to the example of the add template function. Is there something we can do if we want to enforce that this template function is used only for arithmetic types such as integers and floats?

<type_traits> header from metaprogramming library provides us with the std::enable_if template type, which accepts two parameters, a Boolean and a type. If a Boolean is true, the resulting type will have a public typedef member, type. Let's take a look at the following example:

```cpp
#include <type_traits>
template<typename T>
std::enable_if<true, T>::type
add(T a, T b) {
    return a + b;
}
```

In the preceding example, we used std::enable_if in place of the return type of the add template function. As we set the Boolean argument to true, it will have a public typedef type, T, meaning that the return type of the add function template will be T.

We will expand this example using type trait class template std::is_arithmetic<T>, which will have a public Boolean named value set to true if T is an arithmetic type. The preceding example will result in the following code:

```cpp
template<typename T>
std::enable_if<std::is_arithmetic<T>::value, T>::type
add(T a, T b) {
    return a + b;
}
```

In the preceding example, instead of hardcoding true as the condition for std::enable_if, we use the std::is_arithmetic<T>::value. Let's take a look at the main function using this template function and the point type from the previous example:

```cpp
int main() {
    auto a = add(1, 2); // OK
    auto b = add(1.1, 2.1); // OK
    point p_a{1, 2};
    point p_b{2, 1};
    auto p_c = add(p_a, p_b); // compile-error
    return 0;
}
```

If we try to compile this code, the compilation will fail with a lengthy error message containing the following:

```
<source>: In function 'int main()':
<source>:30:17: error: no matching function for call to 'add(point&,
point&)'
   30 |        auto c = add(p_a, p_b); // compile-error
```

```
       |                  ~~~^~~~~~~~~~
<source>:30:17: note: there is 1 candidate
<source>:19:1: note: candidate 1: 'template<class T> typename std::enable_
if<std::is_arithmetic<_Tp>::value, T>::type add(T, T)'
   19 |  add(T a, T b) {
      |  ^~~
<source>:19:1: note: template argument deduction/substitution failed:
<source>: In substitution of 'template<class T> typename std::enable_
if<std::is_arithmetic<_Tp>::value, T>::type add(T, T) [with T = point]':
<source>:30:17:   required from here
   30 |     auto c = add(p_a, p_b); // compile-error
      |                  ~~~^~~~~~~~~~
<source>:19:1: error: no type named 'type' in 'struct std::enable_
if<false, point>'
   19 |  add(T a, T b) {
      |  ^~~
```

The preceding compiler error looks intimidating, and it is hard to read. This is one of those things that templates are notorious for. Before we tackle this concern, let's focus on analyzing what happened in this case.

Template argument deduction/substitution failed as `std::is_arithmetic<point>::value` results in `false`, meaning that the `std::enable_if` template type will not have a public typedef type `T`. Effectively, any attempt at the usage of the `add` template function in this example with a type that's not arithmetic will result in a compiler error, even if `operator+` is defined for that type. We can think of `std::enable_if` as an enabler or disabler of a template function in C++.

Let's modify the `add` template function so that it prints the result of the sum operation. As both integers and floats are arithmetic types, we need to treat them differently. We could use `std::enable_if` and create two template functions using the `std::is_integral` and `std::is_floating_point` type traits as in the following example:

```cpp
template<typename T>
std::enable_if<std::is_integral<T>::value, T>::type
add(T a, T b) {
    T result = a + b;
    printf("%d + %d = %d\r\n", a, b, result);
```

```cpp
    return result;
}


template<typename T>
std::enable_if<std::is_floating_point<T>::value, T>::type
add(T a, T b) {
    T result = a + b;
    printf("%.2f + %.2f = %.2f\r\n", a, b, result);
    return result;
}
```

As you remember, `std::enable_if` is a template enabler or disabler, meaning it will enable the first template function for integer types and print them using `printf` and the `%d` format specifier. Template substitution will fail for the second template function with integer types, but this will not be treated as an error as there is a valid function candidate for integer arguments from the first template. This principle is called **Subsitution Failure Is Not An Error (SFINAE)**. For the floating-point types, the first template function will be disabled, but the second one will be enabled.

Now, the example functions we used are very simple, but let's for a moment pretend that the add function template is doing a heavy-lifting task and that between integer and floating-point versions, the only difference is how we print the result. So, if we used two different function templates, we would copy a lot of the same code. We can avoid this by using `constexpr if`, which will enable or disable certain paths in code at compile time. Let us take a look at a modified example:

```cpp
std::enable_if_t<std::is_arithmetic_v<T>, T>
add(T a, T b) {
    T result = a + b;
    if constexpr (std::is_integral_v<T>) {
        printf("%d + %d = %d\r\n", a, b, result);
    } else if constexpr (std::is_floating_point_v<T>) {
        printf("%.2f + %.2f = %.2f\r\n", a, b, result);
    }
    return a + b;
}
```

In the preceding example, we used the `constexpr` `if` statement to enable certain paths of the program based on the compile-time evaluation of the `std::is_integral_v<T>` and `std::is_floating_point_v<T>` expressions. `constexpr` `if` was introduced in C++17. You can also notice that we used aliases for type traits as `std::enable_if_t<T>`, which is equivalent to `std::enable_if<T>::type`, and `std::is_floating_point_v<T>`, which is equivalent to `std::is_floating_point<T>::value`.

In this example, we used type traits and `std::enable_if` to enable the add function template only for arithmetic types. C++20 introduced concepts, which we can use to put restraints on template types.

Concepts

Concepts are named sets of template parameter requirements. They are evaluated at compile time and are used during overload resolution to select the most appropriate function overload; that is, they are used to determine which function template will be instantiated and compiled.

We will create a concept for arithmetic types and use it in our add template function, as follows:

```cpp
template<typename T>
concept Arithmetic = std::is_arithmetic_v<T>;

template<Arithmetic T>
T add(T a, T b) {
    T result = a + b;
    if constexpr (std::is_integral_v<T>) {
        printf("%d + %d = %d\r\n", a, b, result);
    } else if constexpr (std::is_floating_point_v<T>) {
        printf("%.2f + %.2f = %.2f\r\n", a, b, result);
    }
    return a + b;
}
```

In the preceding code, we created the `Arithmetic` concept and used it in the add function template to put requirements on the T template type. The add template function is now easier to read. It is visible from the template declaration that type T must meet the requirements of the `Arithmetic` concept, which makes the code easier to read and comprehend.

Concepts not only make the code easier to read but also improve readability of compiler errors. If we tried to call the function template add on type point, we would now get an error similar to the following one:

```
<source>: In function 'int main()':
<source>:41:17: error: no matching function for call to 'add(point&,
point&)'
   41 |     auto c = add(p_a, p_b); // compile-error
      |              ~~~^~~~~~~~~~~
<source>:41:17: note: there is 1 candidate
<source>:22:3: note: candidate 1: 'template<class T>  requires
Arithmetic<T> T add(T, T)'
   22 | T add(T a, T b) {
      |   ^~~
<source>:22:3: note: template argument deduction/substitution failed:
<source>:22:3: note: constraints not satisfied
<source>: In substitution of 'template<class T>  requires  Arithmetic<T> T
add(T, T) [with T = point]':
<source>:41:17:   required from here
   41 |     auto c = add(p_a, p_b); // compile-error
      |              ~~~^~~~~~~~~~~
<source>:18:9:   required for the satisfaction of 'Arithmetic<T>' [with T
= point]
<source>:18:27: note: the expression 'is_arithmetic_v<T> [with T = point]'
evaluated to 'false'
   18 | concept Arithmetic = std::is_arithmetic_v<T>;
      |                      ~~~~~^~~~~~~~~~~~~~~~~~~
```

The preceding compiler error is way easier to read and understand what happened than the one we had previously when we didn't use concepts. We can easily trace the origin of the error to the fact that constraints imposed by the Arithmetic concept are not satisfied for the point type.

Next, we will move on to discuss compile-time polymorphism and see how we can utilize concepts to help us enforce strong interfaces.

Compile-time polymorphism

In *Chapter 5*, we discussed dynamic, or runtime, polymorphism. We used it to define an interface for uart, which was implemented by the uart_stm32 class. The gsm_lib class has a dependency on the uart interface only, not on the concrete implementation, which is contained in uart_stm32. This is called **loose coupling** and allows us to have portable code for the gsm_lib class.

We can easily supply gsm_lib with another uart interface implementation on a different hardware platform. This principle is called **dependency inversion**. It says that high-level modules (classes) shouldn't depend on low-level modules and that both should depend on abstractions (interfaces). We can implement this principle by using inheritance and virtual functions in C++.

Virtual functions result in indirection, causing the runtime overhead and increased binary size needed for their implementation. They allow runtime dispatching of function calls, but they come with a price. In embedded applications, we usually know all our types, meaning that we can use templates and overload resolution for the static or compile-time dispatch of function calls.

Using Class Templates for Compile-Time Polymorphism

We can make gsm_lib a class template that has one parameter that we will use for the uart type, as shown in the following example:

```cpp
#include <span>
#include <cstdio>
#include <cstdint>

class uart_stm32 {
public:
    void init(std::uint32_t baudrate = 9600) {
        printf("uart_stm32::init: setting baudrate to %d\r\n", baudrate);
    }
    void write(std::span<const char> data) {
        printf("uart_stm32::write: ");
        for(auto ch: data) {
            putc(ch, stdout);
        }
    }
```

```cpp
};

template<typename T>
class gsm_lib{
public:
    gsm_lib(T &u) : uart_(u) {}
    void init() {
        printf("gsm_lib::init: sending AT command\r\n");
        uart_.write("AT");
    }
private:
    T &uart_;
};

int main() {

    uart_stm32 uart_stm32_obj;
    uart_stm32_obj.init(115200);

    gsm_lib gsm(uart_stm32_obj);
    gsm.init();
    return 0;
}
```

In the preceding example, the compiler will instantiate the gsm_lib template class using the uart_stm32 class as a template argument. This will result in using a reference to an object of the uart_stm32 class in the gsm_lib code. We can still easily reuse gsm_lib by using it with a different type that provides all the methods needed to compile it. In this example, the type that used with the gsm_lib class template must provide a write method accepting std::span<char> as its parameter. But this also means that any type that has such a method will allow us to compile the code.

Dynamic polymorphism requires interface classes implemented in concrete classes and used in high-level code. It makes intended behavior of the code clear when reading it. Can we do something similar using templates? It turns out we can. We can use the **curiously recurring template pattern (CRTP)** to implement compile-time subtype polymorphism.

Curiously recurring template pattern (CRTP)

CRTP is a C++ idiom where the derived class uses a template class instantiated with itself as a base class. Yes, it sounds confusing, so let's jump into the code to better understand this:

```cpp
template<typename U>
class uart_interface {
public:
    void init(std::uint32_t baudrate = 9600) {
        static_cast<U*>(this)->initImpl(baudrate);
    }
};


class uart_stm32 : public uart_interface<uart_stm32> {
public:
    void initImpl(std::uint32_t baudrate = 9600) {
        printf("uart_stm32::init: setting baudrate to %d\r\n", baudrate);
    }
};
```

The preceding code implements CRTP. The `uart_stm32` derived class inherits from the `uart_interface` class template instantiated with the `uart_stm32` class itself. The base class template exposes an interface from which it can access the derived class using `static_cast` on `this` (pointer to itself). It provides the `init` method, which calls `initImpl` on the object of the `uart_stm32` class.

CRTP allows us to define our interface in the base class and implement it in a derived class, similar to the inheritance mechanism we are using for runtime polymorphism. The remaining part to ensure that this interface is used in `gsm_lib` is to create type constraints using concepts, as follows:

```cpp
template<typename T>
concept TheUart = std::derived_from<T, uart_interface<T>>;
```

The preceding code is a concept that we will use to restrain types accepted by the `gsm_lib` class template. It will accept only types that are derived from the `uart_interface` class template instantiated by that type itself. The following is the full code example:

```cpp
#include <span>
#include <cstdio>
#include <cstdint>


template<typename U>
class uart_interface {
```

```cpp
public:
    void init(std::uint32_t baudrate = 9600) {
        static_cast<U*>(this)->initImpl(baudrate);
    }
    void write(std::span<const char> data) {
        static_cast<U*>(this)->writeImpl(data);
    }
};


class uart_stm32 : public uart_interface<uart_stm32> {
public:
    void initImpl(std::uint32_t baudrate = 9600) {
        printf("uart_stm32::init: setting baudrate to %d\r\n", baudrate);
    }
    void writeImpl(std::span<const char> data) {
        printf("uart_stm32::write: ");
        for(auto ch: data) {
            putc(ch, stdout);
        }
    }
};


template<typename T>
concept TheUart = std::derived_from<T, uart_interface<T>>;


template<TheUart T>
class gsm_lib{
public:
    gsm_lib(T &u) : uart_(u) {}
    void init() {
        printf("gsm_lib::init: sending AT command\r\n");
        uart_.write("AT");
    }
private:
    T &uart_;
};


int main() {
```

```cpp
    uart_stm32 uart_stm32_obj;
    uart_stm32_obj.init(115200);

    gsm_lib gsm(uart_stm32_obj);
    gsm.init();
    return 0;
}
```

In the preceding code, we used CRTP to implement compile-time or static subtype polymorphism. uart_stm32 is a concrete class that depends on the interface defined by the uart_interface class template. We used the TheUart concept to constrain high-level code in gsm_lib on types derived from uart_interface. We achieved dependency inversion, and it is clearly defined thanks to CRTP and concepts.

The major benefit of compile-time polymorphism over inheritance (runtime polymorphism) is static binding; that is, there are no virtual functions. This comes at the price of template syntax, which may make the code harder to read and understand.

Summary

In this chapter, we covered template basics, template metaprogramming, concepts, and compile-time polymorphism. While templates are an advanced topic that encompasses many deeper concepts, this chapter aims to serve as a solid starting point for new learners. By understanding the fundamentals covered here, you should be well equipped to explore more complex aspects of templates and leverage their full potential in embedded systems programming.

In the next chapter, we will discuss type safety in C++.

Get This Book's PDF Version and Exclusive Extras

Scan the QR code (or go to packtpub.com/unlock). Search for this book by name, confirm the edition, and then follow the steps on the page.

Note: Keep your invoice handy. Purchases made directly from Packt don't require an invoice.

Improving Type-Safety with Strong Types

C++ is a statically typed language, meaning that every expression is assigned a type at a compile time, either by a developer (in most cases), or deduced by a compiler when using the keyword auto. Still, this doesn't make it a type-safe language.

Both C++ and C allow functions with a variable number of arguments (va_arg), or variadic functions and type casting, and support implicit type conversion. These low-level capabilities that are associated with the performance of C++ and C are often the source of bugs in programs. In this chapter, we will cover good practices used to increase type-safety in C++.

Type-safety is an important aspect of a program in safety-critical systems. That's why safety coding standards provided by organizations such as MISRA and AUTOSAR restrain the usage of features that violate type-safety. In this chapter, we're going to cover the following main topics:

- Implicit conversions
- Explicit conversions
- Strong types

Technical requirements

To get the most out of this chapter, I strongly recommend using Compiler Explorer (https://godbolt.org/) as you read through the examples. Select GCC as your compiler for x86 architecture. This will allow you to see standard output (stdio) results and better observe the code's behavior. As we are using a lot of modern C++ features, make sure to select the C++23 standard, by adding -std=c++23 in the compiler options box.

Compiler Explorer makes it easy to try out the code, tweak it, and immediately see how it affects the output and generated assembly. Most of the examples can also be run in the Renode simulator on Arm Cortex-M0 target and are available on GitHub (https://github.com/PacktPublishing/Cpp-in-Embedded-Systems/tree/main/Chapter09).

Implicit conversion

When you make a call to a function that expects an integer parameter, but you pass a float as an argument, the compiler will happily compile the program. Similarly, if you pass an array of integers to a function that expects a pointer to an integer, the program will also compile. These scenarios have become so normalized in both C and C++ that they are often taken for granted without considering what's happening during the compilation process.

In both described scenarios, the compiler is performing implicit conversions. It converts the float to an integer in the first scenario and passes a pointer to the first element of the array in the second scenario, a process known as **array-to-pointer decay**.

While implicit conversions make the code less verbose and easier to write, they also open the door to a range of type-safety-related issues. Converting a float to an integer leads to precision loss, and assuming that an array always behaves like a pointer can lead to misinterpretations of the array's bounds, potentially causing buffer overflows or other memory issues.

Implicit conversion is performed in the following cases:

- When a function is called with an argument of a type different than the parameter. For example:

```cpp
#include <cstdio>

void print_int(int value) {
    printf("value = %d\n", value);
}
```

```
int main() {
    float pi = 3.14f;
    // int implicitly converts to float
    print_int(pi);
    return 0;
}
```

- When a value specified in a return statement is of a different type than specified by a function declaration. For example:

```
int get_int() {
    float pi = 3.14;
    // float implicitly converts to int
    return pi;
}
```

- In expressions with binary operators provided with operands of different arithmetic types. For example:

```
#include <cstdio>

int main() {
    int int_value = 5;
    float float_value = 4.2;
    // int converts to float
    auto result = int_value + float_value;
    printf("result = %f\n", result);

    return 0;
}
```

- In a `switch` statement to an integral type. For example:

```
char input = 'B';

// implicit conversion from char to int
switch (input) {
    case 65:
        printf("Input is 'A'\n");
```

```cpp
        break;
    case 66:
        printf("Input is 'B'\n");
        break;
    default:
        printf("Unknown input");
}
```

- In an `if` statement, types can be converted to a `bool` type. For example:

```cpp
#include <cstdio>

int main() {
    int int_value = 10;
    // int implicitly converts to bool
    if (int_value) {
        printf("true\n");
    }
    return 0;
}
```

There are different types of implicit conversion that are handled by a compiler, and some of the most important are:

- Numeric promotions and conversions
- Array to pointer conversion
- Function to pointer conversion

Next, we will discuss the above implicit conversions with examples.

Numeric promotions and conversions

Arithmetic types can be promoted or converted to other arithmetic types. Type promotion will not change the value or lose precision. `std::uint8_t` can be promoted to `int`, or `float` can be promoted to `double`. If a type that is being converted can fit entirely to the destination type, without loss of precision, it is being promoted.

Arithmetic operators do not accept types smaller than int. Arithmetic types can be promoted when passed as operands to arithmetic operators. There are specific rules for promotions of integral and floating-point types based on their type:

- Boolean promotion: bool is promoted to int with value 0 if set to false, and 1 if true
- Other integral types, including bitfields, are converted to the smallest type from the following list that can represent all the values of the converted type:

    - int
    - unsigned int
    - long
    - unsigned long
    - long long
    - unsigned long long

- A float can be promoted to double.

To better understand integer promotion rules, we will go over the next example:

```cpp
#include <cstdint>
#include <type_traits>

int main() {
    std::uint8_t a = 1;
    std::uint16_t b = 42;
    auto res1 = a + b;
    static_assert(std::is_same_v<int, decltype(res1)>);
    return 0;
}
```

In the above example, we added uint8_t and uint16_t. According to the promotion rules, both types will be promoted to int, as they can be fully represented by int. The result of the adding is stored in the variable res1, which is declared as auto, meaning that the compiler will deduce its type. We expect it to be an int and we verify that using static_assert and std::is_same_v.

In this example, both types were promoted to the same type. If we had different types after promotion, then they would be converted to a common type under the rules of **usual arithmetic conversion.**

The goal of the usual arithmetic conversion is to yield types to a common type, which is also the type of the result. There are a couple of rules to usual arithmetic conversion:

- If both types are signed or unsigned integers, then the common type is the type of greater integer conversion rank. The ranks are listed below in decreasing order (the ranks of unsigned integers correspond to those of matching signed):

    - `long long`
    - `long`
    - `int`
    - `short`
    - `signed char`

- If one of the types is a signed integer and the other one is unsigned then the following rules apply:

    - If the integer conversion rank of the unsigned type is greater than or equal to the signed type, then the common type is that of the unsigned type.
    - Otherwise, if the signed type can represent all the values of the unsigned type, the common type is that of the signed type.
    - Otherwise, the common type is an unsigned integer of the type of the signed integer.

- If one of the types is a floating type and the other is an integer, the integer is converted to that floating type.

- If both types are the floating type but of different floating-point conversion ranks, the type with the lower conversion rank is converted to the other one. The floating-point conversion rank is listed below in decreasing order:

    - `long double`
    - `double`
    - `float`

Let's go through the following example to better understand the rules of usual arithmetic conversion:

```cpp
#include <type_traits>

int main() {
    struct bitfield{
        long long a:31;
    };
    bitfield b {4};

    int c = 1;
    auto res1 = b.a + c;
    static_assert(sizeof(int) == 4);
    static_assert(sizeof(long long) == 8);
    static_assert(std::is_same_v<int, decltype(res1)>);

    long e = 5;
    auto res2 = e - b.a;
    static_assert(std::is_same_v<long, decltype(res2)>);

    return 0;
}
```

In the above example, we have a `bitfield` of 31 bits with an underlying type of `long long`. We first add `b.a` and variable `c` of type `int`. If we are on a platform where the size of the `int` is 4 bytes, the bitfield will be promoted to the `int`, even though the underlying type `long long` has a size of 8 bytes. The promoted bitfield will be added to int `c`, so the result of this operation will also be int, which we verify by checking the type of res1 using `std::is_same_v`.

In the second part of the example, we subtract the bitfield from `long e`. In this case, the bitfield is first promoted to `int`; then, according to the rules of usual arithmetic conversion, it is converted to `long`, meaning that the resulting type will also be `long`.

You can run the above example from the book's GitHub repo. It is placed under `Chapter09/type_safety` and you can build and run it using the following commands:

```
$ cmake -B build -DMAIN_CPP_FILE_NAME="main_usual_arithmetic_conversion.
cpp"
$ cmake --build build --target run_in_renode
```

The fact that the program builds successfully is enough to confirm the usual arithmetic conversion results, as we used `static_assert` to verify it.

Now, let us take a look at an example whose result may be surprising:

```cpp
#include <cstdio>

int main() {
    int a = -4;
    unsigned int b = 3;
    if(a + b > 0) {
        printf("%d + % u is greater than 0\r\n", a, b);
    }
    return 0;
}
```

If you run this example, the expression within the `if` clause will evaluate to true. As per the rules of usual arithmetic conversion, the signed `int` a will be converted to the `unsigned  int`, meaning that the expression a + b will indeed be greater than 0. Mixing unsigned and signed types in arithmetic expressions can lead to undesired behavior and potential bugs due to implicit conversions.

We can use `-Wconversion` and `-Wsign-conversion` compiler flags with GCC to make it raise a warning when implicit conversion may change a value and sign. Still, mixing signed and unsigned types in arithmetic expressions should be avoided as it can result in wrong results.

Next, we will discuss array-to-pointer conversion and its implications.

Array-to-pointer conversion

An array can be implicitly converted to a pointer. The resulting pointer points to the first element of the array. Many C and C++ functions that work on arrays of data are designed with pointer and size parameters. These interfaces are based on contract design. The contract is the following:

- A caller will pass a pointer that points to the first element of the array
- A caller will pass the size of the array

This is a simple contract, but there is no way to enforce it. Let's take a look at the following simple example:

```cpp
#include <cstdio>
void print_ints(int * arr, std::size_t len) {
    for(std::size_t i = 0; i < len; i++) {
        printf("%d\r\n", arr[i]);
    }
}
  int main() {
    int array_ints[3] = {1, 2, 3};
    print_ints(array_ints, 3);
    return 0;
}
```

In the above example, we have the `print_ints` function with `arr`, a pointer to an `int`, and `len`, a `std::size_t` parameter. In the `main` function, we call the `print_ints` function by passing `array_ints`, an array of 3 integers, and 3 as arguments. The array `array_ints` will be implicitly converted to a pointer that points to its first element. There are a couple of potential issues with the `print_ints` function:

- It expects that the pointer we pass to it is valid. It doesn't verify that.
- It expects that the argument it receives for the `len` parameter is the actual size of the array it operates on. A caller could pass a size that may cause out-of-bounds access.
- As it operates directly on a pointer, there is always a chance of out-of-bound access if pointer arithmetic is used in the function.

To eliminate these potential issues, in C++, instead of using a pointer to work on an array of data, we can use the class template `std::span`. It is a wrapper for a contiguous sequence of objects, with the first element of the sequence at position zero. It can be constructed from a C-style array, it has the `size` method, and we can use range-based for loops on it. Let's write the previous example using the `std::span` instead of the pointer:

```cpp
#include <cstdio>
#include <span>

void print_ints(const std::span<int> arr) {
    for(int elem: arr) {
        printf("%d\r\n", elem);
```

```
        }
    }

    int main() {
        int arr[3] = {1, 2, 3};
        print_ints(arr);
        return 0;
    }
```

In the above example, we can see that the function print_ints looks much simpler now. It accepts std::span of integers and it uses a range-based for loop to iterate over the elements. On the call site, we now just pass arr, an array of 3 integers. It is implicitly converted to std::span.

The class template std::span also has the size method, operator [], and begin and end iterators, meaning we can use it in standard library algorithms. We can also construct a subspan from span. It can be constructed from C-style arrays, but also from containers such as std::array and std::vector. It is a great solution to potential issues of interfaces that usually rely on pointer and size parameters.

Function-to-pointer conversion

A function can be implicitly converted to a pointer to that function. The following example demonstrates this:

```
#include <cstdio>
#include <type_traits>

void print_hello() {
    printf("Hello!\r\n");
}

int main() {
    void(*fptr)() = print_hello;
    fptr();

    fptr = &print_hello;
    (*fptr)();

    static_assert(std::is_same_v<decltype(fptr), void(*)()>);
```

```cpp
    static_assert(std::is_same_v<decltype(print_hello), void()>);
    return 0;
}
```

In the example above, we assign the function `print_hello` to a function pointer `fptr`. In C++, we don't need to use the address-off operator with a function name to assign it to a function pointer. Also, we don't need to dereference a function pointer when making a call to a function through it. Still, `print_hello` and `fptr` are two different types and we confirm this using the `static_assert` and `is_same` type traits.

Implicit conversions in C++ make writing the code easier. They can sometimes lead to undesired behavior and potential issues with our program. To mitigate these concerns, we can explicitly convert types when needed.

Next, we will cover explicit conversion.

Explicit conversion

C++ supports C-style cast explicit conversion, but also functional-style cast and the following casting operators:

- `const_cast`
- `static_cast`
- `dynamic_cast`
- `reinterpret_cast`

We will go through casting operators, starting with `const_cast`.

const_cast

`const cast` is used to cast away constness to work with non-const-correct functions. We will go through the following example to better understand it:

```cpp
#include <cstdio>

void print_num(int & num) {
    printf("num is %d\r\n", num);
}

int main() {
    const int num = 42;
```

```cpp
    print_num(const_cast<int&>(num));

    int & num_ref = const_cast<int&>(num);
    num_ref = 16;

    return num;
}
```

In the above example, we used `const_cast` in two different scenarios. We first used it to cast away constness from `const int  num` to be able to pass it to the `print_num` function. The `print_num` function has a single parameter – a non-const reference to an `int`. As we know that this function is not trying to modify the object that the reference is bound to, we decided to cast away constness so we can pass a reference to a const int to it without the compiler generating an error.

Then, we used `const_cast` to cast away constness from the `num` to be able to assign it to non-const reference `num_ref`. If you run this example in Compiler Explorer, you will see the following output:

```
Program returned: 42
num is 42
```

The program returned 42, that is, the value of num is 42 even though we tried to set it to 16 through `num_ref`. This is due to the fact that modifying the const variable through a non-const reference or a pointer is undefined behavior.

`const_cast` is used mostly to interface with non-const correct functions. Still, this is dangerous and should be avoided as we can't guarantee that the function we are passing a const-cast-away pointer or a reference will not try to modify the object that the pointer is pointing to or the reference it is bound to. Next, we will cover `static_cast`.

static_cast

The most used cast operator in C++ is `static_cast`, and it is used in the following scenarios:

- To upcast and downcast a pointer of base class to derived class and vice versa
- To discard a value expression
- To convert between types with well-known conversion paths such as int to float, enum to an `int`, int to an enum, and similar

We will go through several usages of `static_cast` using the following example:

```cpp
#include <cstdio>


struct Base {
    void hi() {
        printf("Hi from Base\r\n");
    }
};


struct Derived : public Base {
    void hi() {
        printf("Hi from Derived\r\n");
    }
};


int main() {

    // unsigned to signed int
    int a = -4;
    unsigned int b = 3;

    if(a + static_cast<int>(b) > 0) {
        printf("%d + %d is greater than 0\r\n", a, b);
    }
    else {
        printf("%d + %d is not greater than 0\r\n", a,b);
    }

    // discard an expression
    int c;
    static_cast<void>(c);

    Derived derived;
    // implicit upcast
    Base * base_ptr = &derived;
    base_ptr->hi();
```

```cpp
    // downcast
    Derived *derived_p = static_cast<Derived*>(base_ptr);
    derived_p->hi();

    return 0;
}
```

If we run the above example, we will get the following output:

```
-4 + 3 is not greater than 0
Hi from Base
Hi from Derived
```

In the above example, we used `static_cast` to convert an `unsigned int` to a signed int, which helps mitigate the issue of comparing integers with mixed signs introduced by implicit conversion. Still, we would need to make sure that the conversion is safe as `static_cast` doesn't do any runtime checks.

Using `static_cast` to cast the variable c to void is a technique used to suppress compiler warnings about unused variables. It indicates that we are aware of the variable, but we intentionally do not use it.

In the other part of the above example, we can see that an address to an object of the `Derived` class can be implicitly converted to a pointer of the `Base` class. If we call a function `hi` on the pointer of the `Base` class which is pointing to an object of the Derived class, we will actually make a call to a `hi` function defined in the `Base` class. Then we used `static_cast` to downcast `Base` pointer to a `Derived` pointer.

Down-casting using `static_cast` can be dangerous as `static_cast` doesn't do any runtime checks to make sure that the pointer is actually pointing to the converting type. An object of the `Derived` class is also an object of the `Base` class, but the reverse is not true – `Base` is not `Derived`. The following example demonstrates why this is dangerous:

```cpp
#include <cstdio>

struct Base {
    void hi() {
        printf("Hi from Base\r\n");
    }
};
```

```cpp
struct Derived : public Base {
    void hi() {
        printf("Hi from Derived, x = %d\r\n", x);
    }
    int x = 42;
};

int main() {
    Base base;
    Derived *derived_ptr = static_cast<Derived*>(&base);
    derived_ptr->hi();
    return 0;
}
```

In this code, we are trying to access member x of the Derived class on an object of the base class. As we used static_cast, the compiler will not complain and this will result in undefined behavior, as the base class doesn't have member x. One of the possible outputs of this program is shown here:

```
Hi from Derived, x = 1574921984
```

To avoid this problem, we can use dynamic_cast, which we will cover next.

dynamic_cast

dynamic_cast performs runtime checks of types and sets the result to nullptr in case the Base pointer doesn't actually point to an object of the Derived class. We will go through an example to better understand it:

```cpp
#include <cstdio>

struct Base {
    virtual void hi() {
        printf("Hi from Base\r\n");
    }
};

struct Derived : public Base {
    void hi() override {
        printf("Hi from Derived\r\n");
```

```cpp
    }

    void derived_only() {
        printf("Derived only method\r\n");
    }
};

void process(Base *base) {
    base->hi();
    if(auto ptr = dynamic_cast<Derived*>(base); ptr ! = nullptr)
    {
        ptr->derived_only();
    }
}

int main() {
    Base base;
    Derived derived;

    Base * base_ptr = &derived;

    process(&base);
    process(base_ptr);

    return 0;
}
```

In the above example, we have a function process with a pointer to Base as a parameter. The function uses dynamic_cast to downcast the Base pointer to a Derived pointer. In the **if statement with initializer**, we initialize ptr with the result of dynamic_cast<Derived*> on a Base pointer. In the condition of the if statement, we check if ptr is different from nullptr, and if it is we can safely use it as a pointer to an object of the Derived class. Next, we will cover reinterpret_cast.

reinterpret_cast

reinterpret_cast is used to convert between types by reinterpreting the underlying bits. It can be used in the following situations:

- To convert a pointer to an integer large enough to hold all of its values.

- To convert a value of an integer to a pointer. A pointer converted to an integer and back to its original type is guaranteed to have the original value and can be dereferenced safely.

- To convert pointers between different types, such as between T1 and T2. The resulting pointer to T2 can be dereferenced safely only if the resulting pointer is char, unsigned char, std::byte, or T1.

- To convert a function pointer F1 to a pointer to a different function F2. Converting F2 back to F1 will result in the pointer to F1.

To better understand reinterpret_cast, we will go through the following example:

```cpp
#include <cstdio>
#include <cstdint>

int fun() {
    printf("fun\r\n");
    return 42;
}

int main() {
    float f = 3.14f;

    // initialize pointer to an int with float address
    auto a = reinterpret_cast<int*>(&f);
    printf("a = %d\r\n", *a);

    // the above is same as:
    a = static_cast<int*>(static_cast<void*>(&f));
    printf("a = %d\r\n", *a);

    // casting back to float pointer
    auto fptr = reinterpret_cast<float*>(a);
    printf("f = %.2f\r\n", *fptr);
```

```cpp
    // converting a pointer to integer
    auto int_val = reinterpret_cast<std::uintptr_t>(fptr);
    printf("Address of float f is 0x%8X\r\n", int_val);

    auto fun_void_ptr = reinterpret_cast<void(*)()>(fun);
    // undefined behavior
    fun_void_ptr();

    auto fun_int_ptr = reinterpret_cast<int(*)()>(fun);
    // safe call
    printf("fun_int_ptr returns %d\r\n", fun_int_ptr());

    return 0;
}
```

You can run the above example from the book's GitHub repo. It is placed under `Chapter09/type_safety` and you can build and run it using the following commands:

```
$ cmake -B build -DMAIN_CPP_FILE_NAME="main_reinterpret_cast.cpp"
$ cmake --build build --target run_in_renode
```

Running the example in Renode will provide the following output:

```
a = 1078523331
a = 1078523331
f = 3.14
Address of float f is 0x20003F18
fun
fun
fun_int_ptr returns 42
```

The above example demonstrates the usage of `reinterpret_cast`. We first initialized a pointer to an int using the address of a float using `reinterpret_cast<int*>(&f)`. This is equivalent to using `static_cast` as `static_cast<int*>(static_cast<void*>(&f))`. We print the value of the dereference integer pointer, and it is `1078523331`. This is an actual bit pattern contained in the `float` variable f. It is an IEEE-754 floating point representation of `3.14`.

However, dereferencing the integer pointer initialized by an address of a float is not a defined behavior according to the C++ standard. This is called **type punning** – treating an object of one type as if it were another type. Using `reinterpet_cast` for type punning is common, as it proved to yield expected results on most platforms despite the undefined behavior. There are alternatives that we will discuss after going through this example.

If we cast the pointer to the integer back to a pointer to a float, it is safe to dereference the resulting pointer.

Next, we converted the pointer to float to an integer to print the address it contains. We used `std::uintptr_t`, an integer type that is capable of holding a pointer to void. Following this, we initialized `fun_void_ptr` – a pointer to a function that returns void with function `fun`, which returns int. We made a call on the `fun_void_ptr` pointer, which printed the expected output, but it is still undefined. Converting `fun_void_ptr` to a pointer that matches the signature of function fun – `fun_int_ptr` – will make calling fun through the resulting pointer safe.

Next, we will go through type punning in C++ and the alternatives to using `reinterpret_cast` for this task.

Type punning

Using `reinterpret_cast` for type punning is a common practice even though it introduces undefined behavior. Aliasing rules determine how we can access an object in C++, and to put it simply, we can access an object through a pointer and const qualified version of that pointer, a struct or union that contains the object, and through a `char`, `unsigned char`, and `std::byte`.

We will go through the following example to better understand type punning in C++:

```cpp
#include <cstdio>
#include <cstdint>
#include <cstring>
namespace {
struct my_struct {
    int a;
    char c;
};

void print_my_struct (const my_struct & str) {
    printf("a = %d, c = %c\r\n", str.a, str.c);
}
```

```cpp
void process_data(const char * data) {
    const auto *pstr = reinterpret_cast<const my_struct *>(data);
    printf("%s\r\n", __func__);
    print_my_struct(pstr[0]);
    print_my_struct(pstr[1]);
}


void process_data_memcpy(const char * data) {
    my_struct my_structs[2];
    std::memcpy(my_structs, data, sizeof(my_structs));
    printf("%s\r\n", __func__);
    print_my_struct(my_structs[0]);
    print_my_struct(my_structs[1]);
}
};


int main() {
    int i = 42;
    auto * i_ptr = reinterpret_cast<char*>(&i);
    if(i_ptr[0]==42) {
        printf("Little endian!\r\n");
    }
    else {
        printf("Big endian!\r\n");
    }

    my_struct my_structs_arr[] = {{4, 'a'}, {5, 'b'}};
    char arr[128];
    std::memcpy(&arr, my_structs_arr, sizeof(my_structs_arr));

    process_data(arr);
    process_data_memcpy(arr);

    return 0;
}
```

You can run the above example from the book's GitHub repo. It is placed under `Chapter09/type_safety` and you can build and run it using the following commands:

```
$ cmake -B build -DMAIN_CPP_FILE_NAME="main_type_punning.cpp"
$ cmake --build build --target run_in_renode
```

Running the example in Renode will provide the following output:

```
Little endian!
process_data
a = 4, c = a
a = 5, c = b
process_data_memcpy
a = 4, c = a
a = 5, c = b
```

In the example above, we used `reinterpret_cast` to treat an integer i as an array of chars. By checking the value pointed by the first element of the mentioned array, we can determine if we are on a big or little-endian system. As per the aliasing rules, this is a valid approach, but treating an array of chars as some other type would be undefined behavior. We did that in the function void `process_data` where we reinterpreted an array of chars as an array of `my_struct` objects. The output of the program is as we would expect it, even though we introduced undefined behavior. To mitigate this issue, we can use `std::memcpy`.

Type punning – the correct way

Using `std::memcpy` is the only (as of C++23) available option for type punning in C++. In the above example, we demonstrate this in the `process_data_memcpy` function. There is usually a concern of bytes being copied, using additional memory and runtime overhead, but the fact is that the call to `memcpy` is usually optimized away by a compiler. You can verify this by running the above example in Compiler Explorer and by experimenting with different optimization levels.

C++20 introduces `std::bit_cast`, which can also be used for type punning, as in the following example:

```cpp
#include <cstdio>
#include <bit>


int main() {
```

```
    float f = 3.14f;

    auto a = std::bit_cast<int>(f);
    printf("a = %d\r\n", a);

    return 0;
}
```

The output of the above program is:

```
a = 1078523331
```

The above example and the program output demonstrate the usage of std::bit_cast for type punning. The std::bit_cast will return an object. We specify the type that we are converting to as the template argument. This will also be the return type of the std::bit_cast. The size of the converting type and the type we are converting to must be the same. This means std::bit_cast is not an option for interpreting arrays of one type as arrays of another type, and for that we still need to use std::memcpy.

Next, we will see how we can use strong types in C++ to increase type safety.

Strong types

When we talk about type-safety, we should also discuss the safety of interfaces that use commonly available types such as integers and floats to represent physical units such as time, length, and volume. Let us take a look at the following function from a vendor's SDK:

```
/**
 * @brief Start the direct connection establishment procedure.
A LE_Create_Connection call will be made to the controller by GAP with the
initiator filter policy set to "ignore whitelist and
process connectable advertising packets only for the specified
device".
 * @param LE_Scan_Interval This is defined as the time interval from when
the Controller started its last LE scan until it begins the subsequent LE
scan.
Time = N * 0.625 msec.
 * Values:
 - 0x0004 (2.500 ms) ... 0x4000 (10240.000 ms)
```

```
     * @param LE_Scan_Window Amount of time for the duration of the LE scan. LE_Scan_Window
shall be less than or equal to LE_Scan_Interval.
Time = N * 0.625 msec.
   * Values:
   - 0x0004 (2.500 ms)  ... 0x4000 (10240.000 ms)
   * @param Peer_Address_Type The address type of the peer device.
   * Values:
   - 0x00: Public Device Address
   - 0x01: Random Device Address
   * @param Peer_Address Public Device Address or Random Device Address of the device
to be connected.
     * @param Conn_Interval_Min Minimum value for the connection event
interval. This shall be less than or equal to Conn_Interval_Max.
Time = N * 1.25 msec.
   * Values:
   - 0x0006 (7.50 ms)  ... 0x0C80 (4000.00 ms)
   * @param Conn_Interval_Max Maximum value for the connection event
interval. This shall be
greater than or equal to Conn_Interval_Min.
Time = N * 1.25 msec.
   * Values:
   - 0x0006 (7.50 ms)  ... 0x0C80 (4000.00 ms)
   * @param Conn_Latency Slave latency for the connection in number of
connection events.
   * Values:
   - 0x0000 ... 0x01F3
     * @param Supervision_Timeout Supervision timeout for the LE Link.
It shall be a multiple of 10 ms and larger than (1 + connSlaveLatency) *
connInterval * 2.
Time = N * 10 msec.
   * Values:
   - 0x000A (100 ms)  ... 0x0C80 (32000 ms)
   * @param Minimum_CE_Length Information parameter about the minimum
length of connection needed for this LE connection.
Time = N * 0.625 msec.
   * Values:
```

```
      - 0x0000 (0.000 ms)  ... 0xFFFF (40959.375 ms)
      * @param Maximum_CE_Length Information parameter about the maximum
     length of connection needed
     for this LE connection.
     Time = N * 0.625 msec.
      * Values:
      - 0x0000 (0.000 ms)  ... 0xFFFF (40959.375 ms)
      * @retval Value indicating success or error code.
     */

     tBleStatus aci_gap_create_connection(
                               uint16_t LE_Scan_Interval,
                               uint16_t LE_Scan_Window,
                               uint8_t Peer_Address_Type,
                               uint8_t Peer_Address[6],
                               uint16_t Conn_Interval_Min,
                               uint16_t Conn_Interval_Max,
                               uint16_t Conn_Latency,
                               uint16_t Supervision_Timeout,
                               uint16_t Minimum_CE_Length,
                               uint16_t Maximum_CE_Length);
```

This is a well-documented function. Still, it takes a lot of effort to understand all the parameters that it accepts and the exact units of each. Most of the parameters represent time but in a different way.

`LE_Scan_Interval`, `LE_Scan_Window`, `Conn_Interval_Min`, `Conn_Interval_Max`, `Supervision_Timeout`, `Minimum_CE_Length`, and `Maximum_CE_Length` are all time-related parameters, but they represent different units. They are either multiples of 0.625, 1.25, or 10 ms. The vendor of the above function also provided the following macros:

```
#define CONN_L(x) ((int)((x) / 0.625f))
#define CONN_P(x) ((int)((x) / 1.25f))
```

Here is an example of a call to the above function using the provided macros:

```
tBleStatus status = aci_gap_create_connection(CONN_L(80), CONN_L(120),
PUBLIC_ADDR, mac_addr, CONN_P(50), CONN_P(60), 0, SUPERV_TIMEOUT,
CONN_L(10), CONN_L(15));
```

The macros help a bit with readability, but the problem of passing bad values to this function still remains. It is fairly easy to make a mistake, swap the `CONN_L` and `CONN_P` macros, and introduce a hard-to-find bug to the program. Instead of `uint16_t`, we could define and use types `conn_l` and `conn_p`. If we wrap the function with these amendments, we will have the following wrapper function:

```
tBleStatus aci_gap_create_connection_wrapper(
                            conn_l LE_Scan_Interval,
                            conn_l LE_Scan_Window,
                            uint8_t Peer_Address_Type,
                            uint8_t Peer_Address[6],
                            conn_p Conn_Interval_Min,
                            conn_p Conn_Interval_Max,
                            uint16_t Conn_Latency,
                            uint16_t Supervision_Timeout,
                            conn_l Minimum_CE_Length,
                            conn_l Maximum_CE_Length);
```

In the above example, we are using `conn_l` and `conn_p` types instead of `uint16_t`, and we will define these types as follows:

```
class conn_l {
private:
    uint16_t time_;
public:
    explicit conn_l(float time_ms) : time_(time_ms/0.625f){}
    uint16_t & get() {return time_;}
};

class conn_p {
private:
    uint16_t time_;
public:
    explicit conn_p(float time_ms) : time_(time_ms/1.25f){}
    uint16_t & get() {return time_;}
};
```

Using the above strong types conn_1 and conn_p, we can call the wrapper function as shown below:

```cpp
tBleStatus stat = aci_gap_create_connection_wrapper(
        conn_1(80),
        conn_1(120),
        PUBLIC_ADDR,
        nullptr,
        conn_p(50),
        conn_p(60),
        0,
        SUPERV_TIMEOUT,
        conn_1(10),
        conn_1(15)
    );
```

By using the keyword explicit in front of constructors of types conn_1 and conn_p, we make sure that the compiler doesn't perform implicit conversion from integer types. This makes it impossible to pass an integer or a float that can be used to construct conn_1 and conn_p to the aci_gap_create_connection_wrapper.

You can run the entire example from the book's GitHub repo. It is placed under Chapter09/type_safety and you can build and run it using the following commands:

```
$ cmake -B build -DMAIN_CPP_FILE_NAME="main_strong_types.cpp"
$ cmake --build build --target run_in_renode
```

Compiling the example successfully means that we passed all the correct arguments to aci_gap_create_connection_wrapper. As an exercise, try passing integer values instead of conn_1 and conn_p arguments to see how they prevent the compiler from doing implicit conversions. After that, try removing the explicit keyword from the conn_1 and conn_p constructors to see what will happen.

We can further improve the example by introducing a strong-type time that will represent the time duration, and make it a private member of types conn_1 and conn_p. The code would look as follows:

```cpp
class time {
private:
    uint16_t time_in_ms_;
public:
    explicit time(uint16_t time_in_ms) : time_in_ms_(time_in_ms){}
```

```cpp
    uint16_t & get_ms() {return time_in_ms_;}
};

time operator""_ms(unsigned long long t) {
    return time(t);
}

class conn_l {
private:
    uint16_t val_;
public:
    explicit conn_l(time t) : val_(t.get_ms()/0.625f){}
    uint16_t & get() {return val_;}
};

class conn_p {
private:
    uint16_t val_;
public:
    explicit conn_p(time t) : val_(t.get_ms()/1.25f){}
    uint16_t & get() {return val_;}
};
```

In the above example, we created a strong-type time and used it as a private member in types conn_l and conn_p. We also created a user-defined literal with operator""_ms to make the following function call possible:

```cpp
    tBleStatus stat = aci_gap_create_connection_wrapper(
            conn_l(80_ms),
            conn_l(120_ms),
            PUBLIC_ADDR,
            nullptr,
            conn_p(50_ms),
            conn_p(60_ms),
            0_ms,
            4000_ms,
            conn_l(10_ms),
            conn_l(15_ms)
    );
```

In the above example, we are using the user-defined literal `operator""_ms` to create objects of strong-type time that are used to instantiate conn_l and conn_p objects.

The above changes to the original interface improve code readability and compile-time error detection. Using strong types, we make it a lot harder to pass wrong values to the function, increasing the type-safety of our codebase.

Summary

Type safety is an important aspect of any programming language used in critical applications. Understanding potential issues of implicit conversion is important to mitigate type-safety concerns. Type punning is another area that deserves special attention in C++, and we learned how to address it properly. We also learned how to use strong types to mitigate issues of passing wrong values to parameters with the same types.

Next, we will cover lambdas in C++.

Join our community on Discord

Join our community's Discord space for discussions with the author and other readers:

https://packt.link/embeddedsystems

10

Writing Expressive Code with Lambdas

Lambda expressions in C++ allow us to write short blocks of code that encapsulate functionality and capture the surrounding state into a callable object. We can use `operator()` on a callable object to execute the functionality implemented in it.

Common uses of lambdas include passing a function object (also called a functor – an object of a class that overrides `operator()`) to standard library algorithms, or any code expecting a function object, encapsulating small blocks of code that are often used only in a single function, and variable initialization. Their ability to localize functionality without separate functions or class methods modernized C++, making it possible to write cleaner, more expressive code.

In embedded development, lambdas are especially useful for defining actions in response to timer or external interrupts, scheduling tasks, and similar event-driven mechanisms. The goal of this chapter is to learn how to use lambda expressions to write expressive C++ code. In this chapter, we're going to cover the following main topics:

- Lambda expression basics
- Store lambdas using `std::function`
- `std::function` and dynamic memory allocation

Technical requirements

To get the most out of this chapter, I strongly recommend using Compiler Explorer (https://godbolt.org/) as you read through the examples. Select GCC as your compiler and target x86 architecture. This will allow you to see standard output (stdio) results and better observe the code's behavior. As we are using a lot of modern C++ features, make sure to select the C++23 standard by adding `-std=c++23` in the compiler options box.

Compiler Explorer makes it easy to try out the code, tweak it, and immediately see how it affects the output and generated assembly. Most of the examples can also be run in the Renode simulator on the ARM Cortex-M0 target and are available on GitHub (https://github.com/PacktPublishing/Cpp-in-Embedded-Systems/tree/main/Chapter10).

Lambda expression basics

Lambda expressions, or lambdas, were introduced in C++11. They are used to create an instance of an unnamed closure type in C++. A closure stores an unnamed function and can capture variables from its scope by value or reference. We can call `operator ()` on a lambda instance, with arguments specified in the lambda definition, effectively calling the underlying unnamed function. To draw a parallel with C, lambdas are callable in the same way as function pointers.

We will now dive into an example to demonstrate how we can use lambdas in C++ and explain details regarding lambda capturing. Let us process the example below:

```cpp
#include <cstdio>
#include <array>
#include <algorithm>

int main() {
    std::array<int, 4> arr{5, 3, 4, 1};

    const auto print_arr = [&arr](const char* message) {
        printf("%s\r\n", message);
        for(auto elem : arr) {
            printf("%d, ", elem);
        }
```

```cpp
        printf("\r\n");
    };
    print_arr("Unsorted array:");

    std::sort(arr.begin(), arr.end(), [](int a, int b) {
        return a < b;});
    print_arr("Sorted in ascending order:");

    std::sort(arr.begin(), arr.end(), [](int a, int b) {
        return a > b;});
    print_arr("Sorted in descending order:");
    return 0;
}
```

Running the above example, we will get the following output:

```
Unsorted array:
5, 3, 4, 1,
Sorted in ascending order:
1, 3, 4, 5,
Sorted in descending order:
5, 4, 3, 1,
```

What we see are outputs of the lambda print_arr used to print an array arr defined in the main function. Let's go through the print_arr lambda in detail:

- The [&arr] syntax captures the variable arr by reference from the surrounding scope. This means the lambda can access and use arr directly within its body.

- We can capture variables by value, or by reference if we prefix the name of a variable with & as we did for the print_arr lambda.

- Capturing by reference [&arr] allows the lambda to see any changes made to arr outside the lambda after its definition. If we captured by value, the lambda would have its own copy of arr.

- By defining print_arr as a lambda within main, we encapsulate the functionality of printing the array without needing to create a separate function. This keeps related code together and enhances readability.

In the same example, we used lambdas as predicate functions to the `std::sort` algorithm, to sort array `arr` first in ascending, then in descending order. We will go through this use case of lambdas in more detail:

- The `std::sort` algorithm rearranges the elements of `arr` based on the comparator provided.
- The lambda `[](int a, int b) { return a < b; }` acts as a comparator function for `std::sort`. It takes two integers and returns `true` if the first is less than the second, which results in an ascending sort.
- The lambda `[](int a, int b) { return a > b; }` returns `true` if the first integer is greater than the second, resulting in a descending sort.

Defining the comparator directly at the call site of `std::sort` makes the code more concise. It becomes immediately clear how the array is being sorted without needing to look elsewhere in the code.

In the cases of using lambdas with the `std::sort` algorithm, both lambdas are small and simple, making it easy to deduce what they return. Keeping lambdas short and straightforward is considered a good practice as it improves readability and makes the intent of the code immediately clear to others. We can also specify the lambda return type explicitly as in the following example:

```cpp
auto greater_than = [](int a, int b) -> bool {
    return a > b;
};
```

Here, we explicitly defined the return type. This is optional and can be used when we want to be explicit about the type that a lambda returns. Also, note that the capture clause of this lambda is empty square brackets `[]`. This indicates that the lambda is not capturing any variables from the surrounding scope.

When the lambda is capturing a variable by reference, it is important to note that this introduces lifetime dependency – meaning that the object that reference is bound to must exist when we call the lambda – else, we will use a so-called dangling reference, which is undefined behavior. This is especially a concern with asynchronous operations – that is, when a lambda is passed to a function and called later. Next, we will learn how to store lambdas using `std::function` to use them asynchronously.

Storing lambdas using std::function

`std::function` is a class template that allows us to store, copy, and invoke callable objects such as function pointers and lambdas. We will go through a simple code example to demonstrate this:

```cpp
#include <cstdio>
#include <cstdint>
#include <functional>

int main() {
    std::function<void()> fun;
    fun = []() {
        printf("This is a lambda!\r\n");
    };
    fun();

    std::uint32_t reg = 0x12345678;
    fun = [reg]() {
        printf("Reg content 0x%8X\r\n", reg);
    };
    reg = 0;
    fun();

    return 0;
}
```

Let us go through the example:

- In the `main` function, we first create an object fun of type `std::function<void()>`. This specifies that `fun` can store any callable object that returns `void` and takes no arguments. This includes function pointers, lambdas, or any object with an `operator()` that matches the signature.

- We then assign a lambda to `fun` and invoke it, which prints the message "This is a lambda!" to the console.

- Next, we assigned another lambda to the `fun` object. This time the lambda captures the `uint32_t reg` by value from the surrounding scope and prints it. Capturing by value means the lambda makes its own copy of reg at the moment the lambda is defined.

- We change the value of reg to 0 before invoking the callable object stored in `fun` to show it is being captured by value. Calling `fun` prints `Reg content 0x12345678`.

Let's use `std::function` in a more interesting example, where we will use it to store a callback to a GPIO interrupt. The code is below:

```cpp
#include <cstdio>
#include <cstdint>
#include <functional>

namespace hal
{
class gpio
{
public:
    gpio(const std::function<void()> & on_press) {
        if(on_press) {
            on_press_ = on_press;
        }
    }
    void execute_interrupt_handler () const {
        if(on_press_) {
            on_press_();
        }
    }

private:
    std::function<void()> on_press_ = nullptr;
};
```

```cpp
}; // namespace hal

int main () {
    hal::gpio button1([]() {
        printf("Button1 pressed!\r\n");
    });

    // invoke stored lambda
    button1.execute_interrupt_handler();

    return 0;
}
```

In the code above, we created a `hal::gpio` class that represents a GPIO:

The class stores `std::function<void()> on_press_`, which can hold any callable object like a lambda function. It is initialized to nullptr to indicate it holds no callable object.

- It provides the method `execute_interrupt_handler`, which checks if `on_press_` evaluates to true, that is, if it stores a callable object, and executes it if it does.

In the `main` function, we create button1, an object of class `hal::button`:

- We provide the constructor with a simple lambda that prints Button1 pressed!.
- Next, we call the method `execute_interrupt_handler`, which invokes the stored lambda and the program prints `Button1 pressed!`.

In a real firmware, we would call the method `execute_interrupt_handler` from an interrupt service.

The above code is an example of the application of the **command pattern**, which is implemented in a simple and expressive way in C++ thanks to `std::function` and lambda expressions.

The command pattern

The **command pattern** is a behavioral design pattern used to capture a function call together with required arguments – allowing us to execute those functions with a delay.

We will go through a canonical definition of the command pattern. Let us start with a UML diagram of the pattern and explain it afterward:

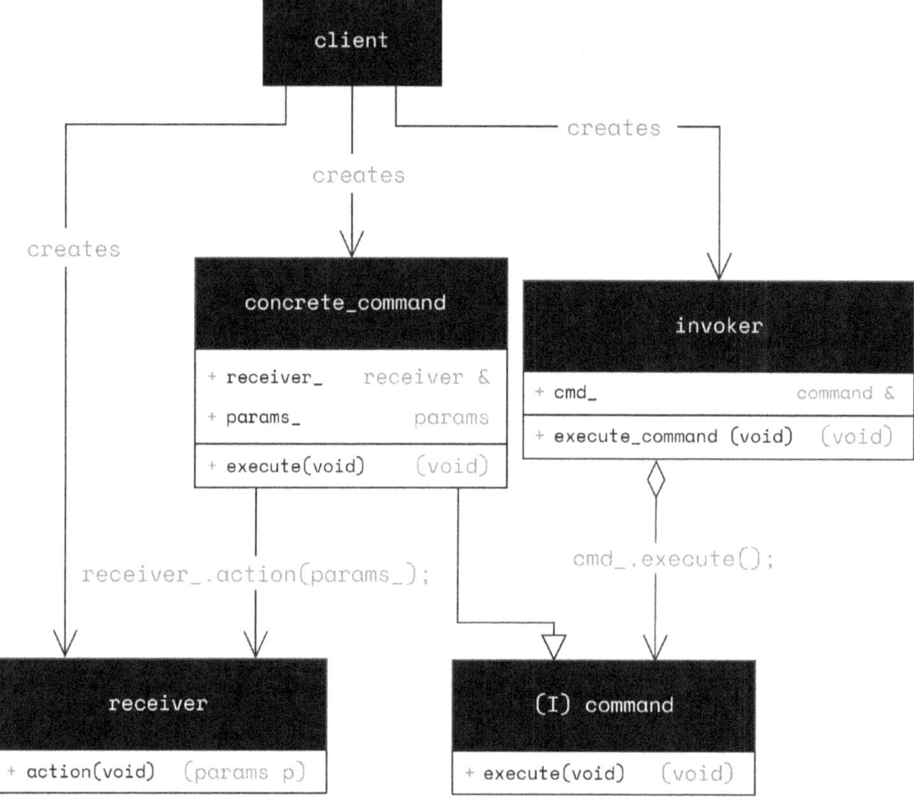

Figure 10.1 – Command pattern – UML diagram

Figure 10.1 depicts a UML diagram of the command pattern. We notice the following entities in the above diagram.

The command interface with a virtual execute method, and a `concrete_command` implementation of the interface.

- `receiver`, stored by a reference in the `concrete_command` implementation. It performs an `action` that takes `params` as arguments.
- `invoker`, which stores a reference to the command interface and executes a command.
- `client`, which creates a `receiver` and passes it to the constructor of `concrete_command`. It passes a reference of a created `concrete_command` to an `invoker`.

By using the command interface, we are able to make different concrete commands and provide them to invokers. Instead of the command interface and concrete commands, we can use class template `std::function` and lambda expressions for the same purpose.

In our previous example, we created the `hal::gpio` class as an invoker from the command pattern. It has a `std::function<void()>` as a member – an equivalent to a command interface. A concrete command is a lambda expression that we stored in `std::function<void()>`.

`receiver` is the lambda body – the `printf` function in our example – and `client` is the `main` function. The client creates a receiver (`hal::gpio button1`) and provides it with a concrete command (lambda expression). We call `execute_interrupt_handler` on the invoker directly from the `main` function.

Next, we will expand this example to call `execute_interrupt_handler` from the interrupt handler on the STM32 platform. The design will support interrupts from multiple pins. We will introduce the `gpio_interrupt_manager` entity, which will be responsible for registering invokers and calling the `execute_interrupt_handler` method on them.

GPIO interrupt manager

We want to utilize the `std::function` class template and lambda expressions to enable an expressive way of creating GPIO interrupt handlers in firmware as in the following code:

```cpp
const hal::gpio_stm32<hal::port_a> button1(hal::pin::p4, [](){
    printf("Button1 pressed!\r\n");
});
```

In the code above, we are creating an object `button1` from the class template `hal::gpio_stm32` parametrized with `hal::port_a`. We are providing a constructor with `hal::pin::p4` and a lambda expression that will be executed on interrupt. This is a goal, an expressive interface for writing interrupt handlers that also allows us to capture surrounding variables if needed, thanks to lambda expressions.

From the code above, we can see both the pin and the port we are configuring and the callback that will be executed on the interrupt. The mechanism that we will create will handle interrupt handler registration to a central entity we will name `gpio_interrupt_manager`. Before we proceed with the design, please run the full example in Renode using the instructions below.

1. Start Visual Studio Code, attach it to the running container, open the `Chapter10/lambdas` project as described in *Chapter 4*, and run the following commands in the Visual Studio Code terminal, or run them directly in the container terminal:

```
$ cd Chapter10/lambdas
$ cmake -B build -DCMAKE_BUILD_TYPE=Debug -DMAIN_CPP_FILE_NAME=main_
std_function_command_pattern.cpp
$ cmake --build build --target run_in_renode
```

2. In Renode, we can simulate button press and release using the following command for `button1` and `button2`:

```
gpioPortA.button1 PressAndRelease
gpioPortA.button2 PressAndRelease
```

3. Entering the above command should result in the following output in the Renode console:

```
Button1 pressed!
Button2 pressed!
```

As you can see, actions provided in lambdas are invoked by interrupts generated by buttons. Let us go through the UML diagram of this example to understand how it works:

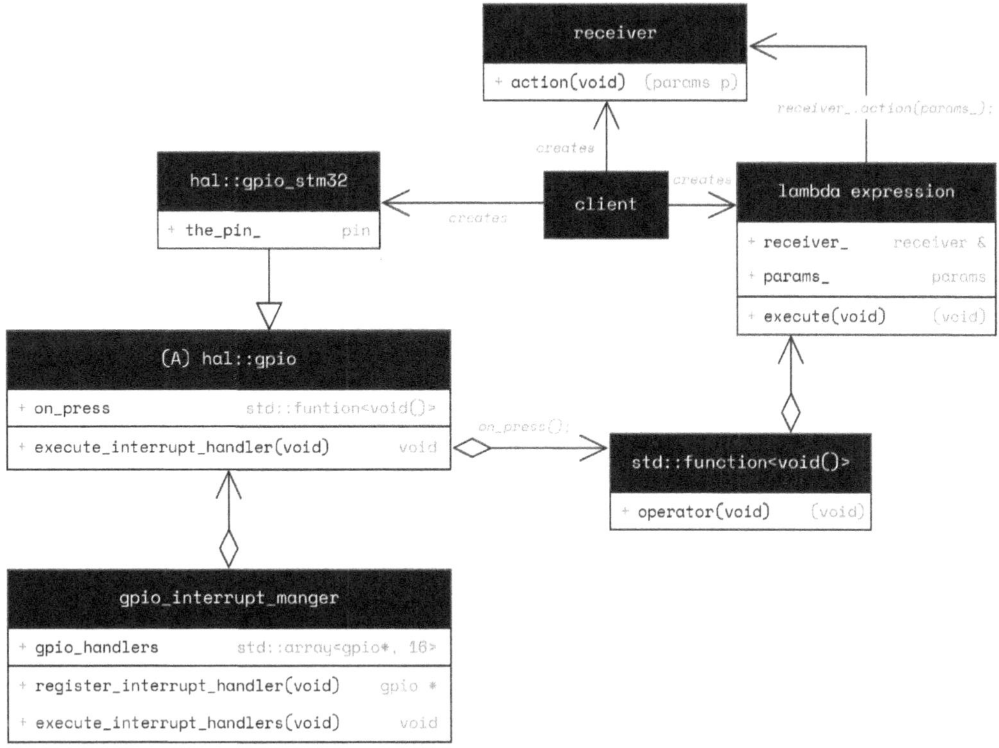

Figure 10.2 – GPIO Interrupt manager UML diagram

In *Figure 10.2*, we see the UML diagram of the GPIO interrupt manager. It is based on the command pattern. We are using `std::function<void()>` in place of the command interface and lambda expression for concrete commands. The invoker is the `hal::gpio` abstract class, which stores the lambda in the member `on_press`. It registers itself with `gpio_interrupt_manager` in the constructor as we can see from the following code:

```
gpio::gpio(const std::function<void()> & on_press) {
    on_press_ = on_press;
    gpio_interrupt_manager::register_interrupt_handler(this)
}
```

gpio_interrupt_manager is a simple struct. It serves as a central entity for the interrupt handling mechanism with the following features:

- It contains an array of hal::gpio pointers – std::array<gpio*, c_gpio_handlers_num> gpio_handlers.

- It provides a static method to register a hal::gpio pointer – void register_interrupt_ handler(gpio * pin).

- It provides a static method that executes interrupt handlers stored in the array – void execute_interrupt_handlers().

The method execute_interrupt_handlers is called from the interrupt service routine as shown below:

```cpp
extern "C" void EXTI4_15_IRQHandler(void) {
    gpio_interrupt_manager::execute_interrupt_handlers();
}
```

EXTI4_15_IRQHandler is an interrupt service routine defined in the vector table (defined in platform/startup_stm32f072xb.s). That's why we used "C" language linkage and implemented it as a global function. The execute_interrupt_handlers method loops through the array of hal::gpio pointers and calls the execute_interrupt_handler method on them as shown below:

```cpp
void gpio_interrupt_manager::execute_interrupt_handlers() {
    for(std::size_t i = 0; i < w_idx; i++) {
        gpio_handlers[i]->execute_interrupt_handler();
    }
}
```

hal::gpio is an abstract class with the following features:

- It implements the execute_interrupt_handler method used by gpio_interrupt_ manager as we saw earlier.

- It defines the pure virtual method [[nodiscard]] virtual bool is_interrupt_ generated() const = 0. This method needs to be overridden by the derived class that implements platform-specific functionality.

- It defines the virtual method virtual void clear_interrupt_flag() const = 0. This method needs to be overridden by the derived class that implements platform-specific functionality.

The code for execute_interrupt_handler is shown below:

```cpp
void gpio::execute_interrupt_handler () const {
    if(is_interrupt_generated()){
        clear_interrupt_flag();
        if(on_press_) {
            on_press_();
        }
    }
}
```

The execute_interrupt_handler method implements the following functionality:

- It checks if the interrupt should be handled by the current object using the virtual method is_interrupt_generated. This method must be overridden by a derived class. The derived class has the data needed to determine if the generated interrupt needs to be addressed by the current object.

- If the interrupt should be addressed by the current object, the interrupt flag is cleared using the virtual method clear_interrupt_flag and on_press_ is called if it stores a callable object.

hal::gpio_stm32 is a class template derived from hal::gpio. We instantiate it with port as a parameter, and it implements platform-specific operations such as GPIO initialization using the vendor-provided C HAL library.

In the example, we instantiated hal::gpio_stm32 with struct port_a, which contains the void init_clock() static function. This allows us to call a static method on the template parameter, instead of defining port as an enum, checking it in runtime, and calling a port-specific function for clock initialization.

The hal::gpio_stm32 class template uses hal::gpio as a base class:

- The constructor takes an enum pin and const reference to a std::function<void()> object that we use to initialize the base class in the initialization list.

- [[nodiscard]] bool is_interrupt_generated() const – the overridden method uses vendor-provided C HAL to determine if the interrupt was generated by the pin provided to the object through the constructor.

- void clear_interrupt_flag() const – the overridden method implements platform-specific code used to clear the interrupt flag.

This sums up the implementation of the GPIO interrupt manager and explains the design. You can refer to other details of the implementation in the source code provided in the `Chapter10/lambdas` folder of the book's GitHub repo.

Next, we will discuss the implications of using `std::function` on dynamic memory allocation.

std::function and dynamic memory allocation

`std::function` needs to store all variables and references that a lambda captures. This behavior is implementation-defined, and implementations usually use heap, which is dynamic memory allocation to store large amounts of variables. If the captured data is small (on some platforms, 16 bytes), it will be stored on the stack. This is called small object optimization. To demonstrate the behavior of the `std::function` class template when capturing data, we will go through the following example:

```cpp
#include <cstdio>
#include <cstdint>
#include <cstdlib>
#include <functional>

void *operator new(std::size_t count) {
  printf("%s, size = %ld\r\n", __PRETTY_FUNCTION__, count);
  return std::malloc(count);
}
void operator delete(void *ptr) noexcept {
  printf("%s\r\n", __PRETTY_FUNCTION__);
  std::free(ptr);
}

int main () {

    std::function<void()> func;

    auto arr = []() {
        constexpr std::size_t c_array_size = 6;
        std::array<int, c_array_size> ar{};
        for(int i = 0; i < ar.size(); i++) {
            ar[i] = i;
        }
```

```cpp
        return ar;
    }();

    auto array_printer = [arr]() {
        for(int elem: arr) {
            printf("%d, ", elem);
        }
        printf("\r\n");
    };

    func = array_printer;
    // invoke stored lambda
    func();
    return 0;
}
```

In the above example, we have overridden the operators new and delete to show that storing a lambda that captures an array of 6 integers will invoke dynamic memory allocation. If you run the above example in Compiler Explorer using x86-64 GCC 14.2, you will see the following output:

```
void* operator new(std::size_t), size = 24
0, 1, 2, 3, 4,
void operator delete(void*)
```

This example also demonstrates the initialization of variable arr by using a lambda to generate members of the array. If you change constexpr std::size_t c_array_size to 4, you will notice that the operators new and delete are no longer invoked, meaning that, in this case, the captured data is stored on the stack.

To get around this problem, we can assign std::reference_wrapper of a lambda object to std::function<void()> fun instead of the object itself as in the following line of code:

```cpp
    func = std::ref(array_printer);
```

This will make the std::function object use a reference wrapper to the lambda object, instead of copying it and storing all the variables that lambda is capturing. Using this approach, we must take care of the lambda object lifetime, meaning that if it goes out of scope and we try to invoke it through the std::function object, we will end up with undefined behavior of the program.

We can also use plain function pointers to store lambdas, but only if they don't capture anything from the surrounding scope, as in the following example:

```cpp
#include <cstdio>
#include <functional>

int main () {
    void(*fun)(void);
    fun = []() {
        printf("Lambda!\r\n");
    };
    fun();
    return 0;
}
```

In the above example, we assign the lambda to a function pointer, making it a possible alternative to storing lambdas to the `std::function` class template in certain applications. This also makes it possible to pass non-capturing lambdas to C functions that expect function pointers.

Summary

Lambda expressions and `std::function` are powerful modern C++ tools that allow us to write expressive code and implement design patterns such as command patterns in an elegant way. We learned about different ways to capture data from the surrounding scope – by value or a reference. We also went through the command pattern design pattern and learned how to apply it to a GPIO interrupt manager.

In the next chapter, we will go through compile-time computation in C++.

Get This Book's PDF Version and Exclusive Extras

UNLOCK NOW

Scan the QR code (or go to `packtpub.com/unlock`). Search for this book by name, confirm the edition, and then follow the steps on the page.

Note: Keep your invoice handy. Purchases made directly from Packt don't require an invoice.

11
Compile-Time Computation

Compile-time computation refers to the ability of a compiler to execute functions at compile time, instead of converting them to machine code. This means that the results of complex operations can be calculated by the compiler and stored in variables that are used at runtime. A compiler can execute a function at compile time only if all arguments of the function are known at compile time.

We can use compile-time computation in C++ firmware to calculate complex math operations, generate lookup tables and arrays in general, and use the generated values at runtime. Performing these operations at compile time will save valuable memory and processor (space and time) resources and make them available for other, more important operations.

The goal of this chapter is to learn how to use compile-time computation in C++ to shift complex operations at compile time and save valuable resources. In this chapter, we're going to cover the following main topics:

- Templates
- The `constexpr` specifier
- The consteval specifier

Technical requirements

To get the most out of this chapter, I strongly recommend using Compiler Explorer (`https://godbolt.org/`) as you read through the examples. Select GCC as your compiler for x86 architecture. This will allow you to see standard output (stdio) results and better observe the code's behavior. As we are using a lot of modern C++ features, make sure to select the C++23 standard by adding `-std=c++23` to the compiler options box.

Compiler Explorer makes it easy to try out the code, tweak it, and immediately see how it affects the output and generated assembly code. Most of the examples can also be run in the Renode simulator on an ARM Cortex-M0 target and are available on GitHub (`https://github.com/PacktPublishing/Cpp-in-Embedded-Systems/tree/main/Chapter11`).

Templates

The first available mechanism for compile-time computation in C++ was **Template Meta-Programming (TMP)**. Using TMP, we can store the results of operations in types, as shown in the following example of computing the factorial:

```cpp
template <unsigned int N>
struct factorial {
    static const unsigned int value = N * factorial<N-1>::value;
};

template <>
struct factorial<0> {
    static const unsigned int value = 1;
};

int main () {
    const int fact = factorial<5>::value;
    return fact;
}
```

If you run this example in Compiler Explorer (even without optimizations), you will see that it returns 120. The generated assembly code is short and does not contain any function calls. It simply places the value 120 in the return register in the main function, meaning the factorial computation was done at compile time. You can see the generated assembly code here:

```asm
main:
        push    rbp
        mov     rbp, rsp
        mov     DWORD PTR [rbp-4], 120
        mov     eax, 120
        pop     rbp
        ret
```

We performed the following steps in the preceding example:

- We defined a class template factorial. It has an unsigned int, N, as the parameter and only one member: `static const unsigned int value = N * factorial<N-1>::value`.
- In the assignment expression of the member `value`, we use recursion at the template level as we calculate it by multiplying N by the `value` from the factorial instantiated with N – 1.
- We define factorial template specialization for 0, making it a base type that will stop recursion, meaning that `factorial<0>::value` will contain 1.

To better understand the recursion at the template level, we will write down the entire recursion chain for the preceding example:

- `factorial<5>::value = 5 * factorial<4>::value;`
- `factorial<4>::value = 4 * factorial<3>::value;`
- `factorial<3>::value = 3 * factorial<2>::value;`
- `factorial<2>::value = 2 * factorial<1>::value;`
- `factorial<1>::value = 1 * factorial<0>::value;`
- `factorial<0>::value = 1;`

If we substitute the base value of `factorial<0>` with 1, back up the chain, we have the following:

- `factorial<1>::value = 1 * 1 = 1`
- `factorial<2>::value = 2 * 1 = 2`
- `factorial<3>::value = 3 * 2 = 6`
- `factorial<4>::value = 4 * 6 = 24`
- `factorial<5>::value = 5 * 24 = 120`

The `main` function computes the factorial of 5 by accessing `factorial<5>::value` and returns it. The recursion is terminated by the specialized template for `factorial<0>`, which provides the base case. The final result is that the program returns `120`, the factorial of 5.

While TMP allows for compile-time computations, it often involves complex recursive patterns that can be difficult to read and maintain. To address these challenges, C++11 introduced the `constexpr` specifier, which has become the preferred mechanism for compile-time computations.

constexpr specifier

Using the constexpr **specifier**, we declare that it is possible to evaluate variables and functions at compile time. There are limitations to what can be evaluated at compile time. A constexpr variable must meet the following requirements:

- It needs to be of a literal type, any of the following:

    - Scalar types such as arithmetic types, enumerations, and pointers
    - Reference types
    - An array of literal types

- Classes that meet specific requirements (such as a trivial constexpr destructor, all of its non-static data members are literal types, or at least one constexpr constructor).
- It must be immediately initialized.
- The entire expression of its initialization needs to be a constant expression.

Let's go through the following example to better understand the requirements for constexpr variables:

```cpp
#include <cmath>
int main () {
    constexpr int ret = round(sin(3.14));
    return ret;
}
```

If you run this example in Compiler Explorer using x86-64 GCC 14.2 compiler, without optimization enabled, we can observe the following:

- The program returns 0.
- The resulting assembly is small, and it just moves 0 to return the register.
- If you change the initialization of the ret variable so that the sine function takes 3.14/2 as the argument, the program will return 1.

Now, if we try to change the compiler in Compiler Explorer to x86-64 clang 18.1.0, we will get the following compiler error:

```
<source>:4:19: error: constexpr variable 'ret' must be initialized by a
constant expression
    4 |     constexpr int ret = round(sin(3.14));
      |                         ^     ~~~~~~~~~~~~~~~~~~
```

```
<source>:4:31: note: non-constexpr function 'sin' cannot be used in a
constant expression
    4 |       constexpr int ret = round(sin(3.14));
```

The compiler reports that we are violating the rule that says that the entire expression of its initialization needs to be a constant expression, as the function sin, in the expression round(sin(3.14)), is non-constexpr. This is because Clang's implementation of math functions is non-constexpr, while GCC implements them as constexpr functions. Many math functions will be constexpr functions in the new C++26 standard.

Although the upcoming C++26 standard mandates that math functions should be constexpr, we will utilize the current GCC implementation because it is the compiler we are using for our STM32 target in the examples throughout this book. All constexpr functions must meet the following requirements:

- Its return type must be of the literal type.
- Each of its parameters must be of the literal type.
- If a function is not a constructor, it must have only one return statement.

To better understand constexpr functions, let us implement the factorial algorithm as a constexpr function in the following example:

```
constexpr unsigned int factorial(unsigned int n) {
    unsigned int prod = 1;
    while(n > 0) {
        prod *= n;
        n--;
    }
    return prod;
}

int main () {
    constexpr int calc_val = 5;
    constexpr unsigned int ret = factorial(calc_val);
    return ret;
}
```

In this example, we implemented the `factorial` algorithm as a simple `constexpr` function. Comparing it to a TMP-based solution, this code looks familiar to many developers with a C background. There is no recursion at the template level and strange syntax. C++11 `constexpr` functions still relied on recursion, but C++14 relaxed constraints on `constexpr` functions and allowed using local variables and loops.

If we run the preceding example in Compiler Explorer using the x86-64 `GCC 14.2` compiler, without optimization enabled, we can observe the following:

- The program returns 120.

- The resulting assembly is small, and it just moves 120 to the return register.

- There is no `factorial` function in the resulting assembly code, meaning that the compiler executed this function at compile time. We supplied a factorial function with a constant expression argument and the compiler evaluated the function at compile time.

- If we remove the `constexpr` specifier from the `calc_val` and `ret` variables declarations, we will see the `factorial` function in the resulting assembly call, and in `main`, we will see a call to this function, meaning that in this case, the `factorial` function is being executed at runtime, and in the case of firmware, it will be part of the binary.

As we can see from this example, the `constexpr` function can be executed at both compile time and runtime, depending on the arguments we supply it with. Next, we will go over practical examples to see how we can apply the `constexpr` specifier in firmware development.

Example 1 – MAC address parser

The **Medium Access Control (MAC)** address is used in the MAC layer of different communication stacks, including Ethernet, Wi-Fi, and Bluetooth. Here, we will create a 48-bit MAC address compile-time parser that will help us convert a common format of a MAC address written as hex numbers separated by a colon into an array of `uint8_t`, which is usually used in software stacks. The code is shown here:

```cpp
#include <array>
#include <cstdint>
#include <string_view>
#include <charconv>

struct mac_address {
    static constexpr std::size_t c_bytes_num = 6;
```

```cpp
    static constexpr std::size_t c_mac_addr_str_size = 17;

    std::array<uint8_t, c_bytes_num> bytes{};
    bool is_valid = false;

    constexpr mac_address(std::string_view str) {
        if (str.size() != c_mac_addr_str_size) {
            return;
        }

        for (size_t i = 0; i < c_bytes_num; ++i) {
            const std::string_view byte_str = str.substr(i * 3, 2);

            uint8_t value = 0;
            auto result = std::from_chars(byte_str.data(), byte_str.data()
                                          + byte_str.size(), value, 16);
            if (result.ec != std::errc()) {
                return;
            }
            bytes[i] = value;
        }
        is_valid = true;
    }
};

int main () {
    constexpr mac_address addr("00:11:22:33:44:55");
    static_assert(addr.is_valid);

    return addr.bytes.at(5);
}
```

In the main function, we create an instance of the struct mac_address, by providing a constructor with "00:11:22:33:44:55". If we run the preceding example in Compiler Explorer using the x86-64 GCC 14.2 compiler, without optimization enabled, we can observe the following:

- The program returns 85 as a decimal number. Converting it to hex format, we will get 0x55, which corresponds to the last byte from the MAC address 00:11:22:33:44:55.

- The resulting assembly is small. It populates the stack with bytes from the MAC address we used in the constructor. There are no calls to the constructor, meaning it is executed at compile time.

- If we change the MAC address provided in the constructor to `"000:11:22:33:44:55"` or `"G0:11:22:33:44:55"`, the compiler will generate an error due to failed `static_assert(addr.is_valid)`.

Let us now explain the `struct mac_address` in more detail:

- The `struct` contains the members `std::array<uint8_t, c_bytes_num>` bytes and `bool is_valid`. It doesn't contain any methods except the constructor.

- The constructor accepts the `std::string_view` class template, which encapsulates a pointer to the first element of the provided string literal, and its size.

- The constructor creates substring views using the `susbstr` method on the `string_view` object and it uses `std::from_char` to convert them to `uint8_t` values, which are stored in the bytes array.

- The constructor sets the `bool is_valid` to true if there are no errors. Using `static_assert`, we can validate at compile time that the provided MAC address string literal was converted successfully. We cannot use asserts in `constexpr` functions. The alternative is to throw an exception, which would result in a compile-time error, but we decided not to use exceptions for our embedded target.

You can also run the preceding example in the Renode simulator on the STM32 target. Start Visual Studio Code, attach it to the running container, and open the `Chapter11/compile_time` project, as described in *Chapter 4*, and run the following commands in the Visual Studio Code terminal, or run them directly in the container terminal:

```
$ cd Chapter11/compile_time
$ cmake -B build -DCMAKE_BUILD_TYPE=MinSizeRel -DMAIN_CPP_FILE_NAME=main_
constexpr_mac_address.cpp
$ cmake --build build --target run_in_renode
```

Here is part of the main function from the `main_constexpr_mac_address.cpp` file:

```cpp
constexpr mac_address addr("00:11:22:33:44:55");
static_assert(addr.is_valid);
const std::array<uint8_t, 6> addr_arr{0x00, 0x11, 0x22, 0x33, 0x44, 0x55};
const auto & mac_ref = addr.bytes;
```

```cpp
//const auto & mac_ref = addr_arr;
```

```cpp
printf("%02X:%02X:%02X:%02X:%02X:%02X\r\n", mac_ref[0], mac_ref[1], mac_
ref[2], mac_ref[3], mac_ref[4], mac_ref[5]);
```

To confirm that all the work of converting a string literal to an array is performed at compile time, you can bind the reference `mac_ref` to `addr_arr` and compare binary sizes in both cases. They are both 6,564 bytes, meaning that the `constexpr` constructor is not included in the binary as it is actually executed at compile time by the compiler.

Next, we will go through an example of creating a lookup table for a temperature thermistor using `constexpr` functions in C++.

Example 2 – Generating a lookup table

Thermistors are resistors whose resistance changes with temperature. They are commonly used in embedded systems. They usually have a non-linear curve. There are different methods to approximate an **Analog-to-Digital Converter** (**ADC**) reading from a thermistor into a temperature. One of the most used methods is the **beta coefficient**. It is calculated by measuring the thermistor's resistance at two temperature points. It is used to calculate temperature using the following equation:

$$\frac{1}{T} = \frac{1}{T_0} + \frac{1}{\beta} \ln\left(\frac{R}{R_0}\right)$$

In this equation, T_0 is a room temperature of 25°C (298.15K) and R_0 is the resistance of a thermistor at room temperature. Using the beta coefficient (a constant provided by the manufacturer) is a simplification of the thermistor's curve as it relies on measuring the curve only at two points.

The Steinhart-Hart equation provides a more accurate curve-fitting method as it relies on four coefficients calculated by measuring the thermistor at four temperature points. The equation is shown here:

$$\frac{1}{T} = A + B \ln(R) + C(\ln(R))^2 + D(\ln(R))^3$$

Coefficients A, B, C, and D are calculated after measuring the thermistor's temperature at four different temperature points – meaning these are constants that are given for a thermistor by the manufacturer. The calculated temperature from the Steinhart-Hart equation is in Kelvins. The drawback of the Steinhart-Hart equation is it is computationally heavy for small, embedded targets.

In this example, we will create a lookup table using the Steinhart-Hart equation and rely on it to determine temperature by reading a value from the ADC in our embedded target. As we can see from the equation, temperature is a function of resistance and given constants. For a selected range of resistance, and with a selected resolution, we will generate a lookup table of temperature values. Then, we will simulate a reading of the thermistor resistance and search the lookup table to determine the temperature.

We will select a range of resistance that we want to base the lookup table on, and the number of points we want to use. For this, we need functionality that will generate an array of numbers in the given range that are evenly spaced, also called linear space. Next, we will use that linear space as an argument to a signal generator. Let's start with implementing this as follows:

1. Here is the code showing the linear space generator:

```cpp
#include <array>
#include <cstdio>

template <typename T, std::size_t N>
struct signal : public std::array<T, N> {
  constexpr signal() {}
  constexpr signal(T begin, T end) {
    static_assert(N > 1, "N must be bigger than 1");
    float step = (end - begin) / (N - 1);

    for (std::size_t i = 0; i < N; i++) {
      this->at(i) = begin + i * step;
    }
  }
};

int main() {

  constexpr signal<float, 10> x_axis(0, 9);
  for(auto elem: x_axis) {
      printf("%.2f, ", elem);
  }
  printf("\r\n");
  return 0;
}
```

If we run this program, it will print 10 numbers in the range of 0 to 10, as shown here:

```
0.00, 1.00, 2.00, 3.00, 4.00, 5.00, 6.00, 7.00, 8.00, 9.00,
```

The numbers printed are generated at compile time by the `signal` struct. To connect this back to our example, imagine that these are the values of resistance for which we want to calculate the temperature using the Steinhart-Hart equation. Let's go through the implementation in detail:

- The `signal` is a class template. Template parameters are typename `T` and `std::size_t N`. They determine the array type that the `struct` is based on.
- The `struct` derives from `std::array<T, N>`. We based it on `std::array` to be able to use range-based for loops easily and standard library algorithms.
- In the `constexpr` constructor, we use `static_assert` to make sure that `N` is greater than 1, and we populate the underlying array with evenly spaced points between begin and end.
- In `main`, we provide `float` and `10` as template arguments to the `struct signal`, and `0` and `9` as begin and end points for the linear space to the constructor. We use a range-based for loop to go through elements of the compile-time-generated object `x_axis` and print its elements.

2. Next, we will expand the `signal` struct with an additional constructor that allows us to create a signal based on another signal and a lambda we will use to provide a math function to generate elements of a new signal. The code for a new constructor is shown here:

```cpp
template <typename T, std::size_t N>
struct signal : public std::array<T, N> {
  // ...

  constexpr signal(const signal &sig, auto fun) {
    for (std::size_t i = 0; i < N; i++) {
      this->at(i) = fun(sig.at(i));
    }
  }
};
```

In this constructor, we initialize elements of a new signal by calling the passed `fun` on elements of the passed signal `sig`.

3. Now we can create a new signal, as shown in this code:

```cpp
int main() {

    const auto print_signal = [](auto sig) {
        for(auto elem: sig) {
            printf("%.2f, ", elem);
        }
        printf("\r\n");
    };

    constexpr signal<float, 10> x_axis(0, 9);
    print_signal(x_axis);

    auto sine = signal(x_axis, [](float x){ return std::sin(x);});
    print_signal(sine);

    return 0;
}
```

If you are following the example using Compiler Explorer, make sure to include the `<cmath>`
header as we are using the `std::sin` function. Running it will give the following output:

```
0.00, 1.00, 2.00, 3.00, 4.00, 5.00, 6.00, 7.00, 8.00, 9.00,
0.00, 0.84, 0.91, 0.14, -0.76, -0.96, -0.28, 0.66, 0.99, 0.41,
```

In this code, we created a new signal named `sine` by passing `x_axis` and the lambda `[]`
`(int x){return std::sin(x);}` to the newly created constructor.

To connect this with the example, now we can generate a lookup table using simple math
functions (such as `std::sin`) and linear space generated with the signal constructor
from *step 1*.

Generating a lookup table

To generate more complex functions, we need to expand the `signal` class with more functionality:

1. First, we will overload the operators * and /, to multiply signals by constants and divide constants by elements of signal. The code is shown here:

```cpp
template <typename T, std::size_t N>
struct signal : public std::array<T, N> {
// ...

  constexpr signal operator*(const T &t) const {
    return signal(*this, [&](T elem)
                  { return elem * t; });
  };


  constexpr signal operator/(const T &t) const {
    return signal(*this, [&](T elem)
                  { return elem / t; });
  };
};
```

   In this code, we overloaded the operators * and /, enabling multiplication and division of a signal with a scalar, as in:

```cpp
auto result = sig * 2.0f;
```

   The preceding code will create a new signal called `result`, which will be the result of the multiplication of every element of signal `sig` by scalar `2.0`.

2. Similarly, we can create a new signal by dividing the existing signal by a scalar, as shown here:

```cpp
auto result = sig / 2.0f;
```

   This code will create a new signal called `result`, which will be the result of the division of every element of signal `sig` by scalar `2.0`.

3. To support scalars from the left side of operators * and /, we need to implement the global operators operator* and operator/. We will do so by declaring them as friends to the struct signal, as shown here:

```cpp
template <typename T, std::size_t N>
struct signal : public std::array<T, N> {
// ...

  friend constexpr signal operator*(const T &t, const signal &sig)
  {
    return sig * t;
  }
  friend constexpr signal operator/(const T &t, const signal &sig)
  {
    signal ret;
    for (std::size_t i = 0; i < N; i++) {
      ret.at(i) = t / sig.at(i);
    }
    return ret;
  }
};
```

The friend function operator* in this code allows scalar multiplication when the scalar is on the left-hand side (scalar * signal), which is not possible with the member function alone. As multiplication has a commutative property ($a * b = b * a$), we simply call the member function operator* and return the result (return sig * t).

4. In the friend function operator/, we perform the following steps:

    1. Create a new signal, ret.

    2. Iterate over the elements of the signal sig, and for each element, the scalar t is divided by the element.

    3. We return the signal ret.

5. By overloading the operators * and / both as global and as member functions, we can now create signals as in the following example:

```cpp
int main() {
  // ...

  constexpr signal<float, 10> x_axis(0, 9);
```

```
    print_signal(x_axis);

    auto linear_fun = 2.f * x_axis;
    print_signal(linear_fun);

    auto linear_fun2 = linear_fun / 2.f;
    print_signal(linear_fun2);

    return 0;
}
```

This code will result in the following output:

```
0.00, 1.00, 2.00, 3.00, 4.00, 5.00, 6.00, 7.00, 8.00, 9.00,
0.00, 2.00, 4.00, 6.00, 8.00, 10.00, 12.00, 14.00, 16.00, 18.00,
0.00, 1.00, 2.00, 3.00, 4.00, 5.00, 6.00, 7.00, 8.00, 9.00,
```

As we can see from this output, the originally created x_axis, representing linear space from 0 to 9.00 with 10 points, is multiplied by 2.0 to create linear_fun. Then we divide linear_fun by 2.0 to create linear_fun2, which matches the x_axis.

6. To be able to write the full Steinhart-Hart equation, we also need to overload operators + and -, as shown here:

```
template <typename T, std::size_t N>
struct signal : public std::array<T, N> {
// ...
  constexpr signal operator+(const T &t) const {
    return signal(*this, [&](T elem)
                  { return elem + t; });
  };
  constexpr signal operator-(const T &t) const {
    return signal(*this, [&](T elem)
                  { return elem - t; });
  };

  constexpr signal operator+(const signal &sig) const {
    signal ret;
    for (std::size_t i = 0; i < N; i++)
```

```cpp
    {
      ret.at(i) = this->at(i) + sig.at(i);
    }
    return ret;
  };

  friend constexpr signal operator+(const T &t, const signal &sig)
  {
    return sig + t;
  }
};
```

In this code, we overload the following operators:

- A member `constexpr signal operator+(const T &t)`, allowing us to add a scalar to a signal (signal + scalar)

- A member `constexpr signal operator-(const T &t)`, allowing us to subtract a scalar from a signal (signal - scalar)

- A member `constexpr signal operator+(const signal &sig)`, allowing us to add two signals, element by element (signal1 + signal2)

- Global `constexpr signal operator+(const T &t, const signal &sig)`, allowing us to add a signal to a scalar (scalar + signal)

Writing a signal representing the Steinhart-Hart equation

Now we have all the elements we need to write a signal that represents the Steinhart-Hart equation, as shown here:

```cpp
int main()
{
  constexpr float A = 1.18090254918130e-3;
  constexpr float B = 2.16884014794388e-4;
  constexpr float C = 1.90058756197216e-6;
  constexpr float D = 1.83161892641824e-8;
  constexpr int c_lut_points = 50;

  constexpr signal<float, c_lut_points> resistance(1e3, 10e3);

  constexpr auto temperature_k =
```

```cpp
                    1 / (A +
        B * signal(resistance, [](float x)
                            { return std::log(x); }) +
        C * signal(resistance, [](float x)
                            { return std::pow(std::log(x), 2); }) +
        D * signal(resistance, [](float x)
                            { return std::pow(std::log(x), 3); }));


    constexpr auto temperature_celsius = temperature_k - 273.15f;


    std::ofstream file("out.csv");
    file << "Resistance[Ohm], Temperature[Celsius]\n";
    for (int i = 0; i < c_lut_points; i++) {
      file << resistance[i] << ", " << temperature_celsius[i] << "\n";
    }
    return 0;
}
```

This code generates points from the Steinhart-Hart equation through the following steps:

1. Define the *A*, *B*, *C*, and *D* coefficients.

2. Create values for resistance in the range 1 to 10 kOhms across 50 points.

3. Calculate values of temperature in Kelvins using the Steinhart-Hart equation in points from the generated resistance signal. We convert temperature to Celsius by subtracting 273.15.

4. Save the values from the generated resistance and temperature signals into a CSV file (file operations require including the `<fstream>` header).

You can run the full example in a Docker container. Start Visual Studio Code, attach it to the running container, and open the `Chapter11/signal_generator` project, as described in *Chapter 4*, and then run the following commands in the Visual Studio Code terminal, or run them directly in the container terminal:

```
$ cd Chapter11/signal_generator
$ cmake -B build
$ cmake --build build
$ ./build/signal_gen
```

Running the example will result in a CSV file being created (out.csv). We can generate an image from the created CSV file using the following command in the terminal:

```
$ graph out.csv -o curve.png
```

We can transfer the generated image using the docker cp command from the host machine:

```
$ docker cp dev_env:/workspace/Cpp-in-Embedded-Systems/Chapter11/signal_
generator/curve.png
```

This command will transfer the generated image curve.png to the host machine. We can also see the same image here:

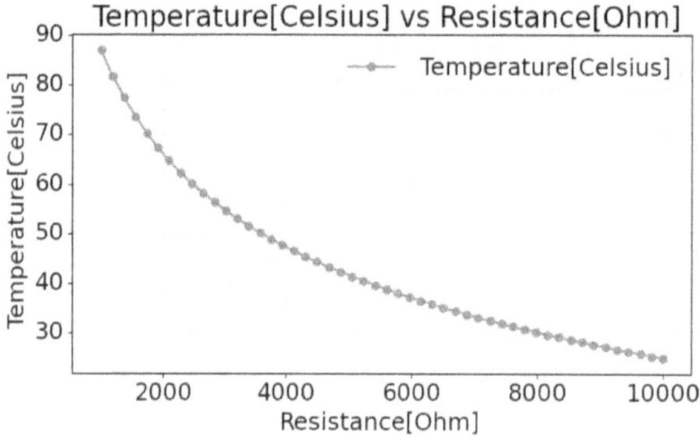

Figure 11.1 – Steinhart-Hart curve

Figure 11.1 depicts the calculated Steinhart-Hart curve. Values for resistance and temperature were generated at compile time using the signal struct. Next, we will use the generated curve in Renode to read a temperature from a simulated thermistor using the ADC. Here is an image of a circuit showing how the thermistor is connected to the microcontroller:

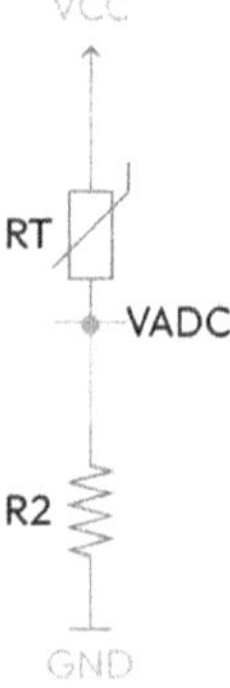

Figure 11.2 – Thermistor circuit

Figure 11.2 depicts a voltage divider with a thermistor. If we measure the voltage on the ADC pin, we can calculate the thermistor's resistance using the following equation:

$$R_T = R_2 \left(\frac{V_{CC}}{V_{ADC}} - 1 \right)$$

In the preceding equation:

- R_T is the calculated resistance of the thermistor.

- R_2 is the resistance of a resistor with a known value.

- V_{CC} is the power supply voltage.

- V_{ADC} is the voltage measured by the ADC.

We can model a voltage divider using a simple `struct` in C++, shown here:

```
struct voltage_divider {
        units::resistance r2;
        units::voltage vcc;

        units::resistance get_r1(units::voltage vadc) {
            return r2 * (vcc/vadc - 1);
        }
    };
voltage_divider divider{10e3_Ohm, 3.3_V};
```

This code shows the `struct voltage_divider`. We will go through its details:

- It uses strong type resistance and voltage defined in namespace units. You can check the implementation details for these strong types in the project folder, `Chapter11/compile_time/util`.

- We instantiate an object of voltage_divider using list initialization as in `voltage_divider divider{10e3_Ohm, 3.3_V}`. `10e3_Ohm` and `3.3_V` are user-defined literals for types resistance and voltage.

- The struct has a single method, `units::resistance get_r1(units::voltage vadc)`. It calculates the R1 value from a voltage divider circuit based on the provided voltage on ADC. In our case, this is the thermistor's resistance.

Analyzing the usage example firmware code

Next, we will go through the firmware code in a while loop in the main function from Chapter11/
compile_time/app/src/main_lookup_table.cpp. It is shown here:

```cpp
auto adc_val = adc.get_reading();
if(adc_val) {
  auto adc_val_voltage = *adc_val;
  auto thermistor_r = divider.get_r1(adc_val_voltage);
  auto it = std::lower_bound(resistance.begin(),
                 resistance.end(), thermistor_r.get());
  if(it != resistance.end()) {
     std::size_t pos = std::distance(resistance.begin(), it);
     float temperature = temperature_celsius.at(pos);

     printf("%d mV, %d Ohm, %d.%d C\r\n",
            static_cast<int>(adc_val_voltage.get_mili()),
            static_cast<int>(thermistor_r.get()),
            static_cast<int>(temperature),
            static_cast<int>(10*(temperature-std::floor(temperature))) );
  }
}
hal::time::delay_ms(200);
```

Let us analyze this code in detail:

1. We are calling the get_reading method on the object adc. It is of type hal::adc_stm32,
    and it returns std::expected<units::voltage, adc::error>. It is an error-handling
    technique that we covered in *Chapter 7*. You can check the implementation details of the
    adc_stm32 class in the project folder, Chapter11/compile_time/hal/adc.

2. If the call to get_reading was successful, we dereference the returned object to get ac-
    cess to the voltage, which we pass to voltage_divider's get_r1 method to calculate the
    thermistor's value.

3. Next, we use the algorithm std::lower_bound to get an iterator to the first element in the
    resistance signal that is not ordered before calculating the thermistor's value. If we find
    such an element, we calculate its position using std::distance, and index temperature_
    celsius to get the temperature value.

4. Finally, we print the ADC's voltage, the thermistor's resistance, and the temperature value. Note that we printed the float value of temperature using `int`s, as printing floats increases the binary size of the firmware.

To run the firmware in the Renode simulator on the STM32 target, start Visual Studio Code, attach it to the running container, and open the `Chapter11/compile_time` project, as described in *Chapter 4*, then run the following commands in the Visual Studio Code terminal, or run them directly in the container terminal:

```
$ cd Chapter11/compile_time
$ cmake -B build -DCMAKE_BUILD_TYPE=MinSizeRel -DMAIN_CPP_FILE_NAME=main_
lookup_table.cpp
$ cmake --build build --target run_in_renode
```

To simulate voltage on the ADC, please enter the following command in the terminal running Renode:

```
$ adc FeedVoltageSampleToChannel 0 1700 3
```

The preceding command will feed a voltage of 1700 mV to the ADC in three successive readings. This will result in the following output:

```
1699 mV, 9412 Ohm, 26.2 C
```

This command shows that for a value of 1700 mV on the ADC, we calculated a thermistor value of 9412 Ohms, resulting in a temperature of $26.2°$C. As an exercise, feed the simulation with different ADC voltage values and compare the results with the curve graph from previous steps.

The `constexpr` specifier is a flexible tool in C++ allowing us to run a function at both compile time and runtime. If we want to make sure that a function is evaluated only at compile time, we can use the `consteval` specifier.

consteval specifier

The **consteval specifier** may be applied only to functions. It specifies that a function is a so-called immediate function and that every call to it must result in a compile-time constant. Let's go through the following simple example:

```
constexpr int square(int x) {
    return x*x;
}

int main() {
```

```cpp
    constexpr int arg = 2;
    int ret = square(arg);
    return ret;
}
```

If you run this example in Compiler Explorer using the x86-64 GCC 14.2 compiler, without optimization enabled, we can observe the following:

- The program returns 4.

- The resulting assembly is small, and it just moves 4 to the return register.

- Removing the constexpr specifier from the variable arg will result in the function square being generated and a call to it in the main function.

Now, let's change the function square constexpr specifier to consteval, as shown here:

```cpp
consteval int square(int x) {
    return x*x;
}

int main() {
    constexpr int arg = 2;
    int ret = square(arg);
    return ret;
}
```

If you run the program in Compiler Explorer, it will return 4 and result in small assembly code. However, if we now remove the constexpr specifier from the variable arg, the compilation will fail with the following error:

```
<source>: In function 'int main()':
<source>:7:21: error: call to consteval function 'square(arg)' is not a
constant expression
    7 |     int ret = square(arg);
      |               ~~~~~~^~~~~
<source>:7:21: error: the value of 'arg' is not usable in a constant
expression
<source>:6:9: note: 'int arg' is not const
    6 |     int arg = 2;
      |         ^~~
```

The consteval specifier ensures that a function is evaluated only at compile time. This prevents the function from being accidentally run at runtime, which could happen with a `constexpr` function.

Summary

In this chapter, we explored techniques for compile-time computation in C++. We covered the basics of TMP and provided an in-depth explanation of the `constexpr` specifier, using examples relevant to embedded systems.

With the knowledge from this chapter, you can generate lookup tables and convert human-readable addresses, UUIDs, and similar data into arrays used by communication stacks, all at compile time. This allows you to write expressive code that generates complex mathematical signals without consuming extra memory or processing time.

Next, we will go over the techniques used in writing a HAL in C++.

Join our community on Discord

Join our community's Discord space for discussions with the author and other readers:

`https://packt.link/embeddedsystems`

Part 4

Applying C++ to Solving Embedded Domain Problems

This part focuses on applying everything you've learned by solving problems from the embedded domain. You will go through writing a type-safe, compile-time checked HAL, learn how to work effectively with C libraries, and study design patterns such as Adapter, State, and Command. You will also learn how to apply RAII to manage resources like the file system. The part wraps up with an overview of libraries and frameworks useful for embedded development and a look at the SOLID principles.

This part has the following chapters:

- *Chapter 12, Writing C++ HAL*
- *Chapter 13, Working with C Libraries*
- *Chapter 14, Enhancing Super-Loop with Sequencer*
- *Chapter 15, Practical Patterns – Building a Temperature Publisher*
- *Chapter 16, Designing Scalable Finite State Machines*
- *Chapter 17, Libraries and Frameworks*
- *Chapter 18, Cross-Platform Development*

12

Writing C++ HAL

A **Hardware Abstraction Layer** (HAL) is a core software component in embedded projects. It simplifies interactions with hardware peripherals by providing an easy-to-use interface that abstracts the hardware details. The HAL manages the reading and writing of memory-mapped peripheral registers, allowing you to use peripherals such as GPIOs, timers, and serial communication interfaces, without dealing directly with low-level hardware specifics. It often supports multiple devices within the same family.

By using a HAL, firmware becomes more portable across different devices and similar families from the same vendor. It hides the register layouts of memory-mapped peripherals, making it easier to reuse drivers and business logic on various devices. The HAL handles platform-specific details, enabling developers to focus on the application rather than hardware nuances. It also manages differences among different series of **microcontrollers** (MCUs).

It's recommended to use vendor-provided HALs, typically delivered as C libraries, because they are well-tested and regularly maintained. Still, in some cases, it may be needed to work directly with memory-mapped peripherals, thus, in this chapter, we will explore C++ techniques that can help you write safer and more expressive HALs. In this chapter, we will cover the following topics:

- Memory-mapped peripherals
- Timers

Technical requirements

The examples from this chapter are available on GitHub (https://github.com/PacktPublishing/
Cpp-in-Embedded-Systems/tree/main/Chapter12). To get the most out of this chapter, run the
examples in the Renode simulator.

Memory-mapped peripherals

Memory-mapped peripherals allow programs to control hardware devices by reading from and
writing to specific memory addresses. Both peripheral registers and RAM are mapped to the same
address space, making communication with hardware registers as simple as writing and reading
to a pointer that points to those locations.

In previous examples in this book, we used an ST-provided HAL written in C, which controls
hardware peripherals through **Common Microcontroller Software Interface Standard (CMSIS)**
headers.

CMSIS is a vendor-independent HAL and software library collection for Arm Cortex-based microcontrollers. Developed by Arm, it standardizes hardware access and configuration, simplifying
software development and improving code portability across different manufacturers. Each microcontroller vendor provides its own CMSIS implementation, adapting the core APIs and drivers to
their specific devices. Next, we will explore CMSIS implementation of access to memory-mapped
peripherals for the STM32F072 microcontroller.

CMSIS memory-mapped peripherals

Access to registers in CMSIS is modeled through pointers to structs that describe register layout.
CMSIS defines macros representing pointers to memory-mapped peripherals.

Structs, according to CMSIS naming conventions, are named using the peripheral name abbre-
viation and _TypeDef postfix. The **reset and clock control (RCC)** peripheral struct is named
RCC_TypeDef. It is defined in example projects in the platform/CMSIS/Device/ST/STM32F0xx/
Include/stm32f072xb.h file, as shown here:

```
typedef struct
{
    __IO uint32_t CR;         /* Address offset: 0x00 */
    __IO uint32_t CFGR;       /* Address offset: 0x04 */
    __IO uint32_t CIR;        /* Address offset: 0x08 */
    __IO uint32_t APB2RSTR;   /* Address offset: 0x0C */
    __IO uint32_t APB1RSTR;   /* Address offset: 0x10 */
```

```c
    __IO uint32_t AHBENR;      /* Address offset: 0x14 */
    __IO uint32_t APB2ENR;     /* Address offset: 0x18 */
    __IO uint32_t APB1ENR;     /* Address offset: 0x1C */
    __IO uint32_t BDCR;        /* Address offset: 0x20 */
    __IO uint32_t CSR;         /* Address offset: 0x24 */
    __IO uint32_t AHBRSTR;     /* Address offset: 0x28 */
    __IO uint32_t CFGR2;       /* Address offset: 0x2C */
    __IO uint32_t CFGR3;       /* Address offset: 0x30 */
    __IO uint32_t CR2;         /* Address offset: 0x34 */
} RCC_TypeDef;
```

In the same header file, along with the `RCC_TypeDef` struct, the following macros are defined:

```c
#define PERIPH_BASE              0x40000000UL

/*!< Peripheral memory map */
#define APBPERIPH_BASE           PERIPH_BASE
#define AHBPERIPH_BASE           (PERIPH_BASE + 0x00020000UL)

/*!< AHB peripherals */
#define RCC_BASE                 (AHBPERIPH_BASE + 0x00001000UL)

/*!< Peripheral_declaration */
#define RCC                      ((RCC_TypeDef *) RCC_BASE)
```

This code is part of the CMSIS header `stm32f072xb.h`, and it's all we need to configure the RCC register. We are setting up clock configuration in the `SystemInit` function, which is called before the `main` function (as you were able to see in *Chapter 4*). The following code snippet is from the `SystemInit` function:

```c
/* Set HSION bit */
RCC->CR |= (uint32_t)0x00000001U;
```

In this code, we are setting up the HSION bit of the clock control register (CR) or the RCC peripheral, and we know we are doing that because of the comment in the code. Also, nothing is preventing us from setting CR to any random value. Here is an example of usage of the clock configuration register (CFGR) from the RCC peripheral:

```c
/* Reset SW[1:0], HPRE[3:0], PPRE[2:0], ADCPRE, MCOSEL[2:0], MCOPRE[2:0]
   and PLLNODIV bits */
RCC->CFGR &= (uint32_t)0x08FFB80CU;
```

This code sets PLL division, various prescaler, and clock settings. It's not quite obvious which settings are applied from the hex value `0x08FFB80CU`.

Even though this approach is common, there are several issues with modeling access to peripherals using register structs and a pointer pointing to the peripheral's base address:

- The first is reduced readability. We can write arbitrary `uint32_t` values in hex format, making the code meaningless and requiring us to refer to reference manuals of micro-controllers.

- As we can write any value we want to a register, we can easily write wrong or even random values.

- Individual registers of a peripheral in a struct must be ordered according to their memory layout. Members named `RESERVERDn` are used to add space into the structure for adjusting the addresses of the peripheral registers and to prevent padding.

- CMSIS headers may contain macros defining bit masks for accessing individual settings in a register, which simplifies access to peripheral registers. Still, these macros are not making the code any safer, just easier to work with.

Let's see how we can utilize C++ to address these concerns, making the code safer and more readable.

Memory-mapped peripherals in C++

We will use the knowledge we gained in previous chapters to create an expressive and type-safe interface to access memory-mapped peripherals in C++. We will create an interface with the following qualities:

- Read and write access control to a hardware register

- Type-safe write to a register

- Expressive and easy to use

Let us start with a basic implementation of an interface representing a memory-mapped register that will match the CMSIS approach in functionality. The code is shown here:

```cpp
struct read_access{};
struct write_access{};
struct read_write_access : read_access, write_access {};

template<std::uintptr_t Address, typename Access = read_write_access,
typename T = std::uint32_t>
```

```cpp
struct reg {

template <typename Access_ = Access>
static std::enable_if_t<std::is_base_of_v<read_access, Access_>, T>
read()
{
    return *reinterpret_cast<volatile T*>(Address);
}

template <typename Access_ = Access>
static std::enable_if_t<std::is_base_of_v<write_access, Access_>, void>
write(T val)
{
    *reinterpret_cast<volatile T*>(Address) = val;
}
};
```

In this code, the class template `reg` models a hardware register. It has the following template parameters:

- `uintptr_t Address`: The memory address of the hardware register
- `typename Access`: The access rights for the register (defaults to `read_write_access`)
- `typename T`: The data type matching the size of the register (defaults to `std::uint32_t`)

The class template `reg` has two static methods: `read` and `write`. These are used to read from and write to a register, respectively. Both methods are enabled or disabled at compile time using SFINAE, which we covered in *Chapter 8*. We are using the following types of access control:

- `struct read_access`
- `struct write_access`
- `struct read_write_access`: This inherits from both `read_access` and `write_access`

To enable and disable `write` and `read` methods at compile time using SFINAE, we made both methods template functions. This allows us to use the class template `enable_if` at the return type of these methods to either enable or disable them, depending on the condition provided to it.

The template parameter for both `write` and `read` is `Access_`, which defaults to `Access`. It ensures that SFINAE works correctly by making the substitution dependent on a template parameter of the function itself.

We are enabling the read method using `std::enable_if_t<std::is_base_of_v<read_access, Access_>, T>`. This means that if `std::is_base_of_v<read_access, Access_>` is true (i.e., if `Access_` is derived from or is the same as `read_access`), `std::enable_if_t` resolves to `T`, and the function is enabled. Otherwise, it results in a substitution failure, and the function is not included in the overload set. We are enabling the `write` method in a similar fashion, by checking whether `Access_` type is derived from or the same as `write_access`.

We use `reinterpret_cast<volatile T*>` to convert the integer template parameter `Address` into a pointer to a volatile variable of type `T` (which defaults to `std::uint32_t`). The volatile keyword informs the compiler that the value at this memory location can change at any time outside the program's control – by hardware. This prevents the compiler from applying certain optimizations that might omit necessary reads or writes to this address.

Without `volatile`, the compiler might assume that multiple reads from the same address yield the same value or that writes to the address can be reordered or even omitted, which can lead to incorrect behavior when interacting with hardware.

As we discussed in *Chapter 9*, casting an integer to a pointer using `reinterpret_cast` is considered an implementation-defined behavior in C++. This means the C++ standard doesn't specify exactly how it should work, and different compilers or platforms might handle it differently. Writing directly to a specific memory location is inherently unsafe and relies on behavior that isn't guaranteed to be portable across all systems. Therefore, we need to be cautious about the portability of this solution, as some platforms may implement pointer conversions differently.

Here are a few examples of using the class template `reg`:

```cpp
using rcc = reg<0x40021000>;
auto val = rcc::read(); // ok
rcc::write(0xDEADBEEF); // ok

using rcc_read = reg<0x40021000, read_access>;
auto val = rcc_read::read(); // ok
rcc_read::write(0xDEADBEEF); // compiler-error, no write access

using rcc_write = reg<0x40021000, write_access>;
auto val = rcc_write::read(); // compiler-error, no read access
rcc_write::write(0xDEADBEEF); // ok
```

These examples demonstrate the usage of the implemented interface for accessing memory-mapped peripherals. When defining types using the class template reg, we provide it with the address of a register and write access if we are working with write-only or read-only registers. The default access type allows us both read and write privileges.

The preceding solution is as effective as the CMSIS approach. You can experiment with the full example and compare binary sizes by running the full example in Renode. Start Visual Studio Code, attach it to the running container, open the Chapter12/cpp_hal project as described in *Chapter 4*, and run the following commands in the Visual Studio Code terminal, or run them directly in the container terminal:

```
$ cmake -B build -DCMAKE_BUILD_TYPE=Release -DMAIN_CPP_FILE_NAME=main_
basic_reg.cpp
$ cmake --build build --target run_in_renode
```

Our current solution still allows us to write arbitrary values to registers. To address this, we will use strong types based on enum classes to model bit fields used to set different settings in registers.

Type-safe memory-mapped peripherals in C++

To prevent arbitrary writings to a register using the class template reg, we will add a new static method, set, which will accept only types meeting certain criteria. We will model these types by creating a BitFieldConcept. We covered concepts in *Chapter 8*. Also, we will remove public access to the write method and put it instead in the private section. The modified code is shown here:

```cpp
template<typename BitField, typename Reg, typename T>
concept BitFieldConcept =
    std::is_same_v<Reg, typename BitField::reg> &&
    std::is_enum_v<typename BitField::value> &&
    std::is_same_v<std::underlying_type_t<typename
BitField::value>, T>;


template<std::uintptr_t Address, typename Access = read_write_access,
typename T = std::uint32_t>
struct reg {

using RegType = T;
    // Type alias for the current instantiation
```

```cpp
using ThisReg = reg<Address, Access, T>;

template<typename BitField>
requires BitFieldConcept<BitField, ThisReg, T>
static void set(BitField::value bits_val)
{
    auto reg_value = read();
    reg_value &= ~BitField::c_mask;
    reg_value |= (static_cast<T>(bits_val) <<
        BitField::c_position) & BitField::c_mask;
    write(reg_value);
}


template <typename Access_ = Access>
static std::enable_if_t<std::is_base_of_v<read_access, Access_>, T>
read()
{
    return *reinterpret_cast<volatile T*>(Address);
}
private:

template <typename Access_ = Access>
static std::enable_if_t<std::is_base_of_v<write_access, Access_>, void>
write(T val)
{
    *reinterpret_cast<volatile T*>(Address) = val;
}
};
```

The template method set has a single template parameter – type BitField. We use BitFieldConcept to impose the following requirements on the BitField:

- Reg must be the same as BitField::reg. This ensures the bit field is associated with the correct register.

- BitField::value must be an enum.

- The underlying type of the BitField::value enum must be T. This ensures that values represented by the enum can fit in the registers.

The set function parameter is `BitField::value bits_val`. The function itself is simple, and it performs the following operations:

- Reads the current register value
- Clears the bits specified by `BitField::c_mask`
- Sets the new bits by shifting `bits_val` to the correct position (`BitField::c_position`) and applying the mask
- Writes the modified value back to the register

To use the set function, we need to define types that describe the register's bit fields and that meet the requirements imposed by the `BitFieldConcept`.

Modeling HSION and HSITRIM bit fields from the RCC register

Let us examine bit fields in the RCC CR register defined in the STM32F0x2 reference manual document, as shown in *Figure 12.1*:

31	30	29	28	27	26	25	24	23	22	21	20	19	18	17	16
Res	Res	Res	Res	Res	Res	PLL RDY	PLLON	Res	Res	Res	Res	CSS ON	HSE BYP	HSE RDY	HSE ON
						r	rw					rw	rw	r	rw

15	14	13	12	11	10	9	8	7	6	5	4	3	2	1	0
HSICAL[7:0]								HSITRIM[4:0]						HSE RDY	HSE ON
r	r	r	r	r	r	r	r	rw	rw	rw	rw	rw		r	rw

Figure 12.1 – RCC CR register

Figure 12.1 depicts bit fields in the RCC CR register. Let us define a struct `hsion` that describes the HSI clock enable bit field from the RCC CR register. It has only one bit on position 0, so we can model it as follows:

```
using rcc = reg<0x40021000>;
struct hsion {
    using reg = rcc;
    using T = reg::RegType;

    static constexpr T c_position = 0U;
    static constexpr T c_mask = (1U << c_position);

    enum class value : T {
        disable = 0U,
```

```
        enable  = 1U,
    };
};
```

In this code, we declare type rcc as an instance of the class template reg by providing it with the address of the RCC register. Then, we create a struct hsion with the following properties:

- A public typedef member reg, which we set to rcc. This "maps" hsion to the rcc register thanks to BitFieldConcept.

- The constexpr variables c_position and c_mask, used for bit manipulation by the set method.

- An enum class value, defining enable and disable.

We can use the hsion struct to enable or disable the HSI clock using the following code:

```
rcc::set<hsion>(hsion::value::enable);
rcc::set<hsion>(hsion::value::disable);
```

This code allows us to safely set bits in a register. It is also expressive: the syntax rcc::set<hsi on>(hsion::value::enable); clearly communicates the intent – setting the hsion bit field to enable on the rcc register.

As we can see in *Figure 12.1*, most of the defined bit fields in the CR register are enable/disable bits. Exceptions are:

- HSICAL[7:0]: HSI clock calibration: These bits are automatically initialized at startup and can be adjusted by software via the HSITRIM setting.

- HSITRIM[4:0]: HSI clock trimming: These bits offer an additional user-programmable trimming value added to the HSICAL[7:0] bits. This setting allows adjustments for voltage and temperature variations that may affect the HSI frequency.

HSICAL bits are initialized at startup, meaning we shouldn't modify them. HSITRIM bits are user-programmable, and they occupy 5 bits. Defining all combinations of 5 bits in the BitField value enum wouldn't be practical, so we will approach this by providing value through a template parameter, as shown in the code here:

```
template<auto Bits>
struct hsi_trim {
    using reg = rcc;
    using T = reg::RegType;
```

```cpp
    static_assert(std::is_same_v<T, decltype(Bits)>);

    static constexpr T c_position = 3;
    static constexpr T c_mask = (0x1F << c_position);

    static_assert(Bits <= 0x1F);

    enum class value : T {
        val = Bits
    };
};
```

In this code, we defined the class template `hsitrim` with the auto template parameter `Bits`. The auto keyword is used to indicate that we are using a non-type template parameter. We use `static_assert` to make sure that the type of provided parameter `Bits` (`decltype(Bits)`) is the same as the underlying registers type to satisfy requirements imposed by `BitFieldConcept`.

We encode the `enum` class value val with the `Bits`. This encodes the value in the type itself and makes it possible to use it with the `reg` struct set method. We also utilize `static_assert` to make sure that the provided value fits in the allocated number of bits – `static_assert(Bits <= 0x1F)`. Again, we are utilizing compile-time operations to ensure type safety. Here is an example of using the `hsitrim` struct:

```cpp
rcc::set<hsi_trim<0xFLU>>(hsi_trim<0xFLU>::value::val);
```

This code sets the `hsitrim` value in the `rcc` register to 0xF. You can experiment with the full example in Renode. Start Visual Studio Code, attach it to the running container, open the Chapter12/cpp_hal project, as described in *Chapter 4*, and run the following commands in the Visual Studio Code terminal, or run them directly in the container terminal:

```
$ cmake -B build -DCMAKE_BUILD_TYPE=Release -DMAIN_CPP_FILE_NAME=main_
type_safe_reg.cpp
$ cmake --build build --target run_in_renode
```

Generic versions of hsion and hsi_trim

To enable the reuse of bit fields that have a single bit (enable/disable) such as `hsion`, we will define the class template `reg_bits_enable_disable`, as shown here:

```
template<typename Reg, uint32_t Pos>
struct reg_bits_enable_disable {
    using reg = Reg;
    using T = reg::RegType;

    static constexpr T c_position = Pos;
    static constexpr T c_mask = (0x1UL << c_position);

    enum class value : T {
        disable = 0,
        enable = 1
    };
};
```

This defined template type, `reg_bits_enable_disable`, could be used to define the `hsion` type, as shown in the following code:

```
using hsion = reg_bits_enable_disable<rcc, 0U>;
```

Next, we will create a generic version of the type used to set multiple fields with a value, such as `hsi_trim`. We will call it `reg_bits`, and the code is shown here:

```
template<auto Bits, typename Reg, uint32_t Mask, uint32_t Pos = 0>
struct reg_bits {

    using reg = Reg; using T = reg::RegType;
    static_assert(std::is_same_v<T, decltype(Bits)>);

    static constexpr T c_position = Pos;
    static constexpr T c_mask = (Mask << c_position);

    static_assert(Bits <= Mask);
```

```cpp
    enum class value : T {
        val = Bits
    };

};
```

We could use the generic type `reg_bits` to define the `hsi_trim` template type, as shown here:

```cpp
template<auto Bits>
using hsi_trim = reg_bits<Bits, rcc, 0x1F, 3U>;
```

Next, we will explore how to use C++ to create templates for peripherals that are similar but also have some implementation differences.

Timers

STM32F072 has multiple timers, including TIM2 and TIM3. TIM2 is a 32-bit timer and TIM3 is a 16-bit timer.

We will create a template class timer that will depend on timer traits structures containing timer-specific details. Here is the code for timer traits structures:

```cpp
struct timer2_traits {
    constexpr static std::uintptr_t base_address = 0x40000000;
    constexpr static IRQn_Type irqn = TIM2_IRQn;

    constexpr static std::uint32_t arr_bit_mask = 0xFFFFFFFF;
};

struct timer3_traits {
    constexpr static std::uintptr_t base_address = 0x40000400;
    constexpr static IRQn_Type irqn = TIM3_IRQn;

    constexpr static std::uint32_t arr_bit_mask = 0xFFFF;
};
```

In this code, `timer2_traits` and `timer3_traits` are traits structures that encapsulate the hardware-specific details of TIM2 and TIM3 timers, respectively. They have the following members:

- `base_address`: The base memory address of the timer's register map

- `irqn`: The interrupt request number associated with the timer

- `arr_bit_mask`: The bit mask for the auto-reload register (ARR):

    - For TIM2, it's `0xFFFFFFFF` (32-bit timer).

    - For TIM3, it's `0xFFFF` (16-bit timer).

Next, let's look at the template class timer:

```cpp
template <typename TimerTraits>
struct timer {
    constexpr static std::uintptr_t base_address =
                                    TimerTraits::base_address;

    using cr1 = reg<base_address + 0x00>;
    using dier = reg<base_address + 0x0C>;
    using sr = reg<base_address + 0x10>;
    using psc = reg<base_address + 0x28>;
    using arr = reg<base_address + 0x2C>;


    template<auto Bits>
    using psc_bits = reg_bits<Bits, psc, static_cast<uint32_t>(0xFFFF)>;

    template<auto Bits>
    using arr_bits = reg_bits<Bits, arr, TimerTraits::arr_bit_mask>;

    using uie = reg_bits_enable_disable<dier, 0UL>;
    using cen = reg_bits_enable_disable<cr1, 0UL>;
    using uif = reg_bits_enable_disable<sr, 0UL>;

    template<std::uint32_t Period>
    static void start() {
```

```cpp
    // a magic number prescaler value
    // for 1ms timer resolution
    constexpr std::uint32_t prescaler = 9999;
    constexpr std::uint32_t auto_reload = Period - 1;

    psc::template set<psc_bits<prescaler>>
                (psc_bits<prescaler>::value::val);
    arr::template set<arr_bits<auto_reload>>
                (arr_bits<auto_reload>::value::val);

    dier::template set<uie>(uie::value::enable);

    NVIC_SetPriority(TimerTraits::irqn, 1);
    NVIC_EnableIRQ(TimerTraits::irqn);

    cr1::template set<cen>(cen::value::enable);
  }
};
```

In this code, we defined a template class timer with template parameter `TimerTraits` – a traits class that provides hardware-specific constants. The timer class template provides a generic interface to configure and control timers, customized for each specific timer via `TimerTraits`.

Please note that for the sake of simplicity of the example, this is the minimum code needed to set up the STM32 timer peripheral.

Within the timer class, we define register type aliases, as follows:

```cpp
constexpr static std::uintptr_t base_address = TimerTraits::base_address;
using cr1 = reg<base_address + 0x00>;
using dier = reg<base_address + 0x0C>;
using sr = reg<base_address + 0x10>;
using psc = reg<base_address + 0x28>;
using arr = reg<base_address + 0x2C>;
```

These type aliases represent the timer's hardware registers, each mapped to a specific memory address. Each register is an instantiation of the reg class template, which provides read/write access to hardware registers.

Next, we define type aliases for `BitFields`:

```cpp
template<auto Bits>
using psc_bits = reg_bits<Bits, psc, static_cast<uint32_t> (0xFFFF)>;
template<auto Bits>
using arr_bits = reg_bits<Bits, arr, TimerTraits::arr_bit_mask>;
using uie = reg_bits_enable_disable<dier, 0UL>;
using cen = reg_bits_enable_disable<cr1, 0UL>;
using uif = reg_bits_enable_disable<sr, 0UL>;
```

In this code, we instantiate bit fields using the class templates `reg_bits` and `reg_bits_enable_disable`.

Finally, we define the template static method `start` in the class template timer. This `static` function sets up the timer with the desired period and starts it. The code executes the following steps:

1. Calculate Prescaler and Auto-Reload values. The function uses the template parameter Period to calculate these values.

2. Set Prescaler (PSC) and Auto-Reload (ARR) registers.

3. Enable the update interrupt on the DIER register. It uses the `uie` bit field to enable the update interrupt in the DIER register.

4. Configure NVIC for timer interrupts using CMSIS functions.

5. Start the timer. It uses the cen bit field to enable the timer counter in the CR1 register.

Let's now see how we can use the provided timer template class:

```cpp
using timer2 = timer<timer2_traits>;
using timer3 = timer<timer3_traits>;


extern "C" void TIM2_IRQHandler(void)
{
    if (timer2::sr::read() & TIM_SR_UIF)
    {
        timer2::sr::set<timer2::uif> (timer2::uif::value::disable);
        printf("TIM2 IRQ..\r\n");
    }
}


extern "C" void TIM3_IRQHandler(void)
```

```cpp
    {
        if (timer3::sr::read() & TIM_SR_UIF)
        {
            timer3::sr::set<timer3::uif> (timer3::uif::value::disable);
            printf("TIM3 IRQ..\r\n");
        }
    }
    int main()
    {
        timer2::start<1000>();
        timer3::start<500>();

        while(true)
        {
        }
    }
```

In this code, we create the type aliases timer2 and timer3 and implement **Interrupt Request (IRQ)** functions for the TIM2 and TIM3 interrupts. In the IRQs, we clear interrupt flags. We make calls to start functions of types timer2 and timer3 in the main function.

You can run the full example in Renode. Start Visual Studio Code, attach it to the running container, open the Chapter12/cpp_hal project, as described in *Chapter 4*, and run the following commands in the Visual Studio Code terminal, or run them directly in the container terminal:

```
$ cmake -B build -DCMAKE_BUILD_TYPE=Release -DMAIN_CPP_FILE_NAME=main_
timer_peripheral.cpp
$ cmake --build build --target run_in_renode
```

In this section, we learned how to create a generic, template-based timer interface by utilizing C++ templates and traits classes. By defining TimerTraits structures (timer2_traits and timer3_traits) that encapsulate hardware-specific details of the TIM2 and TIM3 timers, we can instantiate a flexible timer class template that abstracts the configuration and control of different timers. This approach offers two main benefits: it increases type safety by using templates to enforce correct usage at compile time, and it results in code that is as efficient as traditional C HAL implementations because the use of templates and constexpr allows the compiler to optimize the code thoroughly.

Summary

In this chapter, we learned techniques that we can apply to create safer HAL code in C++. We covered the implementation of memory-mapped peripherals. The design utilizes templates and advanced techniques such as SFINAE, which we discovered in *Chapter 8*. We applied the knowledge from previous chapters in the embedded systems domain.

We also learned how to design classes that implement generic behavior and depend on traits classes to supply them with specific details. The code we developed is as efficient as a hand-coded (CMSIS-based) solution, thanks to the usage of templates and compile-time computations, enabling compiler optimizations.

In the next chapter, we will cover working with C libraries in C++.

Get This Book's PDF Version and Exclusive Extras

Scan the QR code (or go to `packtpub.com/unlock`). Search for this book by name, confirm the edition, and then follow the steps on the page.

Note: Keep your invoice handy. Purchases made directly from Packt don't require an invoice.

13

Working with C Libraries

In *Chapter 6*, we discussed interoperability between C and C++. We learned about language linkage and how to use it to include C libraries in a C++ project. From the technical standpoint, that's all we need to use C in C++.

In this chapter, we'll focus on software development techniques for integrating C libraries into a C++ project to enhance code flexibility. Since many C++ projects still rely on vendor-provided C **hardware abstraction layers (HALs)**, we'll concentrate on how to effectively incorporate these C libraries into our projects.

Additionally, this chapter will cover the **Resource Acquisition is Initialization (RAII)** paradigm and explain why it's particularly beneficial in embedded systems. By automatically managing resource allocation and deallocation, RAII greatly reduces the risk of leaks and other resource misuse issues, which is especially important in resource-limited embedded environments.

In this chapter, we're going to cover the following main topics:

- Using C HAL in C++ projects
- Static classes
- Using RAII for wrapping `LittleFs` C library

Technical requirements

The examples from this chapter are available on GitHub (`https://github.com/PacktPublishing/Cpp-in-Embedded-Systems/tree/main/Chapter13`). To get the most out of this chapter, run the examples in the Renode simulator.

Using C HAL in C++ projects

In *Chapter 12*, we explored the benefits of using C++ for HAL development. However, despite these advantages, target vendors provide HALs as C libraries. These libraries have been thoroughly tested on millions of devices worldwide, and vendors usually maintain them well, offering regular updates. Thus, it makes more sense to use them rather than re-implement the HAL in C++.

Next, we will create an interface-based design for the UART peripheral, which will provide us with a more flexible software design and allow us to decouple components that are using the UART interface from low-level details.

UART interface for flexible software design

In *Chapter 5*, we covered the importance of interfaces for flexible software design. There, we had an uart interface class that was implemented by the uart_stm32 class. The gsm_lib class depended on the uart interface, meaning we can reuse it with different uart interface implementations.

The uart_stm32 class from *Chapter 5* had a simple implementation for demo purposes. It used the printf and putc functions from the C standard library to write messages on standard output. We will now go through the actual implementation of the uart_stm32 class that's already been used in all the examples in the book's GitHub repo, enabling us to see the output in the Renode simulator. Let's start from the uart interface class with the code shown here:

```cpp
#include <cstdint>
#include <span>

namespace hal
{
class uart
{
  public:
    virtual void init(std::uint32_t baudrate) = 0;
    virtual void write(std::span<const char> data) = 0;
};
}; // namespace hal
```

The uart interface is a simple class with two virtual methods:

- `virtual void init(std::uint32_t baudrate)`: A method used to initialize the UART peripheral with a single parameter – baudrate.
- `virtual void write(std::span<const char> data)`: A method used to send data over the UART peripheral. It has a `std::span<const char>` parameter in contrast to the usual C approach with a pointer to the data buffer and length. Using `std::span` increases the memory safety of the code.

Next, let us go through the uart_stm32 class definition:

```cpp
#include <span>
#include <cstdint>

#include <uart.hpp>

#include <stm32f0xx_hal.h>
#include <stm32f072xb.h>

namespace hal
{
class uart_stm32 : public uart
{
  public:
    uart_stm32(USART_TypeDef *inst);

    void init(std::uint32_t baudrate = c_baudrate_default);
    void write(std::span<const char> data) override;

  private:
    UART_HandleTypeDef huart_;
    USART_TypeDef *instance_;
    std::uint32_t baudrate_;
    static constexpr std::uint32_t c_baudrate_default = 115200;
};
}; // namespace hal
```

In the uart_stm32 class definition, we can notice the following:

- Overridden virtual methods init and write from the uart interface.

- A constructor accepting a pointer to USART_TypeDef. This type is a struct that describes the UART peripheral register layout in the CMSIS header stm32f072xb.h.

- Among the private members, we see UART_HandleTypeDef, a type defined in ST HAL in the file stm32f0xx_hal_uart.h.

Next, let us go through the implementation of the constructor and methods from the uart_stm32 class in this code:

```cpp
hal::uart_stm32::uart_stm32(USART_TypeDef *inst): instance_(inst)
{
}
```

In this code, we see the implementation of the uart_stm32 constructor. It just sets the private member USART_TypeDef *instance_ using the initializer list syntax. CMSIS defines the macros USART1, USART2, USART3, and USART4, which specify the addresses of these peripherals and which we can use to initialize the uart_stm32 object.

The uart interface defines the init method, as UART peripheral initialization depends on other hardware initializations (i.e., clock configuration). If we implemented the initialization within the constructor, we might run into issues if someone defines a global or static uart_stm32 object. The init method is shown here:

```cpp
void hal::uart_stm32::init(std::uint32_t baudrate)
{
    huart_.Instance = instance_;
    huart_.Init.BaudRate = baudrate;
    huart_.Init.WordLength = UART_WORDLENGTH_8B;
    huart_.Init.StopBits = UART_STOPBITS_1;
    huart_.Init.Parity = UART_PARITY_NONE;
    huart_.Init.Mode = UART_MODE_TX_RX;
    huart_.Init.HwFlowCtl = UART_HWCONTROL_NONE;
    huart_.Init.OverSampling = UART_OVERSAMPLING_16;
    huart_.Init.OneBitSampling = UART_ONE_BIT_SAMPLE_DISABLE;
    huart_.AdvancedInit.AdvFeatureInit = UART_ADVFEATURE_NO_INIT;
    huart_.MspInitCallback = nullptr;
    HAL_UART_Init(&huart_);
}
```

In the init method, we initialize the member `UART_HandleTypeDef huart_` with the following configuration:

- `instance_`: The address to the UART peripheral selected in the constructor
- baudrate
- 8-bit word length
- 1 stop bit
- Both TX and RX mode
- No hardware control

We also set `MspInitCallback` to `nullptr`. We make a call to the ST HAL `HAL_UART_Init` function providing it with a pointer to `huart_`. Please note that for the sake of example simplicity, there is no error handling. Error handling is an important step, and return codes from HAL should be appropriately handled in code.

Next, we will go through the implementation of the `write` method shown here:

```cpp
void hal::uart_stm32::write(std::span<const char> data)
{
    // we must cast away constness due to ST HAL's API
    char * data_ptr = const_cast<char *>(data.data());
    HAL_UART_Transmit(&huart_,
                      reinterpret_cast<uint8_t *>(data_ptr),
                      data.size(),
                      HAL_MAX_DELAY);
}
```

In the `write` method, we are making a call to `HAL_UART_Transmit` from ST HAL, by passing the data pointer and data size from the `std::span<const char> data` parameter. It's worth noting that we need to cast away constness as the C `HAL_UART_Transmit` function doesn't accept the const pointer to data. This is only safe to do if we are sure that the function we are passing the pointer with cast away constness is not trying to modify its content.

Next, we will analyze this approach from the perspective of software design and patterns used.

The UART interface in the Adapter pattern

The relationship between all the software components in this example (the uart interface, the uart_stm32 implementation of the interface, and the ST HAL) can be represented by the following UML diagram:

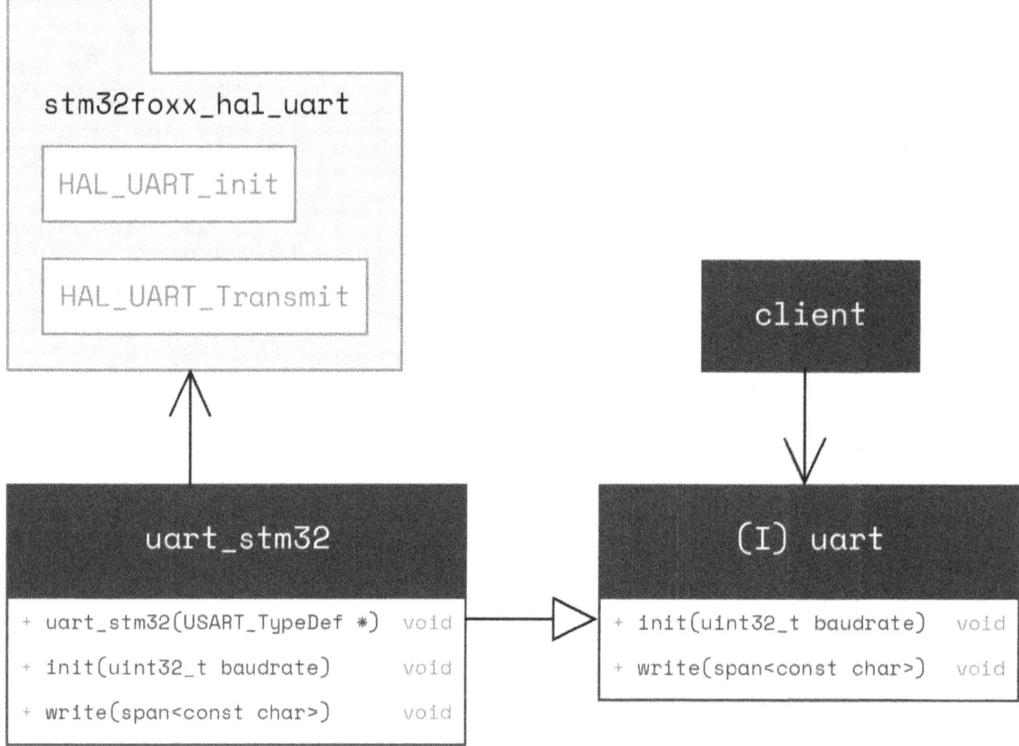

Figure 13.1 – The uart_stm32 class diagram

In *Figure 13.1*, we see the UML class diagram of the uart_stm32 class. This class effectively implements the **Adapter design pattern**, which is a structural design pattern used to allow classes with incompatible interfaces to work together. The Adapter pattern involves creating an adapter class that wraps an existing class (or module) and provides a new interface that the client expects.

In our case, even though stm32f0xx_hal_uart is a C module rather than a C++ class, the uart_stm32 class serves as an adapter by encapsulating the C-based HAL code and exposing it through the C++ uart interface. This adaptation allows other classes or clients in the system, such as a GSM library, to interact with the UART hardware using the standardized C++ interface, without needing to concern themselves with the underlying C implementation details.

Let us analyze this approach from the perspective of the uart interface client, such as a GSM library that is implemented in the gsm_lib class, with this definition:

```
class gsm_lib{
    public:
        gsm_lib(hal::uart &u) : uart_(u) {}
        // other methods
    private:
        hal::uart &uart_;
};
```

In this code, we see an example of a simple client of the uart interface – gsm_lib – with a constructor that initializes the reference hal::uart &uart_. This approach is called **dependency injection**. The dependency of the gsm_lib class is constructed externally and supplied to the class as a reference through the constructor. Depending on the interface also enables loose coupling, which brings the following benefits:

- gsm_lib is not interested in the implementation details of the uart interface. It doesn't need to know about baud rate, hardware settings, etc.
- gsm_lib is not tied to a particular target. We can reuse it on different platforms by implementing the uart interface on those platforms.
- Software testing of gsm_lib is easy as we can mock the uart interface and instantiate the gsm_lib object with the mocked object used in tests.

Instead of directly using the C HAL library in the uart_stm32 class, we can wrap the functions from the C library in a so-called static class with the direct mapping of all parameters.

Introducing static classes

The static class concept that we will discuss here doesn't exist in the C++ language standard. We are borrowing it from languages such as C#, where it is defined as a class that contains only static members and methods. It can't be instantiated. In C#, a static class is declared using the static keyword.

In C++, a static class can be created by defining a class with all static methods and members and by deleting the default constructor. Deleting the constructor ensures that no instances of the class can be created, enforcing this at compile time. Disabling instantiation signals a clear intent to the user: *This is a static class. The functions you're using don't rely on any instance-specific states, as no instances exist. If there's any internal state, it's shared and will affect everyone using the class.*

We will modify the previous example and create a uart_c_hal static class to wrap UART C HAL functions, as shown in this code:

```cpp
struct uart_c_hal {
    uart_c_hal() = delete;

    static inline HAL_StatusTypeDef init(UART_HandleTypeDef *huart)
    {
        return HAL_UART_Init(huart);
    }

    static inline HAL_StatusTypeDef transmit(UART_HandleTypeDef *huart,
                                             uint8_t *pData,
                                             uint16_t Size,
                                             uint32_t Timeout)
    {
        return HAL_UART_Transmit(huart, pData, Size, Timeout);
    }
};
```

In this code, we simply mapped C functions in static methods of the class uart_c_hal. Next, we will modify the uart_stm32 class to use uart_c_hal, as shown here:

```cpp
template <typename HalUart>
class uart_stm32 : public uart
{
  public:
    uart_stm32(USART_TypeDef *inst) : instance_(inst) {}

    void init(std::uint32_t baudrate = c_baudrate_default) override {
      huart_.Instance = instance_;
      huart_.Init.BaudRate = baudrate;
      // ...
      // init huart_ struct
      HalUart::init(&huart_);
    }
    void write(std::span<const char> data) override {
      // we must cast away costness due to ST HAL's API
      char * data_ptr = const_cast<char *>(data.data());
```

```
        HalUart::transmit(&huart_,
                          reinterpret_cast<uint8_t *(data_ptr),
                          data.size(),
                          HAL_MAX_DELAY);
    }

  private:
    UART_HandleTypeDef huart_;
    USART_TypeDef *instance_;
    std::uint32_t baudrate_;
    static constexpr std::uint32_t c_baudrate_default = 115200;
};
```

In this code, we see that uart_stm32 is now a template class that uses the methods init and transmit from the template parameter HalUart. Now we can use the class template, as shown here:

```
uart_stm32<uart_c_hal> uart(USART2);
uart.init();
gsm_lib gsm(uart);
```

The uart_stm32 class template still implements the uart interface, meaning we can still use it with the gsm_lib class. Wrapping C HAL functions in a static class and adjusting uart_stm32 to use it through a template parameter decouples C HAL from the uart_stm32 implementation. This makes it possible to test the uart_stm32 class off-target, as it doesn't depend on platform-specific code anymore.

Static classes are one way of using C libraries in C++ projects. They allow us to encapsulate functions from C libraries in types that can be passed to C++ classes through template arguments, making the code more flexible and easier to test.

Next, we will see how to apply the RAII technique to effectively wrap the **little fail-safe** (littlefs) filesystem C library.

Using RAII for wrapping the littlefs C library

RAII is a simple yet powerful C++ technique used to manage resources through an object's lifetime. Resources can represent different things. Resources are acquired when an object's lifetime begins, and they are released when the object's lifetime ends.

The technique is used to manage resources such as dynamically allocated memory. To ensure that the memory is released and avoid memory leaks, the recommendation is to use dynamic allocation only internally in classes. When an object is instantiated, the constructor will allocate memory, and when the object goes out of scope, the destructor will release the allocated memory.

The RAII technique can be applied to other resources beyond the dynamically allocated memory, such as files, and we will apply it to the `littlefs` filesystem library (https://github.com/littlefs-project/littlefs). We will start with a short overview of `littlefs` – a filesystem designed for microcontrollers.

LittleFS – a filesystem for microcontrollers

The `littlefs` filesystem is designed for microcontrollers featuring the following:

- **Power-loss resilience**: It is built to handle unexpected power failures. In the case of power loss, it will fall back to the last known good state.

- **Dynamic wear leveling**: It is optimized for flash memory, offering wear leveling across dynamic blocks. It also includes mechanisms to detect and bypass bad blocks, ensuring reliable performance over time.

- **Bounded RAM/ROM**: It is optimized for low memory usage. RAM consumption remains constant, regardless of filesystem size, with no unbounded recursion. Dynamic memory is limited to configurable buffers, which can be set up as `static`.

We will first go through the basic usage of `littlefs` and then see how we can apply RAII in a C++ wrapper class. We will go through an example of using `littlefs` that will:

- Format and mount filesystem.

- Create a file, write some content to it, and then close it.

- Open a file, read content from it, and then close it.

The full example is contained in `Chapter13/lfs_raii/app/src/main.cpp`. Let us start with code that formats and mounts the filesystem, as shown here:

```cpp
lfs_t lfs;
const lfs_config * lfs_ramfs_cfg = get_ramfs_lfs_config();
lfs_format(&lfs, lfs_ramfs_cfg);
lfs_mount(&lfs, lfs_ramfs_cfg);
```

This code performs the following steps:

- It declares a filesystem object named lfs of type lfs_t. This object will be used to interact with the littlefs filesystem. It holds the state of the filesystem and is required for all subsequent filesystem operations.

- The function get_ramfs_lfs_config() returns a pointer to the lfs_config structure that contains all the necessary configuration parameters for littlefs to operate on a RAM storage medium. This includes function pointers for reading, writing, and erasing, as well as parameters like block size, block count, and cache size. In the project setup, we are using a portion of RAM as the storage medium. The RAM-based littlefs configuration is defined in the C file Chapter13/lfs_raii/app/src/lfs_ramfs.c.

- It formats the storage medium to prepare it for use with littlefs. The lfs_format function initializes the filesystem structures on the storage medium. This process erases any existing data and sets up the necessary metadata structures. Formatting is typically done once before the first use of the filesystem or when resetting it.

- It mounts the filesystem to make it ready for file operations. The lfs_mount function initializes the filesystem state in RAM based on the existing structures on the storage medium. This step is necessary before performing any file operations like reading or writing.

Next, let us go over creating a file and writing some data to it. The code is shown here:

```cpp
lfs_file_t file;
if(lfs_file_open(&lfs, &file, "song.txt", LFS_O_WRONLY | LFS_O_CREAT) >= 0)
{
    const char * file_content = "These are some lyrics!";
    lfs_file_write(&lfs,
                   &file,
                   reinterpret_cast<const void *>(file_content),
                   strlen(file_content));
    lfs_file_close(&lfs, &file);
}
```

This code performs the following steps:

- Declares a file object named file of type lfs_file_t. This object represents a file within the littlefs filesystem. It holds the state of the file and is required for performing file operations like reading and writing.

- Attempts to open a file named "song.txt" for writing using the function lfs_file_open. The function is provided with the following arguments:

    - &lfs: A pointer to the filesystem object, initialized and mounted earlier.

    - &file: A pointer to the file object that will be associated with the opened file.

    - "song.txt": The name of the file to open.

    - LFS_O_WRONLY | LFS_O_CREAT: Flags specifying to open the file in write-only mode, and to create a file if it doesn't exist already.

    - If the lfs_file_open function returns a non-negative value, the code attempts to write some data to it using the lfs_file_write function.

- We declare the content to write as a file_content string literal.

- The function lfs_file_write is provided with the following arguments:

    - &lfs: A pointer to the filesystem object.

    - &file: A pointer to the file object associated with the opened file.

    - reinterpret_cast<const void *>(file_content): Casts the character string to a const void* pointer as required by the function.

    - strlen(file_content): The number of bytes to write, calculated based on the length of the string.

- Closes the file after writing to ensure data integrity. lfs_file_close flushes any pending writes to the storage medium and releases resources associated with the file.

After writing data to a file, we will attempt to open the same file in read mode and read the data from it. The code for reading a file is shown here:

```cpp
if(lfs_file_open(&lfs, &file, "song.txt", LFS_O_RDONLY)>= 0) {
    std::array<char, 64> buff = {0};
    lfs_file_read(&lfs,
                  &file,
                  reinterpret_cast<void *>(buff.data()),
                  buff.size() - 1);
    printf("This is content from the file\r\n%s\r\n", buff.data());
    lfs_file_close(&lfs, &file);
}
```

This code performs the following steps:

- Attempts to open the file "song.txt" for read-only access using the function `lfs_file_open` and providing it with the flag `LFS_O_RDONLY`.

- If the `lfs_file_open` function returns a non-negative value, the code attempts to read data from the opened file.

- `std::array<char, 64> buff = {0}` declares an array named `buff` with a fixed size of 64 characters and initializes all elements to zero (`'\0'`), ensuring the buffer is null-terminated if treated as a C string.

- Reads data from opened files in the `buff` array using the function `lfs_file_read`. The function is provided with the following arguments:

  - `&lfs`: A pointer to the filesystem object.

  - `&file`: A pointer to the file object associated with the opened file.

  - `reinterpret_cast<const void *>(buff.data())`: Casts the `buff` underlying data array pointer to a const void* pointer as required by the function.

- `buff.size() - 1`: The number of bytes to read from the file. Subtracting 1 reserves space for a null terminator (`'\0'`) at the end of the string.

- Closes the file after reading to ensure data integrity.

You can run the full example in the Renode simulator. Start Visual Studio Code, attach it to the running container, open the `Chapter13/lfs_raii` project, as described in *Chapter 4*, and run the following commands in the Visual Studio Code terminal, or run them directly in the container terminal:

```
$ cd Chapter13/lfs_raii
$ cmake -B build
$ cmake --build build --target run_in_renode
```

Introducing an RAII-based C++ wrapper

Now, we will wrap the `littlefs` functionality in a simple C++ wrapper applying the RAII technique. We will create an `fs` namespace with types `lfs` and `file` in it. Let us start with the `lfs` struct code shown here:

```
namespace fs{

struct lfs {
```

```cpp
    lfs() = delete;

    static inline lfs_t fs_lfs;

    static void init() {
        const lfs_config * lfs_ramfs_cfg = get_ramfs_lfs_config();
        lfs_format(&fs_lfs, lfs_ramfs_cfg);
        lfs_mount(&fs_lfs, lfs_ramfs_cfg);
    }
  };
};
```

The purpose of the struct lfs is to:

- Hold an instance of a filesystem object named fs_lfs of type lfs_t used to interact with the littlefs filesystem.

- Implement the static method init used to initialize the filesystem by calling the lfs_format and lfs_mount functions. The init method must be called before any file operations are performed.

Next, let's go over the file class definition:

```cpp
namespace fs{
class file {
public:
    file(const char * filename, int flags = LFS_O_RDONLY);
    ~file();

    [[nodiscard]] bool is_open() const;

    int read(std::span<char> buff);

    void write(std::span<const char> buff);
private:
    bool is_open_ = false;
    lfs_file_t file_;
  };
};
```

This code shows methods and data members of the class file. Next, we will go through them, starting with the constructor shown here:

```cpp
file(const char * filename, int flags = LFS_O_RDONLY) {
    if(lfs_file_open(&lfs::fs_lfs, &file_, filename, flags) >= 0) {
        is_open_ = true;
    }
}
```

The `file` constructor shown opens a file with the specified `filename` and `flags`. It sets `is_open_` to true if the file opens successfully. Next, let's go over the destructor shown here:

```cpp
~file() {
if(is_open_) {
        printf("Closing file in destructor.\r\n");
        lfs_file_close(&lfs::fs_lfs, &file_);
    }
}
```

The destructor shown will close the file if it's already opened. It calls `lfs_file_close` to close the file and release resources. The constructor and destructor implement the RAII technique – creating an object will acquire resources, and when the object's lifetime ends, the destructor will release them. Next, let's go over the read and write methods:

```cpp
int read(std::span<char> buff) {
return lfs_file_read(&lfs::fs_lfs,
                    &file_,
                    reinterpret_cast<void *>(buff.data()),
                    buff.size() - 1);
}

int write(std::span<const char> buff) {
return lfs_file_write(&lfs::fs_lfs,
                    &file_,
                    reinterpret_cast<const void *>(buff.data()),
                    buff.size());
}
```

The read and write methods are simple wrappers for the `lfs_file_read` and `lfs_file_write` functions. Both read and write use `std::span` as function parameters for increased type safety and better flexibility, as we can simply provide it with `std::array`.

Cleaner file management with RAII

Now, we will see how we can use the `fs` and `file` wrappers to work with the `littlefs` filesystem. The code is shown here:

```cpp
fs::lfs::init();
{
    fs::file song_file("song.txt", LFS_O_WRONLY | LFS_O_CREAT);
    if(song_file.is_open()) {
    song_file.write("These are some lyrics!");
    // destructor is called on song_file object
    // ensuring the file is closed

}
```

We first initialize the filesystem by calling `fs::lfs::init()`. Next, we introduce local scope to demonstrate a call to destructor and perform the next steps:

- Open "`song.txt`" for writing (creating it if it doesn't exist).

- Write a string literal in the file if it was opened successfully.

- Upon exit from the scope, the destructor is called, ensuring the file is closed.

Next, we will open the file and read data from it. The code is shown here:

```cpp
fs::file song_file("song.txt");
std::array<char, 64> buff = {0};
if(song_file.is_open()) {
    song_file.read(buff);
    printf("This is content from the file\r\n%s\r\n",
    buff.data());
}
```

This code performs the next steps:

- Opens "`song.txt`" for reading (default mode).

- Declares `std::array<char, 64> buff`, initialized to zeros.

- Reads the data from the file in `buff` if the file is opened successfully.

You can run the full example in the Renode simulator. Start Visual Studio Code, attach it to the running container, open the Chapter13/lfs_raii project, as described in *Chapter 4*, and run the following commands in the Visual Studio Code terminal, or run them directly in the container terminal:

```
$ cd Chapter13/lfs_raii
$ cmake -B build -DMAIN_CPP_FILE_NAME=main_lfs_raii.cpp
$ cmake --build build --target run_in_renode
```

The simple C++ wrapper we wrote for the littlefs library applies RAII principles, ensuring proper handling of resources as the destructor is called when an object's lifetime ends. This ensures the file is closed even when there are multiple return paths from a code. It also simplifies the development experience as the code is less verbose and cleaner. The usage of std::span increases safety.

Summary

In this chapter, we covered several techniques for using C libraries in C++ projects. By wrapping C code in C++ classes, we can organize our code better in loosely coupled software modules. C++ increases type safety and compile-time features allow us to easily organize C wrappers in static classes.

Applying RAII is simple and provides us with a powerful mechanism that takes care of resource management, as we saw in the example of the littlefs filesystem.

In the next chapter, we will go over super-loop in bare metal firmware and see how we can enhance it with mechanisms such as sequencer in C++.

Join our community on Discord

Join our community's Discord space for discussions with the author and other readers:

```
https://packt.link/embeddedsystems
```

14

Enhancing Super-Loop with Sequencer

Super-loop is the basic software architecture of bare-metal firmware. It is an infinite loop that executes tasks (functions) often conditioned by flags set in an **Interrupt Service Routine (ISR)**. As the complexity of business logic increases, so does the size of a super loop, which can quickly turn into a spaghetti mess. To solve this problem within bare-metal constraints (no operating system), we can use a sequencer.

A **sequencer** stores and executes tasks (functions) in an organized fashion. Instead of setting a flag in an ISR, checking it in a super loop, and executing a function if a flag is set, we simply add a task to a sequencer from the ISR. The super loop then runs the sequencer, which executes the added tasks. Tasks in the sequencer can be prioritized, so the sequencer will execute higher-priority tasks first.

In this chapter, we're going to cover sequencer design and implementation through the following main topics:

- Super-loop and motivation for a sequencer
- Designing a sequencer
- Storing a callable
- Implementing a sequencer

Technical requirements

The examples from this chapter are available on GitHub (`https://github.com/PacktPublishing/Cpp-in-Embedded-Systems/tree/main/Chapter14`). To get the most out of this chapter, run the examples in the Renode simulator.

Super-loop and motivation for a sequencer

Before we get into the design and implementation of a sequencer, we will first analyze the limitations of a super loop. In a usual super-loop scenario, we check flags that are set from an ISR. Below is an example pseudocode of a super loop:

```cpp
bool data_read_ready = false;
bool data_send_timeout = false;

int main() {
    // initialize hardware

    while(1) {
        if(data_read_ready) {
            sensor_data_read_and_buffer();
            data_read_ready = false;
        }

        if(data_send_timeout) {
            data_send_from_buffer();
            data_send_timeout = false;
        }

        if(!data_read_ready && !data_send_timeout) {
            enter_sleep();
        }
    }
}
```

In the preceding pseudocode, we perform the following steps:

1. Check the Boolean flag `data_read_ready` and, if it is set, we execute the function `sensor_data_read_and_buffer`. We then reset the `data_read_ready` flag.

2. Check the Boolean flag `data_send_timeout` and, if it is set, we execute the function `data_send_from_buffer`. We then reset the `data_send_timeout` flag.

3. Both the `data_read_ready` and `data_send_timeout` flags are set from an ISR. In our example, this might be the timer's ISR.

4. Finally, we check if both flags are false, and if they are, we enter sleep mode.

The example we discussed is simple, but as the number of flags grows, so does the size of the super loop, the number of global variables (flags), and the possibility of a mistake such as resetting a flag or forgetting to include it in the `if` statement, which provides the conditions for entering sleep mode.

Now, imagine we wanted to prioritize functions executed in the super loop. Using the current approach would be difficult. Adding a priority variable and checking it in `if` statements might work initially, but the code would quickly become messy and difficult to maintain.

To address issues of a super loop in a bare-metal environment, we will utilize a sequencer. Instead of defining global flags and setting them from an ISR, we will add tasks to the sequencer from an ISR. Each task will include priority information, enabling the sequencer to organize them in an internal queue based on their priority.

In the main loop, the sequencer runs repeatedly. It handles tasks by always picking the highest-priority one from the queue and executing it first, keeping task management efficient and orderly.

Next, we will proceed with the design of the sequencer.

Designing a sequencer

We will base the sequencer design on a command pattern that we covered in *Chapter 10*. In the command pattern, a sequencer will take the role of invoker. In our design, we'll use the term *task* instead of *command*. This *task* is equivalent to a function – it represents a specific unit of functionality – not a task as defined in operating systems.

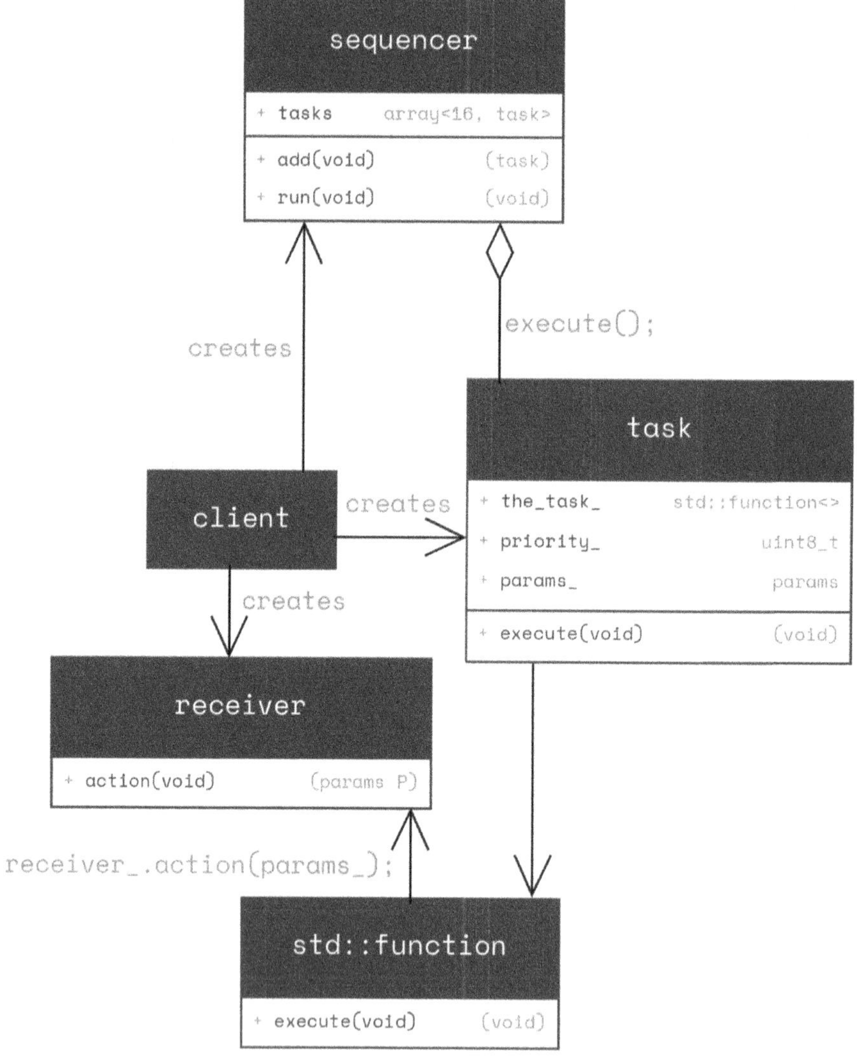

Figure 14.1 – Sequencer design – UML diagram

Figure 14.1 depicts a UML diagram of a sequencer. We can see it takes the role of a sequencer in the command pattern, as described earlier. Instead of a command interface and concrete command, this UML design uses a std::function class template (we used the same approach in the *GPIO Interrupt manager* example of *Chapter 10*).

The sequencer class holds an array of tasks, which are used to store callable objects. The sequencer provides a simple interface, with just two methods:

- void add(task t): The method used to add a task to the sequencer
- void run(): The method used to take a task with the highest priority, execute it, and remove it from the sequencer

Before we go into the implementation of sequencer methods, we will first go over the task class and alternatives to std::array for storing tasks. The task class represents a unit of functionality that will be executed by a sequencer according to priority. It has the following members:

- std::function<void()> the_task_: An actual callable that will be executed
- std::uint8_t priority_: Priority according to which tasks will be sorted in the sequencer's storage

Below is the code that implements the task class:

```cpp
template<typename CallableHolder>
class task {
public:
    constexpr static std::uint8_t c_prio_default = 250;
    constexpr static std::uint8_t c_prio_max = 255;
    constexpr static std::uint8_t c_prio_min = 0;
    task(CallableHolder the_task, std::uint8_t prio = c_prio_default) :
        the_task_(the_task), priority_(prio) {}
    void execute() {
        if(the_task_) {
            the_task_();
        }
    }

    bool operator<(const task &rhs) const
    {
```

```
            return priority_ < rhs.priority_;
    }

private:
    CallableHolder the_task_;
    std::uint8_t priority_ = c_prio_default;
};
```

This code implements the task as a class template, allowing us to use it with different callable holders. The one we introduced in the book previously is std::function. The class template task has the following members:

- A constructor that initializes the the_task_ member, which is type CallableHolder
- The void execute() method, which calls operator() on the_task_
- operator<, which compares task by priority

This code demonstrates the usage of the class template task:

```
using callable_holder = std::function<void()>;

auto fun_a = []() {
    printf("High priority task!\r\n");
};
task<callable_holder> task_a(fun_a, 255);

auto fun_b = []() {
    printf("Low priority task!\r\n");
};
task<callable_holder> task_b(fun_b, 20);

if(task_a < task_b) {
    task_b.execute();
}
else {
    task_a.execute();
}
```

In this example, we instantiate the class template task with `std::function<void()>`. We create two objects, `task_a` and `task_b`, and then execute one with higher priority by using `operator<` to compare them. Task objects in this example are initialized with lambdas, which are internally stored in `std::function<void()>`. If you run the preceding example, you will see the following output:

```
High priority task!
```

As you can see, the task with higher priority was executed thanks to the overloaded `operator<`.

In *Chapter 10*, we saw that the class template `std::function` can resort to dynamic memory allocation to store lambdas that are captured. To mitigate this concern, we will introduce the **Embedded Template Library (ETL)**, a library that defines a set of containers and algorithms whose operations are deterministic and don't use dynamic memory allocation. The ETL will be discussed more in *Chapter 17*.

Storing a callable

Instead of `std::function`, we can use `etl::delegate` – a callable holder from the ETL. One of its limitations is it doesn't work with capturing lambdas. This may affect the code expressiveness, but it provides us with equivalent functionality that allows us to capture different callables. This code demonstrates using the class template task with `etl::delegate`:

```cpp
using callable_etl = etl::delegate<void()>;
using task_etl = task<callable_etl>;

class test {
public:
    test(int x) : x_(x) {}
    void print() const {
        printf("This is a test, x = %d.\r\n", x_);
    }
    void static print_static() {
        printf("This is a static method in test.\r\n");
    }
private:
    int x_ = 0;
```

```cpp
};
test test_1(42);

task_etl task_member_fun(callable_etl::create<test, &test::print>
                                        (test_1));
task_member_fun.execute();

task_etl task_static_fun(callable_etl::create<test::print_static>());
task_static_fun.execute();

task_etl task_lambda([](){
    printf("This is non capturing lambda!\r\n");
});
task_lambda.execute();
```

This code demonstrates how we can use `etl::delegate` to store a callable:

- `callable_etl::create<test, &test::print>(test_1)` creates `etl::delegate` using the template method `create` instantiated with the class `test` and its member `print`

- `callable_etl::create<test::print_static>()` creates `etl::delegate` using the template method `create` instantiated with the static method `print_static`

- `task_lambda([](){ printf("This is non capturing lambda!\r\n");});` initializes `etl::delegate` with the provided non-capturing lambda

Running the preceding example will result in the following output:

```
This is a test, x = 42.
This is a static method in test.
This is non capturing lambda!
```

You can run the full example in the Renode simulator. Start Visual Studio Code, attach it to the running container, open the `Chapter14/sequencer` project, as described in *Chapter 4*, and run the following commands in the Visual Studio Code terminal, or run them directly in the container terminal:

```
cmake -B build -DCMAKE_BUILD_TYPE=MinSizeRel
cmake --build build --target run_in_renode
```

We have alternative implementations for callable storage – `std::function` from the standard library, or the more embedded-friendly `etl::delegate` from ETL. Next, let us consider options for a container for storing the tasks inside the sequencer.

In the UML diagram in *Figure 14.1*, the sequencer is using `std::array` to store tasks. This implies that sorting the elements of an array according to the priority is handled by the sequencer itself. Instead of implementing this manually, we can use `std::priority_queue` – a container adapter from the standard library.

`std::priority_queue` is a template class that is used as an adapter for another container, which provides a random access iterator and the following methods:

- `front()`
- `push_back()`
- `pop_back()`

We could use `std::vector` from the standard library, as it meets all the requirements imposed by `std::priority_queue`. As you know, `std::vector` uses dynamic memory allocation, which doesn't make it a good fit for most of the embedded applications.

ETL provides a fixed-size implementation of a vector with a similar interface as standard library implementation. This makes it compatible with the priority queue. This code demonstrates using `etl::vector` with `std::priority_queue`:

```cpp
std::priority_queue<int, etl::vector<int, 6>> pq{};
pq.push(12);
pq.push(6);
pq.push(16);
pq.push(8);
pq.push(1);
pq.push(10);

printf("priority queue elements:\r\n");
while(!pq.empty()) {
    printf("top element: %d, size: %d\r\n", pq.top(), pq.size());
    pq.pop();
}
```

This code performs the following steps:

1. `std::priority_queue<int, etl::vector<int, 6>> pq{}` defines a priority queue, pq, with the underlying container `etl::vector<int, 6>`, which is a fixed size vector of size 6.

2. `pq.push(12)` inserts an element (12) in the priority queue, pq, and sorts the queue.

3. Using the `push` method, we add 5 more elements in the queue – 6, 16, 8, 1, and 10.

4. With `while(!pq.empty())`, we run a `while` loop until the priority queue is empty.

5. Inside the `while` loop, we print the top element, which we access using the `top()` method, and size using the `size()` method. Then, we pop the top element from the queue using `pop()`.

Running the preceding code will result in the following output:

```
priority queue elements:
top element: 16, size: 6
top element: 12, size: 5
top element: 10, size: 4
top element: 8, size: 3
top element: 6, size: 2
top element: 1, size: 1
```

As you can see from the output, the elements in the priority queue are sorted. This makes it a good solution for storing tasks that can be sorted thanks to the overloaded `operator<`. You can run the full example in the Renode simulator. Start Visual Studio Code, attach it to the running container, open the `Chapter14/sequencer` project, as described in *Chapter 4*, and run the following commands in the Visual Studio Code terminal, or run them directly in the container terminal:

```
cmake -B build -DCMAKE_BUILD_TYPE=MinSizeRel
-DMAIN_CPP_FILE_NAME=main_pq.cpp

cmake --build build --target run_in_renode
```

Now that we have all the elements we need for the sequencer, we will proceed with the implementation.

Implementing a sequencer

In this chapter, we introduced `etl::delegate` – an alternative to `std::function` and fixed size vector implementation from ETL. As ETL avoids dynamic memory allocation, we will use these components for the implementation of the sequencer. Below is an updated UML diagram:

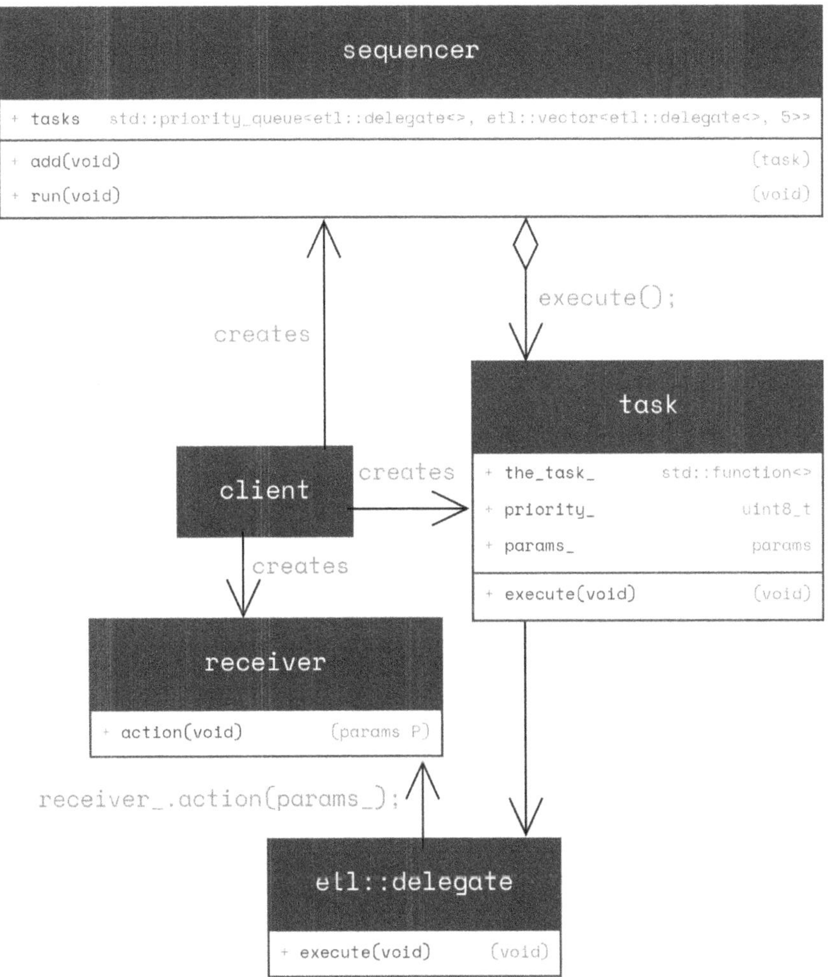

Figure 14.2 – UML sequencer diagram using ETL components

Figure 14.2 depicts a UML diagram of the sequencer using delegate and vector ETL components and the priority queue from the standard library. This code implements sequencer:

```
template<typename Task, std::size_t Size>
struct sequencer {
```

```cpp
    sequencer() = delete;

    static void add(Task task) {
        if(pq.size() < Size) {
            __disable_irq();
            pq.push(task);
            __enable_irq();
        }
    }

    static void run() {
        if(!pq.empty()) {
            __disable_irq();
            auto task = pq.top();
            pq.pop();
            __enable_irq();
            task.execute();
        }
    }

private:
    static inline std::priority_queue<Task, etl::vector<Task, Size>> pq{};

};
```

In this code, sequencer is implemented as a static template class with `Task` and `Size` as template parameters. This allows us to use it with either `std::function` or `etl::function`-based tasks and to define the size of the ETL vector. sequencer has the following members:

- `static inline std::priority_queue<Task, etl::vector<Task, Size>> pq{}`: A private static priority queue based on an ETL vector.
- `static void add(Task task)`: A static method used to add tasks to the queue using the push method, guarded by disabling and enabling interrupts, as it can be called from an ISR.
- `static void run()`: A static method used to take the top element from the queue and execute it. Access to the queue is guarded by disabling and enabling interrupts.

Below is an example of using the sequencer:

```cpp
using callable_etl = etl::delegate<void()>;
using task_etl = task<callable_etl>;


class test {
public:
    test(int x) : x_(x) {}
    void print() const {
        printf("This is a test, x = %d.\r\n", x_);
    }
    void static print_static() {
        printf("This is a static method in test.\r\n");
    }
private:
    int x_ = 0;
};


test test_1(42);


task_etl task_member_fun(callable_etl::create<test, &test::print>
                                        (test_1), 20);


task_etl task_static_fun(callable_etl::create<test::print_static>(), 30);


task_etl task_lambda([](){
    printf("This is non capturing lambda!\r\n");
}, 10);


using seq = sequencer<task_etl, 16>;
seq::add(task_member_fun);
seq::add(task_static_fun);
seq::add(task_lambda);
while(true)
{
    seq::run();
}
```

In this code, we do the following:

- Instantiate the `etl::delegate`-based tasks `task_member_fun`, `task_static_fun`, and `task_lambda`.
- We add tasks to the sequencer using the sequencer `add` method.
- We run the sequencer in the main `while` loop using the method `run()`.

Running the preceding code will result in the following output:

```
This is a static method in test.
This is a test, x = 42.
This is non capturing lambda!
```

As we can see in this code, the tasks are executed according to the assigned priority. You can run the full example in Renode. Start Visual Studio Code, attach it to the running container, open the `Chapter14/sequencer` project, as described in *Chapter 4*, and run the following commands in the Visual Studio Code terminal, or run them directly in the container terminal:

```
cmake -B build -DCMAKE_BUILD_TYPE=MinSizeRel
-DMAIN_CPP_FILE_NAME=main_seq.cpp


cmake --build build --target run_in_renode
```

Running the example in the simulator should provide the same console output. I invite you to explore the sequencer by adding tasks from the timer or external interrupts.

A sequencer offers a better alternative to a super loop by organizing tasks in a strictly sequential, prioritized manner. Deterministic behavior needs to be assured through task implementation. For instance, in the case of real-time requirements, each task must include internal monitoring to guarantee it meets the necessary real-time constraints.

Summary

In this chapter, we examined the common problems with a basic super loop, which motivated our move toward a sequencer design. We covered sequencer design in detail and introduced ETL components `etl::delegate` – callable holder which is an alternative to `std::function` – and a fixed size vector, which are both great fits for embedded applications as they don't use dynamic memory allocation.

In the next chapter, we will learn about the observer pattern and apply it to a temperature-reading application.

15

Practical Patterns – Building a Temperature Publisher

Design patterns are tools for solving common problems. So far, we have covered a few design patterns in this book, such as the Command and Adapter patterns. In this chapter, we will go over the **Observer pattern** and apply it to a common problem in embedded systems – handling temperature readings in different parts of the system.

We will start by looking at the Observer pattern and how it can be implemented at runtime. This pattern is particularly useful when multiple components need to react to changes in data from a central source. Imagine a temperature sensor in an embedded device that reports changes to multiple listeners. This could be part of a smart thermostat, an industrial machine monitor, or an HVAC control board each with components such as a screen, a logger, or a fan controller that react to temperature updates.

Next, we will transition to a compile-time implementation of the same pattern using modern C++ techniques such as variadic templates and fold expressions. By leveraging these techniques, we can generate highly optimized code at compile time, avoiding virtual dispatch, associated with runtime polymorphism. This approach results in a smaller memory footprint and faster code that's better suited to systems with limited resources.

In this chapter, we're going to cover the following main topics:

- The Observer pattern
- Runtime implementation
- Compile-time implementation

Technical requirements

To get the most out of this chapter, I strongly recommend using Compiler Explorer (`https://godbolt.org/`) as you read through the examples. Add an execution pane with GCC as your compiler for x86 architecture. This will allow you to see standard output and better observe the code's behavior. As we are using a lot of modern C++ features, make sure to select C++23 standard, by adding `-std=c++23` in the **compiler options** box, and set the optimization level to -O3. Also, add a compiler pane using `ARM gcc 11.2.1 (none)` to inspect the assembly output of the examples.

You can try the examples from this chapter in the Renode simulator in the Docker container you set up in *Chapter 4*. Make sure that the Docker container is running.

You can find the files for this chapter on GitHub at `https://github.com/PacktPublishing/Cpp-in-Embedded-Systems/tree/main/Chapter15/observer`.

The Observer pattern

The **Observer pattern** is often used in event-driven systems to publish events to subscribed objects, usually by calling a method on them. An object that publishes events is called a **subject** or **publisher**. Objects that receive events from a publisher are called **observers** or **subscribers**. From now on, we will use the terms **publisher** and **subscriber**.

A publisher has an internal list of subscribers and provides an interface to register and unregister a subscriber from the internal list. It also provides the `notify` method, used by its client, which in turn calls `update` methods on subscribers – that's why we say that the publisher notifies subscribers.

An example of a publisher-subscriber mechanism that is common in embedded systems would be a temperature publisher, which notifies the logger, display, and data sender at regular intervals. Before we go on to the implementation of this example, we will first go through a UML diagram of the Observer pattern.

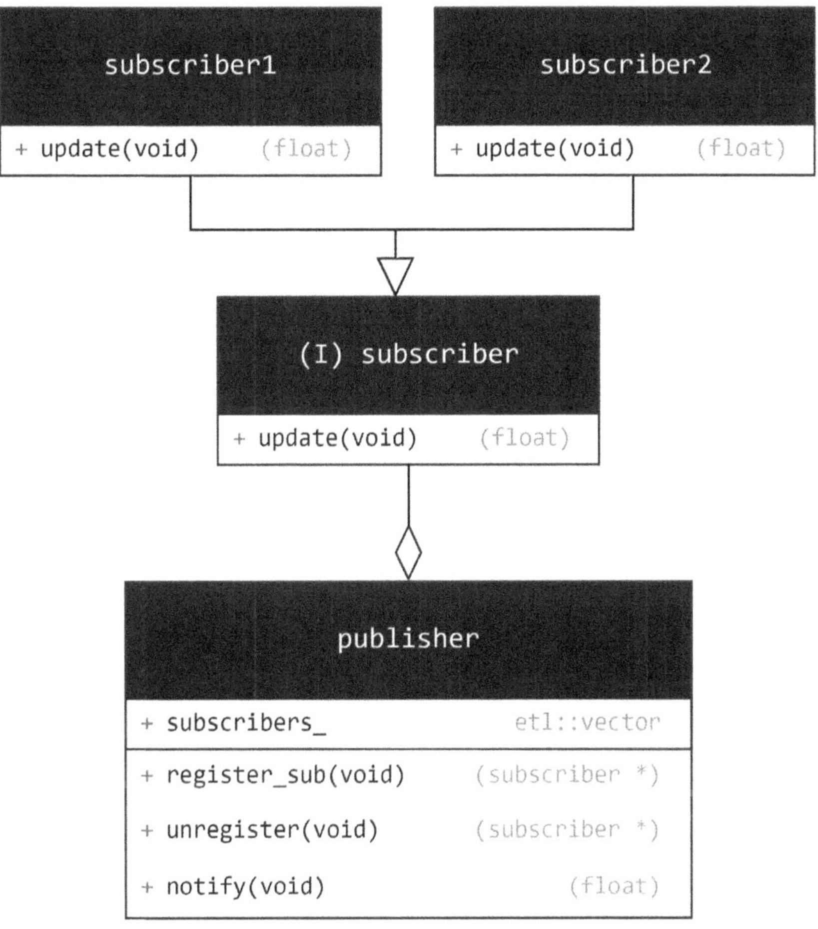

Figure 15.1 – UML diagram of the Observer pattern

Figure 15.1 depicts the UML class diagram of the Observer pattern. In the diagram, we see that the publisher class has the following members:

- `etl::vector<subscribers_, 8>`: Internal list of pointers to the subscriber interface, for which we will use `vector` from ETL.
- `register_sub(subscriber *)`: The method used to register a subscriber. The `register` keyword is reserved in C++ and used as a storage specifier, so we are using `register_sub` as the name for this method.
- `unregister(subscriber *)`: The method used to unregister a subscriber.
- `notify(float)`: The method used by the publisher's client to trigger the updating of subscribers.

The subscriber interface class has one pure virtual method – void update(float). This method is overridden in the concrete implementation of the subscriber class. To see this in action, we will proceed with the runtime implementation of the Observer pattern.

Runtime implementation

We will go through the runtime implementation of the Observer pattern on the example of temperature publisher. Subscribers will be a logger, display, and data sender. The code of the subscriber interface and concrete subscribers is shown here:

```cpp
#include <cstdio>
#include "etl/vector.h"
#include <algorithm>

class subscriber {
public:
    virtual void update(float) = 0;
    virtual ~subscriber() = default;
};

class display : public subscriber {
public:
    void update(float temp) override {
        printf("Displaying temperature %.2f \r\n", temp);
    }
};

class data_sender : public subscriber {
public:
    void update(float temp) override {
        printf("Sending temperature %.2f \r\n", temp);
    }
};

class logger : public subscriber {
public:
    void update(float temp) override {
        printf("Logging temperature %.2f \r\n", temp);
```

```cpp
    }
};
```

The preceding code defines the `subscriber` interface and concrete subscriber classes: `display`, `data_sender`, and `logger`. Concrete classes override the pure virtual `update` method from the interface class. For the sake of simplicity of the example, all concrete implementations are printing temperature to standard output.

Using the interface class allows the publisher to depend on the interface. The publisher maintains an internal container of pointers to the subscriber interface. This makes it possible to add different implementations of the subscriber interface through the pointer on the base interface class. The code for the `publisher` class is provided here:

```cpp
class publisher {
public:
    void register_sub(subscriber * sub) {
        if(std::find(subs_.begin(), subs_.end(), sub) == subs_.end())
        {
            subs_.push_back(sub);
        }
    }

    void unregister(subscriber * sub) {
        if(auto it = std::find(subs_.begin(), subs_.end(),
                                sub); it != subs_.end())
        {
            subs_.erase(it);
        }
    }

    void notify(float value) {
        for(auto sub: subs_) {
            sub->update(value);
        }
    }

private:
    etl::vector<subscriber*, 8> subs_;
};
```

In the preceding `publisher` class, we see the following members:

- `etl::vector<subscriber*, 8> subs_`: A private container used to maintain subscribers. If you are running this example in Compiler Explorer, make sure to add the ETL library using the **Libraries** option.

- `void register_sub(subscriber * sub)`: A method used to register the subscriber. It uses the `std::find` algorithm to check if a subscriber has already been added.

- `void unregister(subscriber * sub)`: A method used to unregister a subscriber. It uses the `std::find` algorithm to check if a subscriber is added before the calling method `erase` to remove it from a vector. The method `erase` is provided by the iterator returned by `std::find` if it is different from `subs_.end()`.

- `void notify(float value)`: Loops through registered subscribers and calls the method `update` on them.

Now, let us see how to use the preceding publisher and subscribers in the following code:

```cpp
int main() {
    logger temp_logger;
    display temp_display;
    data_sender temp_data_sender;

    publisher temp_publisher;
    temp_publisher.register_sub(&temp_logger);
    temp_publisher.register_sub(&temp_display);
    temp_publisher.notify(24.02f);

    temp_publisher.unregister(&temp_logger);
    temp_publisher.register_sub(&temp_data_sender);
    temp_publisher.notify(44.02f);
    return 0;
}
```

In the code, we perform the following steps:

1. Instantiate the following concrete subscribers: `temp_logger`, `temp_display`, and `temp_data_sender`.

2. Instantiate the publisher `temp_publisher`.

3. Register the subscribers `temp_logger` and `temp_display`.

4. Call `notify(24.02f)` on `temp_publisher`.

After these steps, we expect the following output:

```
Logging temperature 24.02
Displaying temperature 24.02
```

Next, we perform the following steps:

1. Unregister the subscriber `temp_logger`.

2. Register the subscriber `temp_data_sender`.

3. Call `notify(44.02f)` on `temp_publisher`.

After these steps, we expect the following output:

```
Displaying temperature 44.02
Sending temperature 44.02
```

As an *exercise*, create a new subscriber class `eeprom_writer` that records temperature if it goes under or above a set threshold.

You can run the full example in Renode. Start Visual Studio Code, attach it to the running container, open the `Chapter15/observer` project as described in *Chapter 4*, and run the following commands in the Visual Studio Code terminal, or run them directly in the container terminal:

```
$ cmake -B build
$ cmake --build build --target run_in_renode
```

Next, we will go through the compile-time implementation of the Observer pattern.

Compile-time implementation

In most embedded applications, we know a lot about the system's behavior at compile time. This means that when using the Observer pattern, we already know all the subscribers. If we assume that subscribers are only registered once and never unregistered, we can create a compile-time version of the Observer pattern.

To enable this, we'll first break down the key C++17 features that make compile-time implementation feasible.

Leveraging variadic templates

We will base the implementation on variadic templates. We will start with a simplified implementation to explain variadic templates, parameter packs, and fold expressions – C++ features
that will allow us to create a compile-time version of the Observer pattern. Let us proceed with
the following code:

```cpp
#include <cstdio>

struct display {
    static void update(float temp) {
        printf("Displaying temperature %.2f \r\n", temp);
    }
};

struct data_sender {
    static void update(float temp) {
        printf("Sending temperature %.2f \r\n", temp);
    }
};

struct logger {
    static void update(float temp) {
        printf("Logging temperature %.2f \r\n", temp);
    }
};

template <typename... Subs>
struct publisher {
    static void notify(float temp) {
        (Subs::update(temp), ...);
    }
};

int main() {

    using temp_publisher = publisher<display,
    data_sender,
```

```
    logger>;
    temp_publisher::notify(23.47);
    return 0;
}
```

In the code above, we have subscribers structs `display`, `data_sender`, and `logger`. All structs implement the static method `update`, which takes `temperature` as a parameter and prints it.

The struct `publisher` is a variadic class template. A **variadic template** is a template with at least one **parameter pack**. A template parameter pack is a template parameter that accepts zero or more template arguments. `typename...` `Subs` is a type template parameter pack named `Subs`, meaning we can instantiate the struct `publisher` with zero or more different types. To sum it up:

- `publisher` is a variadic class template as it has a template parameter pack `typename...` `Subs`.
- We can instantiate it with a variable number of types provided as template arguments. This is the way to register subscribers to the publisher.

In the main function, we create the alias `temp_publisher` as `publisher<display, data_sender, logger>`. We call the `notify` method on this alias, which will result in calls to update functions in types provided through the template parameter pack, thanks to the fold expression in the `notify` method.

The final piece of the puzzle is the fold expression `(Subs::update(temp), ...)`. This is a fold expression that uses the comma operator as the folding operator. It expands to: `(display::update(temp), data_sender::update(temp), logger::update(temp))`.

The fold expression ensures that `display::update(temp)` is called first, then `data_sender::update(temp)`, then `logger::update(temp)`. The order of evaluation is strictly left to right for the operands of the comma operator. Each `update(temp)` call returns a value (likely void).

The comma operator discards all return values except the last one, so only the final `logger::update(temp)` determines the fold's result. If they all return void, the whole expression also returns void.

Fold expressions were introduced in C++17 and using the comma operator is a concise way to call a function on each type in the parameter pack. Before that, a recursion was needed to iterate through types and call a function on them.

When examining the disassembly output in Compiler Explorer, you'll notice that the generated assembly code is relatively brief, approximately 30 lines in total, as shown here:

```
.LC0:
        .ascii  "Displaying temperature %.2f \015\012\000"
.LC1:
        .ascii  "Sending temperature %.2f \015\012\000"
.LC2:
        .ascii  "Logging temperature %.2f \015\012\000"
main:
        push    {r4, r5, r6, lr}
        mov     r4, #-536870912
        ldr     r5, .L3
        mov     r2, r4
        mov     r3, r5
        ldr     r0, .L3+4
        bl      printf
        mov     r2, r4
        mov     r3, r5
        ldr     r0, .L3+8
        bl      printf
        mov     r2, r4
        mov     r3, r5
        ldr     r0, .L3+12
        bl      printf
        mov     r0, #0
        pop     {r4, r5, r6, lr}
        bx      lr
.L3:
        .word   1077377105
        .word   .LC0
        .word   .LC1
        .word   .LC2
```

In this assembly code, we can see that there are no calls to the static update methods from the display, data_sender, and logger structs. This means the compiler was able to optimize these calls out, along with the registration of subscribers and the call to the publisher's notify method, resulting in direct calls to the printf function.

The result is a small memory footprint and fast performance. This example demonstrates the zero-cost abstraction design principle: we have abstractions for the publisher and subscribers, yet there is zero overhead, as the compiler is able to optimize the code to be as efficient as if it were written by hand.

Compare the assembly output of the compile-time implementation with that of the runtime implementation using the same optimization level (-03). It is clear that the compile-time implementation uses less memory and is faster as the compiler optimized away most of the function calls, and there is no indirection caused by virtual functions.

As we analyze the assembly code, let's take the opportunity to better understand fold expressions. To prevent GCC from optimizing away calls to the update methods, we can use the __attribute__ ((noinline)) function attribute, e.g. `static void __attribute__((noinline)) update(float temp)`. Add this attribute to the static update method of the `display`, `data_sender`, and `logger` structs, and observe the generated assembly code. You'll see how the call to the `notify` method in the `main` function results in parameter pack expansion and generates calls to the `update` methods of the `display`, `data_sender`, and `logger` structs.

You can run the full example in Renode. Start Visual Studio Code, attach it to the running container, open the `Chapter15/observer` project as described in *Chapter 4*, and run the following commands in the Visual Studio Code terminal, or run them directly in the container terminal:

```
$ cmake -B build
-DMAIN_CPP_FILE_NAME=main_observer_ct_basic.cpp
$ cmake --build build --target run_in_renode
```

Simplified compile-time implementation of the Observer pattern has a couple of limits:

- Subscribers can only be registered.
- All subscribers are registered when the publisher is instantiated. They cannot be registered after the publisher is instantiated.

Next, we will tackle the last point, as registering all subscribers in a single line of code may be cumbersome and not always practical. This will provide us with a more flexible compile-time design.

Improving the compile-time implementation

We will not change the interface of the publisher template struct. Instead, we will allow it to receive other publishers as arguments. The code is below:

```cpp
template<typename T>
concept Updatable = requires (T, float f) {
    { T::update(f) } -> std::same_as<void>;
};


template<typename T>
concept Notifiable = requires (T, float f) {
    { T::notify(f) } -> std::same_as<void>;
};


template <typename... Subs>
struct publisher {
    static void notify(float temp) {
        (call_update_or_notify<Subs>(temp), ...);
    }
private:
    template<typename T>
    static void call_update_or_notify(float temp) {
        if constexpr (Updatable<T>) {
            T::update(temp);
        } else if constexpr (Notifiable<T>) {
            T::notify(temp);
        }
        else {
            static_assert(false, "Type is not Updatable or Notifiable");
        }
    }
};
```

In the code above, we defined the following concepts:

- Updatable: This describes a type that has a static method update that accepts a float
- Notifiable: This describes a type that has a static method notify that accepts a float

We covered concepts in more detail in *Chapter 8*. The variadic template class publisher has a new method – call_update_or_notify. It is called on every type in the parameter pack typename... Subs in the method notify using the fold expression and the comma operator.

In the method call_update_or_notify, we use if constexpr to check, at compile-time, if the type is Updatable or Notifiable and call the update or notify static method on it respectively.

Below is an example of using the new version of the Observer pattern:

```
using temp_publisher = publisher<display, data_sender>;
temp_publisher::notify(23.47);


using temp_publisher_new = publisher<temp_publisher, logger>;
temp_publisher_new::notify(42.42);
```

In the code above, we instantiate temp_publisher by providing the variadic class template publisher with types display and data_sender, which are both subscribers are Updatable.

Next, we instantiate temp_publisher_new by providing publisher with the previously instantiated temp_publisher and the subscriber logger. Below is the output of the above example:

```
Displaying temperature 23.47
Sending temperature 23.47
Displaying temperature 42.42
Sending temperature 42.42
Logging temperature 42.42
```

You can run the full example in Renode. Start Visual Studio Code, attach it to the running container, open the Chapter15/observer project as described in *Chapter 4*, and run the following commands in the Visual Studio Code terminal, or run them directly in the container terminal:

```
$ cmake -B build -DMAIN_CPP_FILE_NAME=main_observer_ct.cpp
$ cmake --build build --target run_in_renode
```

This implementation of the Observer pattern allows us to register subscribers in a more flexible manner. To make it more generic, as an exercise, you can modify it so that the notify method is able to take a variable number of arguments.

Summary

In this chapter, we went through the Observer pattern, both runtime and compile-time implementations.

Compile-time implementation is utilizing what we know about the application during compile-time. It is based on variadic template classes and fold expressions. The result is super compact and fast code, as we are not storing information about subscribers in a container, nor do we need to iterate through the container to make a call to update methods.

In the next chapter, we will cover **Finite State Machines (FSM)** and the implementation of the State patterns in C++.

Join our community on Discord

Join our community's Discord space for discussions with the author and other readers:

`https://packt.link/embeddedsystems`

16
Designing Scalable Finite State Machines

A **Finite State Machine** (FSM) is an abstract computational module used to represent a system that can be in exactly one of a finite number of states at any given time. An FSM can transition from one state to another on a given input, and it can perform an action during the transition.

In control theory, there is a classification of Moore and Mealy machines. Moore's FSM output depends only on a state, that is, the FSM uses only entry actions. Mealy's FSM output depends on the input and current state, that is, the action it performs is determined by both the current state and the input.

The FSMs that we will cover in this chapter are a combination of both Moore and Mealy FSMs as they support both actions performed during transitions and entry and exit actions that depend only on a current state. FSMs are also called **Unified Modeling Language** (UML) state machines and are used in real-life applications in embedded systems to describe and control machines. For example, FSMs are commonly used to control washing machines, elevator systems, or communication protocols in networking devices, for managing complex sequences of operations based on various inputs. Understanding FSMs will help you design more predictable and maintainable embedded systems.

In this chapter, we're going to cover the following main topics:

- FSM – a simple implementation
- FSM – implementation using the State pattern
- State pattern implementation using tag dispatching
- Boost SML (State Machine Language)

Technical requirements

To get the most out of this chapter, I strongly recommend using Compiler Explorer (`https://godbolt.org/`) as you read through the examples. Select GCC as your compiler and target x86 architecture. This will allow you to see standard output (`stdio`) results and better observe the code's behavior. As we are using a lot of modern C++ features, make sure to select the C++23 standard, by adding `-std=c++23` in the compiler options box.

Compiler Explorer makes it easy to try out the code, tweak it, and immediately see how it affects the output and generated assembly. Most of the examples can also be run in a Renode simulator on an ARM Cortex M0 target and are available on GitHub (`https://github.com/PacktPublishing/Cpp-in-Embedded-Systems/tree/main/Chapter16`).

FSM – a simple implementation

We will jump straight into an example of an FSM handling **Bluetooth Low Energy (BLE)** device connection states, analyze its shortcomings, and see how we can improve it using the State design pattern.

The example FSM will be simplified for the purpose of clarity and easier understanding. We will have three states – `idle`, `advertising`, and `connected`. Here is a state diagram of the example FSM:

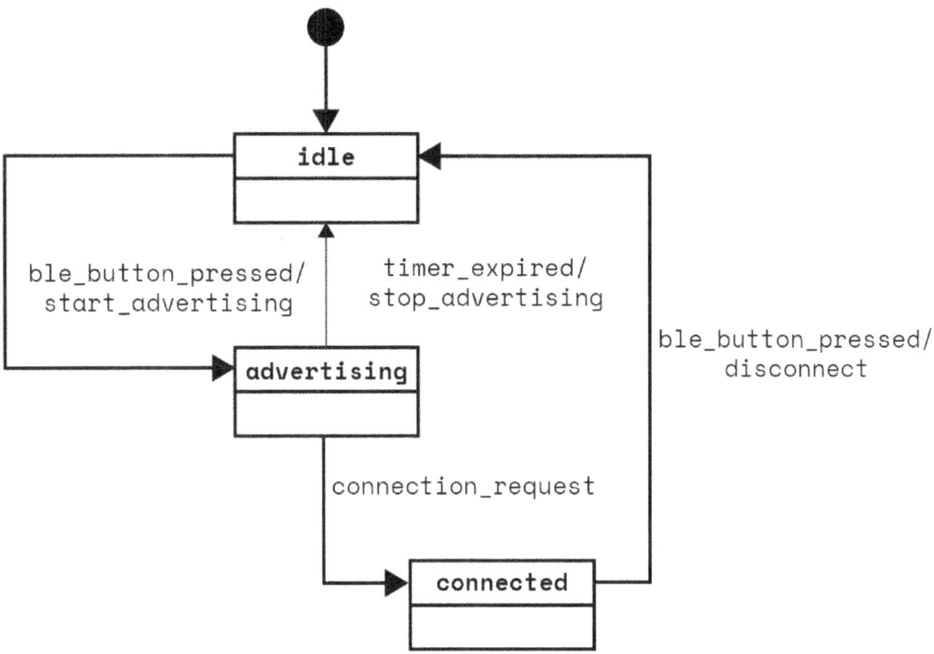

Figure 16.1 – BLE device connection state diagram

Figure 16.1 depicts the state diagram of the BLE device connection FSM. The diagram depicts transitions between states and actions described as follows:

- The default state is idle. It transitions to the advertising state on a ble_button_pressed event. During the transition, the start_advertising action is executed. In simple words, this means that if the device is in an idle state and a user presses a designated button, it will start advertising and change state.

- From the advertising state, the FSM can transition to connected on a connection_request event or go back to idle on the timer_expired state while stopping the advertising by executing the stop_advertising action.

- When in the connected state, the FSM can go only to idle on the ble_button_pressed event while executing the disconnect action.

Keep in mind that this is an extremely simplified FSM we are using for the purpose of an example, and a real-life FSM would include more states and events to properly describe the connecting behavior of a BLE device.

An FSM can also be described using state transition tables. This table shows the state to which the FSM moves based on the current state and input (received event), as well as the action it performs during the transition. Here is the transition table for the BLE device FSM we are analyzing in this chapter:

Current State	Event	Next State	Action
idle	ble_button_pressed	advertising	start_advertising
advertising	timer_expired	idle	stop_advertising
advertising	connection_request	connected	
connected	ble_button_pressed	idle	disconnect

Table 16.1 – BLE device state transition table

Table 16.1 describes the BLE device FSM by listing transitions in rows. It serves as an alternative to the state diagram for describing FSM behavior. We will start with the implementation of this FSM first by defining states and events.

Describing states and events

We will model states and events as enumerators, as shown in the following code:

```
enum class ble_state {
    idle,
    advertising,
    connected
};

enum class ble_event {
    ble_button_pressed,
    connection_request,
    timer_expired
};
```

The preceding enumerators describe states and events for our BLE device FSM.

Tracking current state and handling events — the FSM class

Next, we will define a class `ble_fsm` that will keep track of the current state and provide a public method, `handle_event`, which we will use to feed the FSM with events. The code is as follows:

```cpp
class ble_fsm {
public:
    void handle_event(ble_event event);
    ble_state get_state() const {
        return current_state_;
    }

private:
    ble_state current_state_ = ble_state::idle;

    void start_advertising() {
        printf("Action: start_advertising()\n");
    }

    void stop_advertising() {
        printf("Action: stop_advertising()\n");
    }

    void disconnect() {
        printf("Action: disconnect()\n");
    }
};
```

In the code above, we define the class ble_fsm with the following members:

- `ble_state current_state_` – A private member with the default value `ble_state::idle`. We use it to track the current state, and the initial value is set to `idle`.
- `void start_advertising()` – A private method used to implement an action.
- `void stop_advertising()` – A private method used to implement an action.
- `void disconnect()` – A private method used to implement an action.
- `ble_state get_state() const` – A private method used to retrieve the current state.
- `void handle_event(ble_event event)` – A public method used to respond to events by executing actions and changing the current state depending on the `current_event_`.

The `handle_event` method implements the actual behavior of the FSM, and the code for it is shown here:

```cpp
void ble_fsm::handle_event(ble_event event) {
switch (current_state_) {
    case ble_state::idle:
    if (event == ble_event::ble_button_pressed)
    {
        start_advertising();
        current_state_ = ble_state::advertising;
    }
    break;

    case ble_state::advertising:
    if (event == ble_event::connection_request)
    {
        current_state_ = ble_state::connected;
    }
    else if (event == ble_event::timer_expired)
    {
        stop_advertising();
        current_state_ = ble_state::idle;
    }
    break;

    case ble_state::connected:
    if (event ==ble_event::ble_button_pressed)
    {
        disconnect();
        current_state_ = ble_state::idle;
    }
    break;

    default:
    break;
}
}
```

The preceding code shows the implementation of the handle_event method for the ble_fsm class. It uses a switch statement on current_state_ to handle the event according to it and receive the event. The event is handled by calling an appropriate action and changing the state as described by the FSM.

Next, we will see how to use the ble_fsm class.

Using the ble_fsm class

We will first define a helper function, state_to_string, used to debug our FSM. The code is shown here:

```cpp
static const char* state_to_string(ble_state state) {
    switch (state) {
        case ble_state::idle:        return "idle";
        case ble_state::advertising: return "advertising";
        case ble_state::connected:   return "connected";
        default:                     return "unknown";
    }
}
```

The state_to_string function returns a string literal for a given state enum.

Next, let us see how to use the ble_fsm class, as shown in the following code:

```cpp
int main() {
    ble_fsm my_ble_fsm;

    const auto print_current_state = [&]() {
        printf("Current State: %s\n",
            state_to_string(my_ble_fsm.get_state()));
    };

    print_current_state();

    my_ble_fsm.handle_event(ble_event::ble_button_pressed);
    print_current_state();

    my_ble_fsm.handle_event(ble_event::connection_request);
    print_current_state();
```

```cpp
    my_ble_fsm.handle_event(ble_event::ble_button_pressed);
    print_current_state();

    return 0;
}
```

The preceding code in the `main` function creates an object, `my_ble_fsm`, of the `ble_fsm` type, and it feeds it with events in the following order:

1. It first passes `ble_event::ble_button_pressed` to the FSM handle_event method. The initial state of the FSM is `idle`, and after this event, it will transition to `advertising`.

2. Next, it passes the `ble_event::connection_request` event to the FSM, which will make it transition to the `connected` state.

3. Finally, it passes the `ble_event::ble_button_pressed` event to the FSM for the second time, making it transition back to the `idle` state.

The code above uses the `state_to_string` function to get the string literal from the state enum, and it uses it to print the current state of the FSM after it feeds it with an event.

Analyzing the output

Running the full example will provide the following output:

```
Current State: idle
Action: start_advertising()
Current State: advertising
Current State: connected
Action: disconnect()
Current State: idle
```

The preceding output shows FSM states and the executed actions.

You can run the full example in the Renode simulator from the book's GitHub repo. It is placed under `Chapter16/fsm`, and you can build and run it using the following commands:

```
$ cmake -B build
$ cmake --build build --target run_in_renode
```

The approach for implementing an FSM we just went through works well for simple FSMs. In real-life applications, FSMs are more complex – they have more states, actions, and events. The handle_event method in ble_fsm doesn't scale well as it is implemented using switch-case and if-else logic. Adding more states, and handling more events and actions, makes it less readable and harder to maintain.

Next, we will see how we can utilize the State design pattern to mitigate these issues.

FSM – implementation using the State pattern

Building on our switch-based approach, we will now refactor the BLE device connection FSM using the State design pattern. This pattern is "state-centric," meaning each state is encapsulated as its own class. A common base class interface will allow the FSM to store pointers to these concrete state classes in a container.

In a typical FSM, states change dynamically at runtime in response to external interrupts and timers. In our example, we will continue using an enum to differentiate states and store the current one in a private member variable. This enum-based approach still works well with the State pattern, since it lets us quickly locate and switch between the concrete state objects that the FSM manages. We will start the implementation with the state class interface.

Understanding state class interfaces

The state class interface is shown in the following code:

```
class state {
public:
    virtual ble_state handle_event(ble_event event) = 0;
    virtual ble_state get_state_enum() = 0;
};
```

In the preceding code, we see that the state interface is simple and has two pure virtual methods:

- `virtual ble_state handle_event(ble_event event)` – A method intended to be implemented by a derived class to handle an actual event. It returns a ble_state enum to signal a new state to an FSM. If handling an event doesn't cause transition, it should return the enum that corresponds to the current state.

- `virtual ble_state get_state_enum()` – A method used to return a ble_state enum corresponding to an actual state.

Next, we will go over the implementation of concrete state classes: `idle`, `advertising`, and `connected`. We will start with the `idle` class, as shown in this code:

```cpp
class idle : public state{
public:
    ble_state handle_event(ble_event event) {
        if (event == ble_event::ble_button_pressed) {
            start_advertising();
            return ble_state::advertising;
        }
        return get_state_enum();
    }

    ble_state get_state_enum() {
        return ble_state::idle;
    }
private:
    void start_advertising() {
        printf("Action: start_advertising()\n");
    }
};
```

In the preceding code, we see that the `idle` class implements pure virtual methods defined in the state interface class:

- `ble_state handle_event(ble_event event)` – The `idle` class checks whether the received event is `ble_event::ble_button_pressed` and calls `start_advertising` if it is and returns the `ble_state::advertising` enum. In the case that it receives any other event, it returns the state provided with `get_state_enum`.
- `ble_state get_state_enum()` – This returns the `ble_state` enum corresponding to the `idle` class, which is `ble_state::idle`.

Next, we will go through the derived class `advertising`, as shown in the following code:

```cpp
class advertising : public state{
public:
    ble_state handle_event(ble_event event) {
        if (event == ble_event::connection_request) {
            return ble_state::connected;
        }
```

```cpp
        if (event == ble_event::timer_expired) {
            stop_advertising();
            return ble_state::idle;
        }
        return get_state_enum();
    }


    ble_state get_state_enum() {
        return ble_state::advertising;
    }
private:
    void stop_advertising() {
        printf("Action: stop_advertising()\n");
    }
};
```

In this code, the advertising class implements pure virtual methods defined in the state interface class by handling the events appropriately.

Next, we will go over the connected concrete class:

```cpp
class connected : public state{
public:
    ble_state handle_event(ble_event event) {
        if (event == ble_event::ble_button_pressed) {
            disconnect();
            return ble_state::idle;
        }
        return get_state_enum();
    }


    ble_state get_state_enum() {
        return ble_state::connected;
    }
private:
    void disconnect() {
        printf("Action: disconnect()\n");
    }
};
```

As we can see in the preceding code, the connected class implements a state interface and implements the virtual methods handle_event and get_state_enum appropriately.

Next, we will refactor the ble_fsm class to use the state class interface to store pointers to concrete class objects in a container.

Refactoring the ble_fsm class

We will start with refactoring the ble_fsm class, as shown in the following code:

```cpp
class ble_fsm {
public:
    void handle_event(ble_event event) {
        if(auto the_state = get_the_state(current_state_)) {
            current_state_ = the_state->handle_event(event);
        }
    }
    ble_state get_state() const {
        return current_state_;
    }

    void add_state(state *the_state) {
        states_.push_back(the_state);
    }

  private:
    ble_state current_state_ = ble_state::idle;
    etl::vector<state*, 3> states_;

    state* get_the_state(ble_state state_enum); };
```

Let us break down the implementation of the ble_fsm class:

- ble_state current_state_ – A private member with the default value ble_state::idle. We use it to track the current state, as we did previously.

- etl::vector<state*, 3> states_ – A container used to hold pointers to the state interface. If you are following this example using Compiler Explorer, you can replace it with std::vector (and include a <vector> header).

- `state* get_the_state(ble_state state_enum)` – A private method used to get an actual state using the `ble_state` enum.

- `void handle_event(ble_event event)` – A public method used to handle events. It calls the `get_the_state` method provided with `current_state_` to get a pointer to the actual state object. If the pointer is valid, it calls `handle_event` on the state object and stores the return value in `current_state_`.

Next, let us go through the `get_the_state` method implementation, as shown here:

```cpp
state* ble_fsm::get_the_state(ble_state state_enum) {
const auto is_state_enum = [&](state* the_state) {
        return the_state->get_state_enum() == state_enum;
};

auto it = std::find_if(states_.begin(), states_.end(), is_state_enum);

if (it != states_.end()) {
    return *it;
}

return nullptr;
}
```

In the `get_the_state` method, we use the `std::find_if` function (from the `<algorithm>` header) to search for a pointer to a `state` object that matches the given `state_enum`. The search uses the `is_state_enum` lambda as a predicate, which compares each state's enum value. If a matching state is found, the method returns a pointer to it; otherwise, the `nullptr`.

Next, let us see how to use the refactored `ble_fsm` class, the `state` interface, and the concrete classes `idle`, `advertising`, and `connected` to implement the FSM.

Implementing the State pattern

Next, we will see how to use the above implementation of the State pattern in the following code:

```cpp
int main() {
    ble_fsm my_ble_fsm;

    idle idle_s;
    advertising advertising_s;
```

```cpp
    connected connected_s;

    my_ble_fsm.add_state(&idle_s);
    my_ble_fsm.add_state(&advertising_s);
    my_ble_fsm.add_state(&connected_s);

    const auto print_current_state = [&]() {
        printf("Current State: %s\n",
            state_to_string(my_ble_fsm.get_state()));
    };

    print_current_state();

    my_ble_fsm.handle_event(ble_event::ble_button_pressed);
    print_current_state();

    my_ble_fsm.handle_event(ble_event::connection_request);
    print_current_state();

    my_ble_fsm.handle_event(ble_event::ble_button_pressed);
    print_current_state();

    return 0;
}
```

In this code, we see that after creating an object my_ble_fsm of the ble_fsm type, we create instances of concrete states: idle, advertising, and connected. Then, we add pointers to the concrete states to the my_ble_fsm object using the add_state method. Next, we use the FSM as we did in the initial implementation and feed it with events.

You can run the full example in the Renode simulator from the book's GitHub repo. It is placed under Chapter16/fsm, and you can build and run it using the following commands:

```
$ cmake -B build -DMAIN_CPP_FILE_NAME=main_fsm_state_pattern.cpp
$ cmake --build build --target run_in_renode
```

The example we just went through is using the State design pattern. Next, we will go through the generic form of the State design pattern.

State design pattern

Let us go over the UML diagram of the BLE device connection FSM, as shown in *Figure 16.2*:

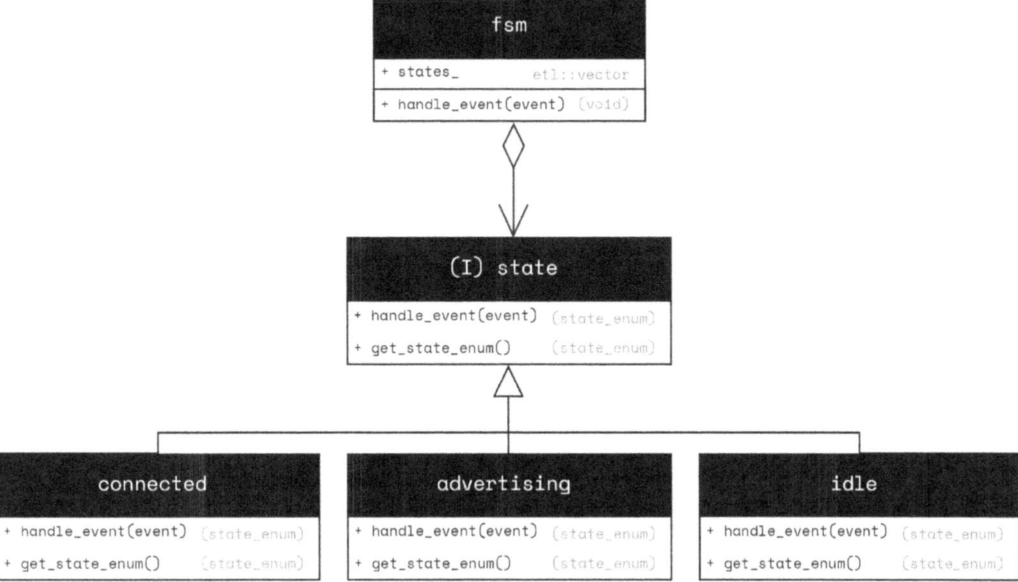

Figure 16.2 – BLE device connection FSM – UML diagram

Figure 16.2 depicts a UML diagram of the BLE device connection FSM. We already went through applying the State design pattern to the FSM implementation. Let us summarize it:

- The FSM class holds pointers to the state class interface in a container.
- The FSM keeps track of the current state.
- The FSM delegates handle_event calls to a current concrete state.
- Concrete states implement the state interface.
- Concrete states implement actions and call them appropriately when handling events.
- Concrete states return a new state from the handle_event method. This allows the FSM to update the current state.

The state design pattern is a simple yet effective pattern that allows us to break down complex switch statements into more manageable code. Still, as we were able to see in the previous example, concrete states handle events using if-else logic. With the increasing complexity of an FSM, the handle functions can also clutter. To mitigate this, we can apply the tag-dispatching technique.

State pattern implementation using tag dispatching

In the previous example (in the previous sections), the program flow in event handlers was determined at runtime using `if-else` logic. Next, we will use the tag-dispatching technique to decouple event handling of different events in separate methods. We will rely no longer on the `ble_event` enum, and will create empty types as events instead, as shown in the following code:

```cpp
struct ble_button_pressed{};
struct connection_request{};
struct timer_expired{};
```

Now, the class `state` will overload `handle_event` virtual methods for every defined event, as shown here:

```cpp
class state {
public:
    virtual ble_state handle_event(ble_button_pressed) {
        return get_state_enum();
    }
    virtual ble_state handle_event(connection_request) {
        return get_state_enum();
    }
    virtual ble_state handle_event(timer_expired) {
        return get_state_enum();
    }
    virtual ble_state get_state_enum() = 0;
};
```

In this code, we see that the class `state` is no longer an interface but an abstract class (as not all virtual methods are pure). It overloads the `handle_event` function for types `ble_button_pressed`, `connection_request`, and `timer_expired`. It implements all overloads by returning the value generated by `get_state_enum` – a pure virtual method that will be implemented by derived classes, that is, concrete states.

Next, let us see the implementation of the `advertising` class:

```cpp
class advertising : public state{
public:
    ble_state handle_event(connection_request cr){
        return ble_state::connected;
```

```cpp
    }

    ble_state handle_event(timer_expired te){
        stop_advertising();
        return ble_state::idle;
    }

    ble_state get_state_enum() {
        return ble_state::advertising;
    }
private:
    void stop_advertising() {
        printf("Action: stop_advertising()\n");
    }
};
```

In this code, we see that the advertising class implements the following overloads of the virtual method handle_event:

- `ble_state handle_event(connection_request cr)` returns `ble_state::connected`.
- `ble_state handle_event(timer_expired te)` calls `stop_advertising` and returns `ble_state::idle`.

By using overloaded functions, we can implement the handling of different events in separate methods and easily dispatch calls to them by calling handle_event with different types. To complete the implementation, we also need to overload the handle_event method in the FSM for all possible events. We can do this easily by making it a template method, as shown in the following code:

```cpp
class ble_fsm {
public:
    template<typename E>
    void handle_event(E event) {
        if(auto the_state = get_the_state(current_state_))
        {
            current_state_ = the_state->handle_event(event);
        }
    }
    //...
};
```

The preceding code shows the template method `handle_event` from the `ble_fsm` class, which makes our tag-dispatching technique application complete.

You can run the full example in the Renode simulator from the book's GitHub repo. It is placed under `Chapter16/fsm`, and you can build and run it using the following commands:

```
$ cmake -B build
-DMAIN_CPP_FILE_NAME=main_fsm_state_pattern_tag_dispatch.cpp
$ cmake --build build --target run_in_renode
```

Until this point, we saw three approaches in this chapter to implement an FSM in C++. We started with a simple switch and if-else-based approach, applied the State design pattern, and then utilized tag dispatching. Each step provided us with more flexibility in the design – making code more readable and easier to manage, which is important when working with complex FSMs.

There are other approaches to implementing an FSM, based on a state transition table, which describes transitions in a single place. Boost **State Machine Language (SML)** uses a table-based approach to describe an FSM using descriptive syntax.

Boost SML

Boost SML is a highly expressive C++14 single header library used to implement FSMs. We will jump straight ahead in using it by implementing the same BLE device connection FSM. Here is the code:

```cpp
#include "sml.hpp"
namespace sml = boost::sml;

struct ble_button_pressed{};
struct connection_request{};
struct timer_expired{};

constexpr auto start_advertising = [](){
    printf("Action: start_advertising()\n");
};

constexpr auto stop_advertising = [](){
    printf("Action: stop_advertising()\n");
};

constexpr auto disconnect = [](){
```

```cpp
        printf("Action: disconnect()\n");
  };


  struct ble_fsm {
    auto operator()() const {
      using namespace sml;
          return make_transition_table(
          *"idle"_s + event<ble_button_pressed>
          / start_advertising                              = "advertising"_s,
          "advertising"_s  + event<connection_request> = "connected"_s,
          "advertising"_s  + event<timer_expired>
          / stop_advertising                              = "idle"_s,
          "connected"_s + event<ble_button_pressed>
          / disconnect                                    = "idle"_s
      );
    }
  };
```

Let us break down this example:

- The events are modeled as structs, the same as in our tag-dispatching implementation.

- Actions are defined as `constexpr` lambdas.

- We define the type `ble_fsm` as a struct with an overloaded `operator()`, which returns the result of a call to `make_transition_table` from the namespace `sml`.

The code in `make_transition_table` allows SML to extract transition definitions, and within it, we are using the following syntax: `src_state + event [ guard ] / action = dst_state`. Here is a breakdown of the syntax:

- `src_state` – This is the state from which the transition starts.

- `+ event` – This is the event that triggers checking for a possible transition. If the event arrives and the guard is satisfied, then the transition proceeds.

- `[ guard ]` – The guard is an optional bool predicate that must evaluate to true for the transition to occur. If omitted, the transition happens unconditionally at the specified event.

- `/ action` – The action is an optional lambda to execute whenever the transition takes place.

- `= dst_state` – The destination state is where the FSM will go if the transition occurs.

The transition syntax is the essence of SML. By writing multiple lines of these rules inside the operator(), we fully describe the FSM's behavior in a declarative, human-readable way.

Let us now see how to use the FSM we discussed using Boost SML:

```cpp
sm<ble_fsm> my_ble_fsm{};
const auto print_current_state = [&]() {
    printf("Current State: ");
    if(my_ble_fsm.is("idle"_s)) {
        printf("idle\n");
    }
    if(my_ble_fsm.is("advertising"_s)) {
        printf("advertising\n");
    }
    if(my_ble_fsm.is("connected"_s)) {
        printf("connected\n");
    }
};
print_current_state();


my_ble_fsm.process_event(ble_button_pressed{});
print_current_state();


my_ble_fsm.process_event(connection_request{});
print_current_state();


my_ble_fsm.process_event(ble_button_pressed{});
print_current_state();
```

In this code, we create an object my_ble_fsm of the type sm<ble_fsm>. Then, we use the process_event method to send an event to it. You can run the full example in the Renode simulator from the book's GitHub repo. It is placed under Chapter16/fsm, and you can build and run it using the following commands:

```
$ cmake -B build -DMAIN_CPP_FILE_NAME=main_fsm_boost_sml.cpp
$ cmake --build build --target run_in_renode
```

Boost SML is a highly expressive library that reduces boilerplate code from the previous implementations of an FSM. It also offers features such as guard variables and composite states. Here is a project link where you can explore more: `https://github.com/boost-ext/sml`.

Boost SML is not only an expressive library but also highly performant, thanks to its use of compile-time template metaprogramming to aggressively optimize code. Event dispatching relies on tag dispatching (resolved at compile time) paired with minimal runtime lookups, avoiding costly branching or indirection. This approach typically outperforms both manual switch-enum-based solutions and State pattern-based implementations (which incur virtual call overhead). For concrete performance comparisons, see the benchmark at the following link: `https://github.com/boost-ext/sml?tab=readme-ov-file#benchmark`.

Summary

In this chapter, we went through FSM implementation starting from the simple switch-case-based approach, to the State pattern, tag dispatching, and using the Boost SML library for highly expressive code.

The most basic, switch-based implementation is suitable for small FSMs with a limited number of states and transitions. When the complexity of an FSM increases, it gets hard to read and manage. Moving to a State pattern-based solution increases code readability and makes changes easier. Boost SML offers ultimate expressiveness, providing us with a human-readable syntax that allows us to write very complex FSMs in a concise manner.

In the next chapter, we will go through an overview of libraries and frameworks in C++ usable for embedded systems development.

Get This Book's PDF Version and Exclusive Extras

Scan the QR code (or go to `packtpub.com/unlock`). Search for this book by name, confirm the edition, and then follow the steps on the page.

Note: Keep your invoice handy. Purchases made directly from Packt don't require an invoice.

17

Libraries and Frameworks

While the C++ standard library offers a vast array of containers and algorithms, certain aspects – such as dynamic memory allocation – can pose challenges in constrained environments. In *Chapter 2*, we explored some of these issues and ways to address them. However, specialized libraries, like the **Embedded Template Library (ETL)**, offer deterministic behavior and fixed memory footprints, making them well suited for embedded systems.

Embedded applications depend on **Hardware Abstraction Layers (HALs)** provided by vendors as C libraries. In *Chapter 12*, we examined how to use interfaces to decouple application-level C++ code from the underlying C-based hardware interactions. Wrapping entire HALs in C++ is a lot of work, but luckily, there are projects such as Google's Pigweed that are tackling exactly that, while offering additional functionality and flexibility for embedded development.

In *Chapter 11*, we explored how C++ can perform computations at compile time, reducing memory footprint. In *Chapter 15*, we learned about the Observer pattern and examined its compile-time implementation. Intel's **Compile-time Initialization and Build (CIB)** elevates these ideas even further, enabling a declarative approach to configuring firmware applications at compile time. In this chapter, we will go through the following C++ libraries:

- Standard library
- Embedded template library
- Pigweed
- Compile-time Initialization and Build

Technical requirements

You can try the examples from this chapter in the Renode simulator in the Docker container you set up in *Chapter 4*. Make sure that the Docker container is running.

You can find the files for this chapter on GitHub at `https://github.com/PacktPublishing/Cpp-in-Embedded-Systems/tree/main/Chapter17`.

Standard library

The C++ standard defines two types of standard library implementation – hosted and freestanding:

- A freestanding implementation is designed to run without relying on services typically provided by an OS, such as filesystem access or multi-threading support. As a result, the C++ standard specifies only a limited subset of standard library headers that must be provided by a freestanding implementation.

- A hosted implementation requires a globally defined main function, and the environment is responsible for invoking this function at startup. In a freestanding implementation, the startup routines and the entry point of the program are implementation-defined, allowing developers greater flexibility in specifying the initialization and execution flow of their applications.

Although the standard makes a clear distinction between hosted and freestanding implementation in terms of the globally defined main function, the configuration in some examples in this book blurs the line between the two.

Freestanding and hosted implementations in GCC

Even though we operate in a freestanding environment (no OS), some examples in this book use components from the C++ standard library (e.g., `std::function`), which are typically associated with hosted implementations. This is possible because:

- As we observed in *Chapter 4*, we set the program entry point in the linker script to `Reset_Handler`.

- `Reset_Handler`, implemented in the assembler startup script, performs low-level initialization and explicitly calls `main`.

- We use nano specs (*Chapter 7*), linking against a size-optimized subset of the C++ standard library. This allows limited use of hosted features like `std::function` while avoiding dependencies on an OS.

This hybrid approach leverages GCC's flexibility to combine freestanding execution (custom entry point, no OS) with hosted library features (standard headers, utilities) in a bare-metal environment.

To explicitly request GCC to use a freestanding implementation of the standard library, the compiler flag `-ffreestanding` should be used. The C++ standard library provides many components that are "pay only for what you use" and can be very useful even in resource-constrained environments. In previous chapters, you've already worked with many parts of the standard library, so you have a solid understanding of its capabilities. Here, we'll provide an overview of the parts that are best suited for resource-constrained environments and point out which ones should be used with caution or avoided.

Numeric and math

Embedded systems are often employed in automation and process control, requiring precise control over numeric types, their ranges, and math operations. The C++ standard library provides the `<cstdint>`, `<limits>`, and `<cmath>` headers to define fixed-width integers, query numeric limits, and perform mathematical computations, helping ensure predictable behavior, portability, and efficiency in resource-constrained environments.

<cstdint>

The `<cstdint>` header provides fixed-width integer types such as `std::int8_t`, `std::uint32_t`, and other well-known C types defined in `stdint.h`. These types are useful in embedded contexts where integer size and bit width are important for direct hardware register access, predictable overflow behavior, and memory usage considerations. By using them, you explicitly document your intention for a variable's size, thereby improving code portability and preventing potential surprises when moving between platforms with different native integer widths.

<limits>

The header provides the `std::numeric_limits` template, which describes properties of fundamental numeric types (like minimum and maximum values, sign, and precision). This is especially useful in embedded contexts for handling overflow. Typical usage occurs at compile-time or through trivial inlining by the compiler, resulting in minimal runtime overhead. By using functions like `std::numeric_limits::max()`, you avoid scattering magic constants or architecture-specific assumptions, aiding portability and maintainability.

\<cmath\>

The `<cmath>` header provides standard math functions such as `std::sin`, `std::cos`, `std::sqrt`, and more. In embedded environments, especially those without floating-point hardware, these functions can be relatively expensive in terms of both runtime performance and code size. Carefully consider whether you really need floating-point math, and if so, whether approximations or fixed-point routines might be sufficient and more efficient.

Containers and algorithms

Embedded systems often manage structured data and require efficient ways to process it under tight resource constraints. The C++ standard library offers container and algorithm headers such as `<array>`, `<span>`, and `<algorithm>` to organize data and perform common operations like searching, sorting, and transforming, enabling more readable and maintainable code.

std::array

The only fixed-size container in the standard library that avoids dynamic allocation is `std::array`. We covered it in *Chapter 1*, when we discussed generic types. In the same chapter, we based the ring buffer implementation on `std::array`, which allowed us to create ring buffers of different types and sizes using the same generic code.

`std::array` is typically implemented as a wrapper around a C-style array. Besides being a generic type, it also offers the at method for index-based access with runtime bounds checking, making it a safer alternative to raw arrays. If an out-of-bounds index is requested, the at method will throw an exception. If exceptions are disabled, it may call `std::terminate` or `std::abort`, depending on the library implementation. These behaviors should be handled according to your system requirements by implementing appropriate terminate and signal handlers.

std:: priority_queue

`std::priority_queue` is a container adapter that provides priority queue functionality. By default, it uses `std::vector` as the underlying container. However, as shown in *Chapter 14*, you can substitute it with `etl::vector` from ETL, avoiding issues with dynamic memory allocation.

std:: span

As shown in *Chapter 9*, `std::span` is a lightweight, non-owning wrapper around a contiguous sequence of objects, where the first element is at position 0. It provides essential functionality such as the `size()` method, `operator[]` for element access, and the `begin()` and `end()` iterators, allowing it to integrate seamlessly with standard library algorithms.

`std::span` can be constructed from C-style arrays as well as containers like `std::array` and `std::vector` or `etl::vector`. This makes it a practical alternative to using separate pointer and size parameters, which is especially useful when interfacing C++ code with C libraries such as those used in HAL.

Iterators

Iterators are abstractions that act like generalized pointers, providing a uniform way to traverse and access elements within a container. For example, standard library containers implement the `begin()` and `end()` methods, which return iterators marking the start and one-past-the-end of their sequence. This consistent interface allows algorithms to work generically over different container types, enhancing code reusability and clarity.

Let us go through the following example using `std::array`:

```cpp
#include <array>
#include <algorithm>
#include <cstdio>

int main() {
    std::array<int, 5> arr = {5, 3, 4, 1, 2};
    std::array<int, 5>::iterator start = arr.begin();
    auto finish = arr.end();
    std::sort(start, finish);
    for (auto it = arr.begin(); it != arr.end(); ++it) {
        printf("%d ", *it);
    }
    printf("\n");
    return 0;
}
```

This example demonstrates how to use iterators with a standard library container:

- The iterator `start` is explicitly declared as `std::array<int, 5>::iterator` to illustrate the full type name, while the iterator `finish` is declared using `auto` for conciseness, allowing the compiler to deduce its type.
- The `std::sort` algorithm is applied using the iterators `start` and `finish`, obtained from `arr.begin()` and `arr.end()`, to sort the array in ascending order.
- The loop uses `auto` to declare the iterator `it`, which makes the code more concise. The loop traverses the sorted array, and `printf` is used to print each element.

Iterators are used to traverse containers. They not only promote generic programming but also make it easy to switch container types without changing the algorithmic logic.

Algorithms

Algorithms from the standard library offer a consistent way to solve common problems across different containers, making the code more expressive and easier to maintain. They allow you to perform operations like searching, sorting, copying, and accumulating data using a uniform interface. Some of the most used algorithms are listed here:

- `std::sort`: Sorts a range of elements in ascending order by default, using the less-than operator for comparison. It can also accept a custom comparator to sort based on different criteria, such as descending order or a specific object property.

- `std::find`: Searches for the first occurrence of a given value in a range and returns an iterator to it. If the value is not found, it returns the end iterator, signaling that the search failed.

- `std::for_each`: Applies a specified function or lambda to each element in a range.

- `std::copy`: Copies the elements of one range into another destination range.

- `std::copy_if`: Copies only elements that satisfy a specified predicate, making it useful for filtering data as you copy.

- `std::min` and `std::max`: Return the smaller or larger of two values, respectively, using the less-than operator by default (or a provided comparison function). They're handy for quick comparisons where you just need the minimum or maximum of two values.

- `std::min_element` and `std::max_element`: Return an iterator to the smallest or largest element in a range. These are useful when you need to find the position of an extreme value in a container (instead of comparing just two values).

- `std::accumulate`: Iterates over a range and combines the elements with an initial value using a binary operation (default is addition). This allows for summing values, computing products, or performing any custom aggregation you define.

Template metaprogramming

As discussed in *Chapter 8*, C++ type traits are compile-time predicates and transformations that allow the compiler to enforce constraints based on a type's properties. They are used for writing generic, robust code without incurring runtime overhead. In *Chapter 12*, we used type traits to create type-safe register access, preventing invalid type usage at compile time and reducing the risk of subtle errors.

Here are some concrete type traits we've utilized in the chapters mentioned in this section:

- `std::enable_if`: Enables or disables function templates based on a Boolean compile-time expression
- `std::is_same`: Checks if two types are exactly the same
- `std::is_enum`: Checks if a type is an enumeration type
- `std::underlying_type`: Retrieves the underlying integer type of an enum
- `std::is_arithmetic`: Checks if a type is an arithmetic type (integral or floating-point)
- `std::is_integral`: Checks if a type is an integral type
- `std::is_floating_point`: Checks if a type is a floating-point type

Parts of the standard library to avoid in embedded applications

Many containers from the standard library, such as `std::vector`, `std::list`, and `std::string`, use dynamic memory allocation. If dynamic memory allocation is not allowed in your embedded application, these should be avoided.

The `iostream` library, included with header `<iostream>`, requires significant memory resources and also relies on dynamic allocation. That's why we used the `<cstdio>` header and the `printf` function for console output.

In *Chapter 10*, we covered `std::function` from the `<functional>` header. There, we outlined that in some scenarios, `std::function` can use dynamic memory allocation, meaning if used, it should be used with caution. Note that `std::function` is not available in a freestanding implementation.

Next, we will give a short overview of ETL that compliments the standard library in the context of restricted embedded environments.

Embedded template library

In *Chapter 2*, we saw that `std::vector` uses dynamic memory allocation by default. We also saw that we can use `std:: polymorphic_allocator` and a monotonic buffer to make it use statically allocated memory. This approach is still not bulletproof as `std::vector` in some cases can resort to dynamic memory allocation even with this approach.

To address some of the challenges posed by the standard library in embedded contexts, ETL provides a set of templated containers and algorithms that closely mimic the interfaces of standard library counterparts but are tailored for systems with limited resources.

Fixed-size containers

One of the primary advantages of ETL is that its containers (such as `etl::vector`, `etl::list`, `etl::string`, and others) allow you to specify a fixed maximum size at compile time. Container implementations ensure that no dynamic memory allocation is performed at runtime as memory is reserved up front as atomic or static storage.

As ETL containers are designed to mimic standard library containers, and they implement iterators, they can be used with most algorithms and container adapters from the standard library. This allows us to leverage components from the standard library without worrying about dynamic allocation.

ETL also offers `etl::array` for platforms that do not support C++11, since `std::array` was introduced in C++11.

Storing a callable with etl::delegate

As shown in *Chapter 14*, you can use `etl::delegate` instead of `std::function` to store a callable. However, `etl::delegate` is non-owning, so you must handle potential dangling references carefully.

Other utilities provided by ETL

Besides fixed-size containers and `etl::delegate`, ETL also provides utilities such as a messaging framework – a collection of messages, message routers, message buses, and finite state machines. It also offers CRC calculations, checksums, and hash functions.

ETL allows you to configure error handling. It can be configured to throw exceptions or send errors to the user-defined handler. This allows greater flexibility and project-based configuration depending on system requirements.

You can learn more about ETL at the website `https://www.etlcpp.com/`.

Next, we will discuss Pigweed – a collection of lightweight, modular C++ libraries for embedded systems, developed by Google, offering components like logging, assertions, and Bluetooth connectivity to simplify development and improve code reuse.

Pigweed

One of the biggest challenges in embedded systems development is portability. For code to be truly portable, it must depend on interfaces. To run it on different hardware targets, someone needs to implement those interfaces on different targets. Maintaining consistent interfaces across various projects and devices can be difficult. Google's Pigweed project aims to solve this by providing software modules for embedded applications, with hardware interfaces already implemented for many targets.

Pigweed is intended for complex projects and large-scale teams. Besides the hardware interfaces, it also:

- Packs software modules built on top of them, such as logging, serial communication (SPI, I2C, and UART), Bluetooth **Host Controller Interface (HCI)**, interactive console, **Remote Procedure Call (RPC)** system, and more.

- Provides embedding-friendly alternatives to standard library components: fixed-size strings and containers.

- Manages the entire toolchain out of the box and simplifies setting up your development environment.

- Provides an entire framework – `pw_system` – which pulls together many modules across Pigweed to construct a working system with RPC, logging, and more.

As you can see, Pigweed is not only a library – it is an entire development ecosystem. It can be used as a framework, but you can also cherry-pick individual modules that suit your needs. As stated on the documentation website – `https://pigweed.dev/` – Pigweed is still in its early stages; some modules are still in development stages, while some are stable and used on devices that are already on the market. As with any library, you need to evaluate it for potential use in your projects.

We'll go through Pigweed's Sense tutorial to demonstrate some of its capabilities – mainly the interactive console and **RPC** system.

Pigweed's Sense tutorial

The Sense project is a demo project that utilizes many Pigweed components and shows how they work together.

Sense is a simplified version of an air quality sensor that only includes some of the functions of a full product. The goal is to give you practical experience with working with Pigweed by following these steps:

1. First, make sure the Docker daemon is running. Start a Docker image in network host mode and attach it to Bash. You can use the following commands in a Linux environment:

```
$ sudo systemctl start docker
$ docker run --network=host -d -it --name dev_env mahmutbegovic/
cpp_in_embedded_systems
$ docker exec -it dev_env /bin/bash
```

For the Windows-based host, use the following command to forward the ports needed to run the tutorial:

```
$ docker run -d -it --name dev_env -p 33000:33000 -p 8080:8080
mahmutbegovic/cpp_in_embedded_systems
```

2. Next, clone the Sense repo:

```
$ git clone https://pigweed.googlesource.com/pigweed/showcase/sense
```

3. Next, start Visual Studio Code, attach to the running container, and open the `/workspace/sense` folder. If you see a pop-up message in **Visual Studio Code** recommending the installation of the Pigweed extension, accept it; otherwise, go to **Extensions**, search for Pigweed, and install it.

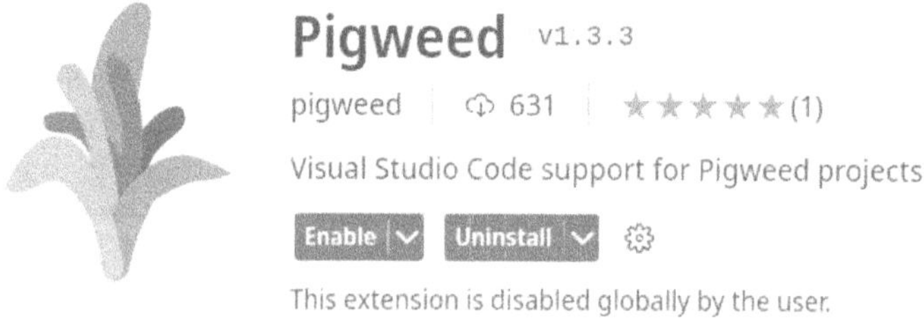

Figure 17.1 – Visual Studio Code extension

Figure 17.1 depicts the Visual Studio Code Pigweed extension.

4. After the installation of the extension, go to Explorer view and expand the **BAZEL BUILD TARGETS** node. Click on the **Refresh Target List** button.

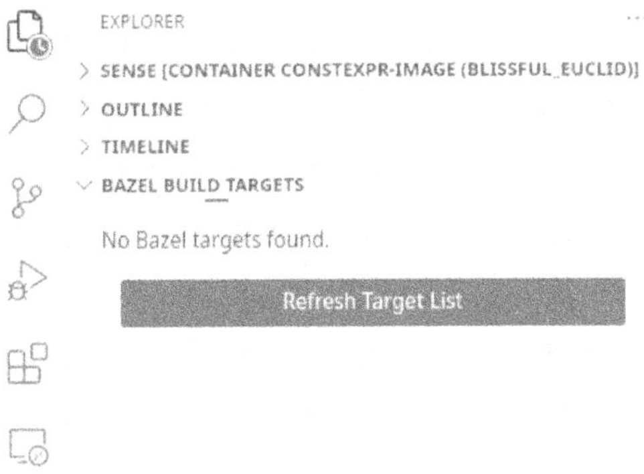

Figure 17.2 – BAZEL BUILD TARGETS node

Refreshing the target list can take between 30 seconds and a couple of minutes. Pigweed uses Bazel for build automation. The refreshed target list should look similar to the following:

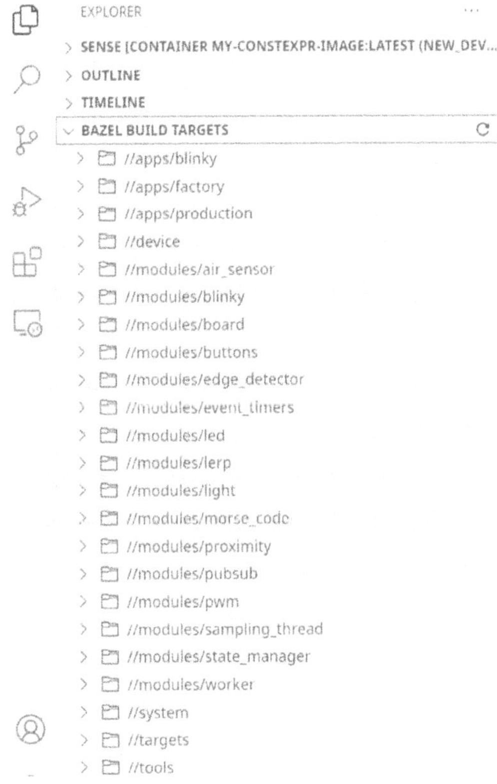

Figure 17.3 – BAZEL BUILD TARGETS

Figure 17.3 depicts Bazel build targets.

5. Next, expand the **//apps/blinky** node.

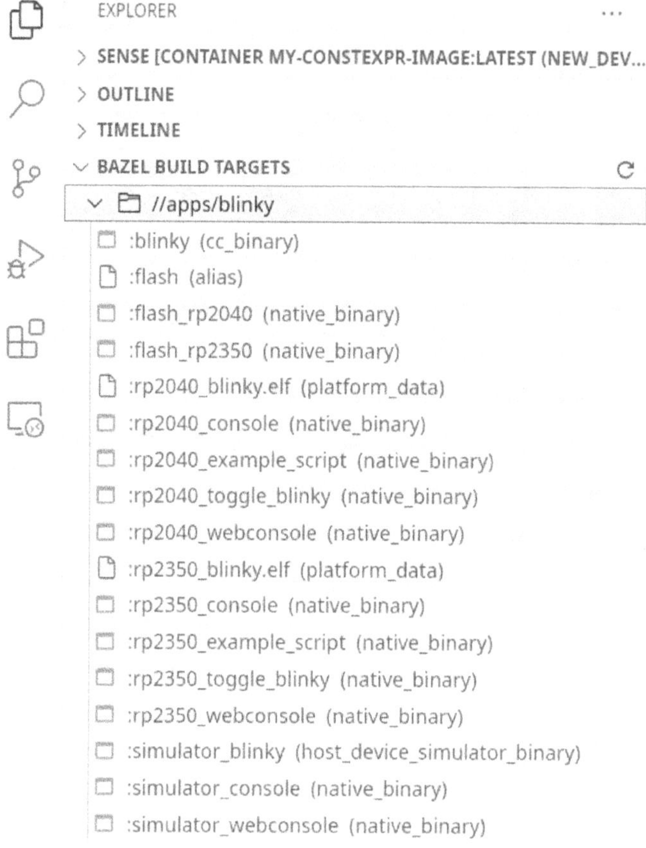

Figure 17.4 – //apps/blinky targets

6. Now, we will build a version of the app that runs on the host. Right-click **simulator_blinky (host_device_simulator_binary)** and then click **Build Target**. The build can take around 10 minutes. When completed, you should see a message similar to this one:

```
INFO: Analyzed target //apps/blinky:simulator_blinky (241 packages loaded, 16300 targets configured).
INFO: Found 1 target...
Target //apps/blinky:simulator_blinky up-to-date:
  bazel-bin/apps/blinky/simulator_blinky
INFO: Elapsed time: 40.067s, Critical Path: 0.57s
INFO: 1 process: 1741 action cache hit, 1 internal.
INFO: Build completed successfully, 1 total action
```

Figure 17.5 – Successful build

7. After a successful build, we will start the app. Right-click **simulator_blinky (host_device_simulator_binary)** and then **Run Target**. If successful, you should see the following message in the terminal: **Awaiting connection on port 33000**.

8. Next, right-click **simulator_console (native_binary)** and then **Run Target**. This will build a console and connect it to the running simulator. If successful, you should see the following screen:

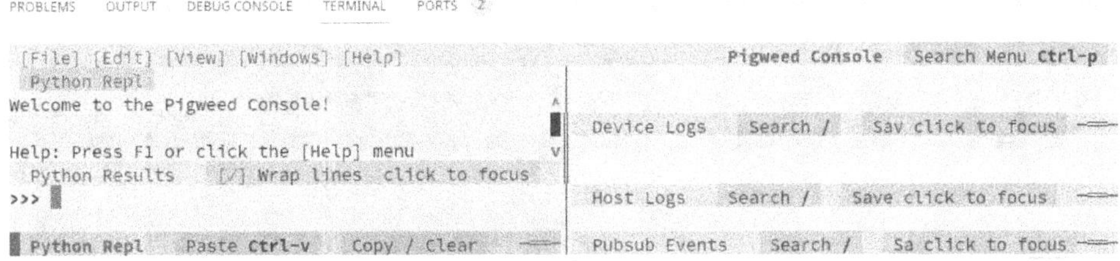

Figure 17.6 – Interactive console running in terminal view

In *Figure 17.6*, you can see the interactive console running in the terminal view in Visual Studio Code.

9. To make the console easier to work with, right-click on **Run //apps/blinky:simulator_console** and select **Move Terminal into New Window**. This will move the console into a separate window, as shown in this image:

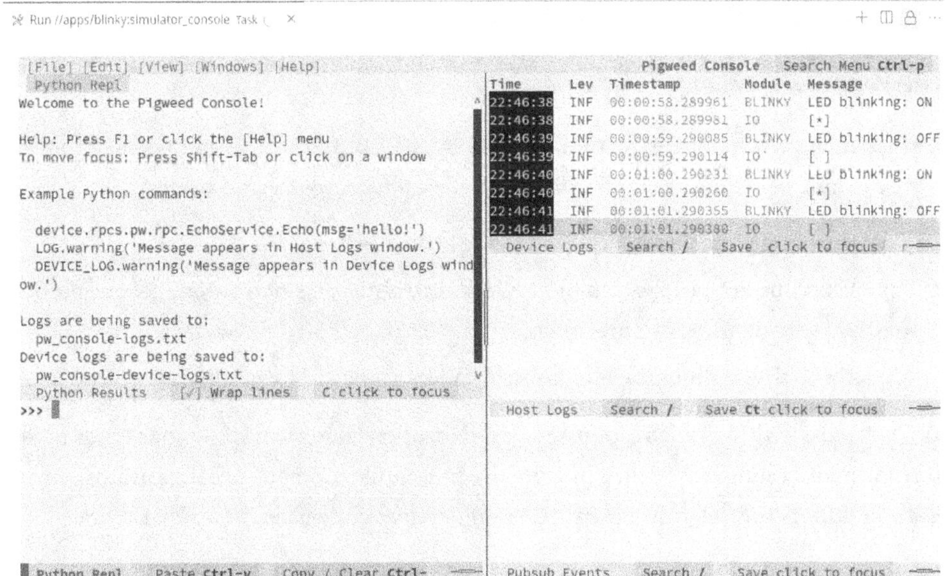

Figure 17.7 – Interactive console running in a separate window

In *Figure 17.7*, in the top-right pane, **Device Logs**, we can see logs coming from the simulated device (app running on the host). It sends **LED blinking** messages every second.

10. Next, we will send a message to the device using the RPC protocol, to retrieve the temperature measured by the device. Enter the following command in the bottom-left pane – **Python Repl**:

```
$ device.rpcs.board.Board.OnboardTemp()
```

You should see the following response:

```
$ (Status.OK, board.OnboardTempResponse(temp=20.0))
```

11. Next, send a message that will toggle the LED:

```
$ device.rpcs.blinky.Blinky.Blink(interval_ms=200, blink_count=3)
```

This call will make the LED blink three times at a 200 ms interval and afterward stop the **LED blinking** messages. This shows us that we can also provide arguments to RPC calls.

Next, we will go through Pigweed's RPC in more detail.

RPC and Protocol Buffers

Pigweed's RPC system is based on Protocol Buffers – a platform-neutral mechanism used for data serialization. Protocol Buffers is a language with its own syntax, which can be compiled into a targeted language such as C++ on our Sense device and the Python code we used in the Python **Read Eval Print Loop (REPL)**.

So, why use an extra layer of abstraction, such as Protocol Buffers, in an embedded application? There are a couple of benefits a standardized serialization brings to your projects:

- Compact binary messages – they add very little overhead.
- A precise contract (a `.proto` file) between different parts of a system, ensuring that all parties agree on the structure and meaning of the exchanged data.
- Updates to the communication protocol can be managed by modifying a proto file.

In short, instead of writing serialization and deserialization code in multiple code bases (C++ and Python) and maintaining it as such, you write the communication protocol in a proto file and use the Protocol Buffers compiler to generate C++ and Python code used for serialization.

Let us examine a part of the `modules/blinky/blinky.proto` file describing the Blinky service used in the *Pigweed's Sense tutorial* section to blink the LED three times at 200 ms intervals in the following code:

```proto
syntax = "proto3";
package blinky;
import "pw_protobuf_protos/common.proto";
service Blinky {
  // Toggles the LED on or off.
  rpc ToggleLed(pw.protobuf.Empty) returns(pw.protobuf.Empty);
  // Blinks the board LED a specified number of times.
  rpc Blink(BlinkRequest) returns (pw.protobuf.Empty);
}
message BlinkRequest {
  // The interval at which to blink the LED, in milliseconds. uint32
  interval_ms = 1;
  // The number of times to blink the LED.
  optional uint32 blink_count = 2;
}
```

This proto file defines a service called `Blinky` for controlling an LED, using Protocol Buffers version 3 (`syntax = "proto3"`). It imports a common proto file and defines two methods:

- `ToggleLed`: A simple method that switches the LED on or off, using an empty request and response.
- `Blink`: A method that blinks the LED with a configurable `interval_ms` and optional `blink_count` (members of `BlinkRequest`). The use of the `optional` keyword means this parameter can be omitted when calling the method.

This is a short explanation of the blinky.proto file. A more thorough guide to Protocol Buffers can be found at the following website: `https://protobuf.dev/programming-guides/proto3/`.

For each service in a `blinky` proto file, Pigweed's code generator will generate a corresponding C++ class. The generated `Blinky` class resides in a dedicated `pw_rpc::nanopb` sub-namespace within the file's package: `blinky::pw_rpc::nanopb::Blinky::Service`.

The generated class serves as a base class that must be inherited to implement the service's methods. It is templated on the derived class. The BlinkyService class implements the base class. The following code is part of its definition from the modules/blinky/service.h file:

```cpp
class BlinkyService final : public ::blinky::pw_
rpc::nanopb::Blinky::Service {
public:
    pw::Status ToggleLed(const pw_protobuf_Empty&, pw_protobuf_Empty&);
    pw::Status Blink(const blinky_BlinkRequest& request, pw_protobuf_Empty&);
private:
    Blinky blinky_;
};
```

BlinkyService bridges the generated RPC interface with the concrete implementation for controlling the LED. It has a private object, blinky_, of type Blinky, which is used to control an LED, as shown in the implementation of the ToggleLed and Blink methods in the following code block from the modules/blinky/service.cc file:

```cpp
pw::Status BlinkyService::ToggleLed(
const pw_protobuf_Empty&,
pw_protobuf_Empty&)
{
    blinky_.Toggle();
    return pw::OkStatus();
}
pw::Status BlinkyService::Blink(
const blinky_BlinkRequest& request,
pw_protobuf_Empty&)
{
    uint32_t interval_ms = request.interval_ms;
    uint32_t blink_count = request.has_blink_count;
    return blinky_.Blink(blink_count, interval_ms);
}
```

In this code, the methods ToggleLed and Blink use the blinky_ object to control the LED. When binary proto messages for the blinky service are received over a transport layer, they are converted into actual calls to the code used to control hardware, which is the essence of RPC.

As an exercise, expand the `blinky` service by adding the `BlinkTwice` method. You already know the files where you need to make changes – the proto file and the `BlinkyService` implementation files.

Pigweed uses **nanopb** (`https://github.com/nanopb/nanopb`) to compile proto files in C files and then wrap them in C++. There is a pure C++ implementation of Protocol Buffers designed especially for microcontrollers – Embedded Proto. It is an object-oriented implementation that only uses static memory allocation. It has been developed using the MISRA C++ guidelines. These traits together make Embedded Proto suitable for applications with a wide range of requirements, from low memory usage to safety concerns. You can find more about it on the GitHub page: `https://github.com/Embedded-AMS/EmbeddedProto`.

Pigweed has a steep learning curve and should be carefully evaluated based on your system requirements. It is better suited for larger, more complex projects due to the learning overhead. Additionally, evaluate the hardware support and take into consideration the memory overhead some modules may introduce.

In contrast to Pigweed, Intel's **CIB** library leverages C++ compile-time capabilities. This approach minimizes memory overhead while enhancing flexibility and expressiveness. Next, we will cover the CIB library.

Compile-time Initialization and Build

One of C++'s major advantages in embedded systems is its ability to perform compile-time computation. In most cases, we have significant knowledge about the application beforehand, allowing us to configure it at compile time. Intel's CIB library provides a declarative interface for configuring firmware components during compilation.

As you saw in *Chapter 15*, the Observer design pattern is commonly used in event-driven systems to decouple the source of events (publisher) from the entities that react to those events (observers or subscribers). By using a subscriber interface, observers can register themselves with the event source, which then notifies them of changes or events without needing to know details about the observers' implementations.

This decoupling allows for greater flexibility and modularity in system design, as components can be added, removed, or modified without tightly coupling them to the event generator. This property is leveraged by the CIB library, which implements a compile-time observer pattern to provide a declarative interface for configuring firmware applications. By resolving dependencies and establishing event-driven relationships at compile time, CIB eliminates runtime overhead while keeping components loosely coupled and efficiently interconnected.

We will start exploring the CIB library on a simple example of a temperature publisher. The entire example is available at `https://github.com/PacktPublishing/Cpp-in-Embedded-Systems/tree/main/Chapter17/cib`. You can run it using the following commands:

```
$ cmake -B build
$ cmake --build build --target run_in_renode
```

You can use `app/src/main.cpp` to follow through the example, as CIB, at the time of writing, is not available as a library in Compiler Explorer.

Using CIB in a temperature publisher example

Let's begin with the following steps:

1. We first need to declare a service (publisher) as an empty struct that inherits from `callback::service`, a variadic class template, provided with types that will be accepted by subscribers, as shown in the following code:

    ```cpp
    struct send_temperature : public callback::service<float> {};
    ```

2. Next, we will create the subscribers (also called components in the context of the CIB library) `display_temperature_component` and `data_sender_component`, as shown in this code:

    ```cpp
    struct display_temperature_component {
    constexpr static auto display_temperature = [](float temperature) {
        printf("Temperature is %.2f C\r\n", temperature);
    };

    constexpr static auto config = cib::config(
        cib::extend<send_temperature>(display_temperature)
    );
    };
    struct data_sender_component {
    constexpr static auto send_temp = [](float temp) {
        printf("Sending temperature %.2f C\r\n", temp);
    };
    constexpr static auto config = cib::config(
        cib::extend<send_temperature>(send_temp)
    );
    };
    ```

The preceding code defines two components, which do the following:

- Provide handlers for the `send_temperature` service in the `constexpr` lambdas `display_temperature` and `send_temp`.

- Define the `constexpr static auto config` member through which they extend the service (subscribe to the events).

Config members are instances of variadic template class `cib::config`, and they are used by the CIB library to wire the application at compile time, that is, to connect services (event generators, publishers) with software components that extend those services (observers). Compile-time initialization and the build process are performed by `cib::nexus`, which needs to be supplied with the project configuration. Here is the code for configuration for this simple project:

```cpp
struct my_project {
constexpr static auto config = cib::config(
    cib::exports<send_temperature>,

    cib::components<display_temperature_component,
                    data_sender_component>
);
};
```

This project configuration is a simple struct, `my_project`, with the `constexpr` member `config`, which is provided with the following:

- `cib::exports<send_temperature>`: Used to declare services (publishers)

- `cib::components<display_temperature_component, data_sender_component>`: Used to declare software components that can extend services

3. Next, let's see how we use all of this in a firmware application in the following code:

```cpp
int main() {
    cib::nexus<my_project> nexus{};
    nexus.init();
    for(int i = 0; i < 3; i++)
    {
        nexus.service<send_temperature>(42.0f);
    }
    return 0;
}
```

In this code, we perform these steps:

- `cib::nexus<my_project> nexus{};`: Create an instance of the class template `cib::nexus` provided by the project configuration `my_project`.

- `nexus.init();`: Initialize Nexus.

- `nexus.service<send_temperature>(42.0f);`: Access the service and provide it with the float argument (temperature). This will trigger calls to lambdas in components that extend the `send_temperature` service.

Extending the temperature publisher example

Next, we will extend this simple example with two components – a dummy temperature sensor and I2C components that we will name `temperature_sensor_component` and `i2c`. We will also introduce two new services – `runtime_init` and `main_loop`:

1. Let's start with defining new services in this code:

    ```cpp
    struct runtime_init : public flow::service<> {};
    struct main_loop : public callback::service<> {};
    ```

    Here, we define two services:

    - `runtime_init`: Derives from the variadic class template `flow::service`, allowing us to sequence actions

    - `main_loop`: Derives from `callback::service`, which will be called in the main `while` loop

2. We will move now to implementations of I2C components, as shown in this code:

    ```cpp
    struct i2c {
    constexpr static auto init = flow::action<"i2c_init">(
        [](){
            printf("I2C init ...\r\n");
        });

    constexpr static auto config = cib::config(
        cib::extend<runtime_init>(*init)
    );
    };
    ```

This code defines a new component – i2c – as a struct with:

- constexpr static auto init: A lambda wrapped in flow::action that implements the initialization of the I2C peripheral.

- constexpr static auto config: Adds the above action to the runtime_init flow service. The * operator explicitly adds an action to the flow. Without it, the action is referenced but never added, causing a compile-time error.

3. Next, let's go through the temperature sensor component shown in the following code:

```cpp
struct temperature_sensor_component {
constexpr static auto init = flow::action<"temp_sensor_init">(
    []() {
        printf("Initializing temperature sensor ... \r\n");
    });

constexpr static auto read_temperature = []() {
    float temperature = 23.4f;

    cib::service<send_temperature>(temperature);
};

constexpr static auto config = cib::config(

    cib::extend<main_loop>(read_temperature),

    cib::extend<runtime_init>(i2c::init >> *init)
);
};
```

The preceding code shows the struct temperature_sensor_component with the following members:

- constexpr static auto init: A flow_action that implements the initialization of the temperature sensor

- constexpr static auto read_temperature: A lambda that implements periodic readings of a temperature sensor and uses cib::service<read_temperature> to publish the read value

- `constexpr static auto config`: Extends the `main_loop` service with the `read_temperature` lambda and the `runtime_init` flow with `i2c::init >> *init`, indicating that `i2c::init` precedes `init`

4. Next, we need to modify the `my_project` struct to export new services and add new components, as shown in this code:

```
struct my_project {
constexpr static auto config = cib::config(
    cib::exports<runtime_init,
                 main_loop,
                 send_temperature>,

    cib::components<i2c,
                    temperature_sensor_component,
                    display_temperature_component,
                    data_sender_component>
);
};
```

In this code, we simply added:

- The `runtime_init` and `main_loop` services to `cib::exports`
- `i2c` and `temperature_sensor_component` to `cib::components`

5. Finally, let us see the new main function, as shown here:

```
int main() {
    cib::nexus<my_project> nexus{};
    nexus.init();
    nexus.service<runtime_init>();
    for(int i = 0; i < 3; i++)
    {
        nexus.service<main_loop>();
    }
    return 0;
}
```

As previously, we first create a `cib::nexus` instance and initialize it. Then, we perform the following steps:

1. `nexus.service<runtime_init>()`: This will run all actions in the flow `runtime_init` and ensure the specified order of actions.

2. `nexus.service<main_loop>()`: This is a call in the main loop executing all lambdas that are extending this service.

This structure is typical for many firmware applications: initialize all components (including hardware peripherals), then repeatedly call relevant services in the main loop. Any changes to the application are done in the `my_project` struct in a declarative way – by extending services and adding or removing components. All initialization is performed in the components themselves, meaning the main function does not need to know the details of individual components and their dependencies.

The CIB library also includes logging, interrupt, message, and string constant libraries – all leveraging C++'s compile-time computation. You can find more information about CIB on GitHub: `https://github.com/intel/compile-time-init-build`.

You can run the full CIB example in Renode. Start Visual Studio Code, attach it to the running container, open the `Chapter17/cib` project, as described in *Chapter 4*, and run the following commands in the Visual Studio Code terminal, or run them directly in the container terminal:

```
$ cmake -B build
$ cmake --build build --target run_in_renode
```

Running the above example will generate the output shown here:

```
I2C init ...
Initializing temperature sensor ...
Sending temperature 23.40 C
Temperature is 23.40 C
Sending temperature 23.40 C
Temperature is 23.40 C
Sending temperature 23.40 C
Temperature is 23.40 C
```

This example demonstrates the usage of the CIB library in an event-driven system with loosely coupled components, where some generate events and others react to them. The wiring of publishers and subscribers happens at compile time, minimizing the memory footprint and reducing runtime overhead, while the declarative project configuration improves readability.

Summary

In this chapter, we saw an overview of the libraries used throughout this book – the C++ standard library and ETL. You also got an insight into Google's Pigweed library and its capabilities and Intel's CIB library.

In the next chapter, we will go through cross-platform development.

Join our community on Discord

Join our community's Discord space for discussions with the author and other readers:

https://packt.link/embeddedsystems

18

Cross-Platform Development

In the previous chapters, we explored practical examples of designing and implementing software components for embedded systems. Each example demonstrated good software design practices and guided you through the implementation using modern C++ techniques.

The design practices we have followed throughout the book have helped us create portable, cross-platform code. Writing cross-platform code is important because it enables the reuse of software components across different hardware configurations. As we conclude this journey, let's recap the key practices demonstrated in earlier chapters.

In this chapter, we will cover the following topics:

- Importance of writing portable code
- SOLID design principles
- Testability

Technical requirements

This chapter focuses on cross-platform development. The code shown here runs on multiple platforms, including common desktop architectures.

You can use Compiler Explorer (`https://godbolt.org/`) to run the examples. All source code is available on GitHub at `https://github.com/PacktPublishing/Cpp-in-Embedded-Systems/tree/main/Chapter18`.

Importance of writing portable code

Hardware projects mature, evolve, and adapt to market needs and supply chain conditions. Between 2020 and 2022, the global semiconductor industry faced a severe supply chain crisis, primarily triggered by the COVID-19 pandemic and worsened by several factors. Lockdowns disrupted production, while soaring demand for electronics (e.g., laptops, servers) collided with miscalculations in the automotive sector. Carmakers initially canceled chip orders, then scrambled to restock as demand rebounded.

As a result, many components became scarce, overpriced, or unavailable altogether. Products had to adapt by replacing electronic components such as sensors, drivers, communication modules, or even microcontrollers. This, in turn, required firmware modifications to match the new hardware.

For well-written firmware, this adaptation was relatively straightforward and involved implementing only hardware-specific interfaces. For example, if a product used an accelerometer and needed to replace it, a well-designed firmware architecture would require just implementing the interface for the new component, leaving the business logic unchanged.

Cross-platform code can also run in a simulated environment on a host. In *Chapter 17*, we ran Pigweed's demo application on a host. This was possible, thanks to Pigweed's well-structured interface design, which allowed host implementations of low-level hardware interfaces. The same business application code can run on multiple targets, including the host, where inputs and outputs are simulated.

Well-structured code is easier to read, change, and maintain. Good design principles keep projects flexible even as requirements evolve. Next, we will examine the five SOLID principles.

SOLID design principles

The examples throughout this book are aligned with **SOLID** design principles, originally described by Robert C. Martin in his 2000 paper *Design Principles and Design Patterns*. They serve as a recognized guide for writing code that remains adaptable and easy to work with over time. Although the SOLID principles were originally introduced in object-oriented programming, their focus on creating modular, maintainable, and extensible code can be applied in broader software design contexts. Each letter in the SOLID mnemonic acronym stands for one principle:

- **Single Responsibility Principle (SRP)**: A class should have only one responsibility, giving it a single reason to change.

- **Open/Closed Principle (OCP)**: A class should be open for extension but closed for modification. A new functionality is added by extending the class through dynamic or static polymorphism, rather than modifying it.

- **Liskov Substitution Principle (LSP)**: Derived classes should be usable in place of their parent classes without breaking the software's behavior.

- **Interface Segregation Principle (ISP)**: Interface classes should remain small and concise so that derived classes implement only methods they need.

- **Dependency Inversion Principle (DIP)**: High-level modules (e.g., an accelerometer) should not depend on low-level modules (e.g., I2C). Both should rely on abstractions (interfaces) rather than concrete implementations.

Next, we'll go through an example of designing an accelerometer interface, explain how to use it, and show how it aligns with SOLID principles and why that alignment matters. First, we will design an accelerometer interface class. The code is shown here:

```cpp
#include <cstdio>
#include <cstdint>

class accelerometer {
public:
struct data {
    float x;
    float y;
    float z;
};
enum class sampling_rate {
    c_20_hz,
    c_50_hz,
    c_100_hz,
};
enum error {
    ok,
    not_supported
};
virtual error set_sampling_rate(sampling_rate) = 0;
virtual data get_data() = 0;
};
```

The interface class accelerometer shown in the preceding code will be implemented by the adxl_345 class, which will use the i2c interface to communicate with the actual accelerometer hardware (the ADXL345 integrated circuit is a small accelerometer with an I2C digital interface). Also, we will run the code on the STM32 platform, so we will create a (stubbed) implementation of the i2c interface – i2c_stm32. The code is shown here:

```cpp
class i2c {
public:
virtual void write() = 0;
};


class i2c_stm32 : public i2c {
public:
void write() override {
    printf("i2c::write...\r\n");
}
};


class adxl_345 : public accelerometer {
public:
adxl_345(i2c &i2c_obj) : i2c_(i2c_obj) {}
error set_sampling_rate(sampling_rate) override {
    printf("adxl_345: setting sampling rate\r\n");
    i2c_.write();
    return error::ok;
}
data get_data() override {
    return data{0.02f, 0.981f, 0.03f};
}
private:
i2c &i2c_;
};
```

Next, we will design a simple `tap_detection_algo` class that uses an accelerometer interface to collect motion data and identify short, sudden movements, typically referred to as taps. The taps are quick spikes in acceleration that can be used as user input or trigger events in the application. A boilerplate for the tap-detection class is shown in the following code:

```cpp
class tap_detection_algo {
public:
tap_detection_algo(accelerometer &accel) : accel_(accel) {
    auto err = accel_.set_sampling_rate(
        accelerometer::sampling_rate::c_100_hz);
    if(err == accelerometer::error::not_supported) {
        // try another sampling rate and adapt

    }
}
bool run () {
    auto accel_data = accel_.get_data();
    printf("algo: x = %.2f, y = %.2f, z = %.2f\r\n", accel_data.x,
                                                     accel_data.y,
                                                     accel_data.z);

    // process data
    return false;
}
private:
    accelerometer &accel_;
};
```

Finally, we will write code for the `main` function that instantiates an accelerometer and runs a tap detection algorithm:

```cpp
int main() {
    i2c_stm32 i2c1;
    adxl_345 accel(i2c1);

    tap_detection_algo algo(accel);
    algo.run();

    return 0;
}
```

The preceding code is depicted in the following UML diagram:

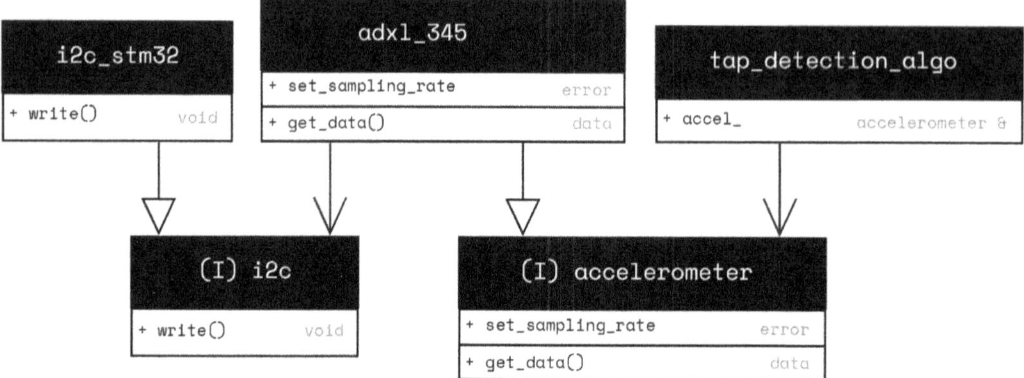

Figure 18.1 – Tap detection algorithm UML diagram

Figure 18.1 shows the architecture of the software components we designed. The code for the classes shown in the UML diagram is simplified, and it serves to demonstrate the following SOLID principles.

Single Responsibility Principle (SRP)

The accelerometer class is an interface class with all virtual methods. Its single responsibility is to define an interface that will be used by higher-level components and implemented by concrete accelerometer implementations such as adxl_345.

The adxl_345 class implements the accelerometer interface and it's only responsible for implementing communication with the ADXL 345 accelerometer over a serial interface such as I2C or SPI. The only reason for this class to change is bug fixing related to the communication with the sensor itself on the higher protocol level, not the serial bus itself.

The i2c class is an interface class with the responsibility of defining an interface for different implementations of the I2C peripheral, while i2c_stm32 implements this interface. The only reason for the concrete implementation to change is bug fixing or optimization related to the serial hardware peripheral.

The tap_detection_algo class takes accelerometer data and implements a tap detection algorithm using the collected data. The only reason to change this class is to fix or optimize the algorithm.

Open/Closed Principle (OCP)

An interface-based design for the I2C and accelerometer components lets us extend the software without modifying any existing code. For example, if we want to run this code on a Texas Instruments microcontroller, all we need to do is implement the i2c interface for that platform. Likewise, if we change the accelerometer sensor (e.g., to an ST LSDO6), we only have to implement the accelerometer interface for the new sensor.

The Liskov Substitution Principle (LSP)

The LSP was introduced by Barbara Liskov in 1987. The LSP focuses on designing robust contracts between base classes and their subclasses. Any client code that relies on a base class's contract should work correctly when using any derived class, without unexpected behavior.

In this example, a contract violation by `adxl_345` would occur if it silently fails when an unsupported sampling rate is requested, rather than handling it in a way that respects the base class contract (e.g., returning an error status).

The Interface Segregation Principle (ISP)

The ISP is about splitting large, monolithic interfaces into more focused ones so that each class only implements the methods it actually needs. An example of a violation of this principle would be having a broad **Inertial Measurement Unit (IMU)** interface that includes gyroscope and magnetometer functions, as `adxl_345` is only an accelerometer and would be forced to provide methods it cannot meaningfully support.

The Dependency Inversion Principle (DIP)

The example code we discussed clearly demonstrates the **Dependency Inversion Principle (DIP)**. By using an interface-based design, software components are cleanly decoupled:

- The `tap_detection_algo` class depends on the `accelerometer` interface, which is implemented by `adxl_345`
- The `adxl_345` class depends on the `i2c` interface, which is implemented by `i2c_stm32`

SOLID principles allow us to write highly decoupled software and create reusable, hardware-independent code. Decoupled code is more flexible, and it is easier to add new features.

As an exercise, add an accelerometer data logging capability without modifying the existing classes.

Good software design also improves software testability, which we will explore next.

Testability

Interface-based design leads to decoupled software, which improves testability. Let us analyze the former example and see how decoupled design helps with testing. We'll focus on the tap detection algorithm.

In this example, we create a simple algorithm that detects a tap when the difference between the current sample and the previous sample on any axis exceeds a predefined threshold. This oversimplified implementation is shown in this code:

```cpp
#include <cmath>
#include <algorithm>
class tap_detection_algo {
public:
tap_detection_algo(accelerometer &accel)
                    : accel_(accel), first_sample_(true) {}

bool run() {
    auto current = accel_.get_data();

    if (first_sample_) {
        prev_ = current;
        first_sample_ = false;
        return false;
    }

    bool tap = (std::fabs(current.x - prev_.x) > c_threshold) ||
            (std::fabs(current.y - prev_.y) > c_threshold) ||
                (std::fabs(current.z - prev_.z) > c_threshold);

    prev_ = current;
    return tap;
}

private:
static constexpr float c_threshold = 0.5f;
accelerometer &accel_;
accelerometer::data prev_;
bool first_sample_ = true;
};
```

The preceding code implements a simple tap detection algorithm. It accepts an accelerometer reference and, on each call to run(), retrieves the current sensor data. If it's the first sample, it stores the value and returns false (no tap detected). On subsequent calls, it compares the current reading with the previous one on each axis. If the absolute difference on any axis exceeds a constant threshold, it signals a tap by returning true, then updates the previous sample.

For unit testing, we'll create a fake_accel class that simulates a sequence of accelerometer readings. This way, we can control the input data to check if tap_detection_algo works. The code for the fake_accel class is shown here:

```cpp
class fake_accel : public accelerometer {
public:
fake_accel(const std::vector<data>& samples)
: samples_(samples), index_(0) {}

error set_sampling_rate(sampling_rate) override {
    return error::ok;
}
data get_data() override {
    if (index_ < samples_.size()) {
        return samples_[index_++];
    }
    return samples_.back();
}
private:
std::vector<data> samples_;
size_t index_;
};
```

This class, fake_accel, is a test double for the accelerometer interface. It simulates accelerometer data by:

- Accepting a vector of predefined data samples through its constructor.
- Implementing set_sampling_rate to always return a successful result.
- Returning each sample in order via get_data(), and once all samples are used, it repeatedly returns the last sample.

This makes it useful for testing components that depend on accelerometer readings. Let us see how to use it to test the tap detection algorithm using the GoogleTest framework in the code shown here:

```cpp
TEST(TapDetectionAlgoTest, DetectTapOnSuddenChange) {
std::vector<accelerometer::data> samples = {
    {0.0f, 1.0f, 0.0f}, // initial reading
    {0.0f, 1.0f, 0.0f}, // no change -> false
    {0.0f, 2.0f, 0.0f} // significant change
};
fake_accel fakeAccel(samples);
tap_detection_algo algo(fakeAccel);

EXPECT_FALSE(algo.run());
EXPECT_FALSE(algo.run());
EXPECT_TRUE(algo.run());
}
```

This test verifies that the tap detection algorithm correctly identifies a sudden change in accelerometer data as a tap. The test sets up a fake accelerometer with three samples:

- First sample: {0.0f, 1.0f, 0.0f} – used for initialization (no tap detection).
- Second sample: {0.0f, 1.0f, 0.0f} – no change compared to the first sample, so no tap is detected.
- Third sample: {0.0f, 2.0f, 0.0f} – a significant change on the y axis (a difference of 1.0, which exceeds the threshold of 0.5) triggers tap detection.

The test expects the first two calls to run() to return false and the third call to return true. Thanks to interface-based design, we can pass a fake_accel reference to the tap_detection_algo constructor since fake_accel implements the accelerometer interface. We supply the fake_accel constructor with a vector container of samples to feed into the algorithm. This allows us to easily test the algorithm with a test dataset.

The full example can be found at GitHub (https://github.com/PacktPublishing/Cpp-in-Embedded-Systems/tree/main/Chapter18). Make sure you add the GoogleTest library to Compiler Explorer when running it.

Summary

In this chapter, we learned why writing portable, cross-platform code is important for embedded development. It allows you to easily reuse software components and adapt to hardware changes, and it improves testability.

You also learned about SOLID principles and how they apply to the design of software components in embedded systems using C++. Code readability and flexibility are some of the most important traits of well-designed software.

We humans read the code, and the human who reads your code may be the future you. So, having easy-to-read code should be a priority. Sacrifice readability and optimize for performance only when absolutely needed. Having flexible code allows you to adapt to changes or add new features easily.

With this chapter, our journey comes to an end. We began by exploring common myths about C++ and debunking them. From there, we covered many important aspects of modern C++ and learned how to apply them in embedded application development.

We explored how to use lambdas to write expressive code and took advantage of compile-time computation to generate lookup tables, conserving memory and processing power. We also leveraged C++ type safety to implement a type-safe HAL.

Next, we learned how to apply design patterns such as Adapter, Observer, and State to solve typical problems in embedded systems. We explored the C++ Standard Library, ETL, Pigweed, and cib and learned how to use them in embedded applications.

Throughout all the examples in this book, we focused on writing readable, maintainable, and loosely coupled code to strengthen our software design and development skills.

I hope you enjoyed this journey and wish you happy coding!

Get This Book's PDF Version and Exclusive Extras

Scan the QR code (or go to `packtpub.com/unlock`). Search for this book by name, confirm the edition, and then follow the steps on the page.

Note: Keep your invoice handy. Purchases made directly from Packt don't require an invoice.

packtpub.com

Subscribe to our online digital library for full access to over 7,000 books and videos, as well as industry leading tools to help you plan your personal development and advance your career. For more information, please visit our website.

Why subscribe?

- Spend less time learning and more time coding with practical eBooks and Videos from over 4,000 industry professionals
- Improve your learning with Skill Plans built especially for you
- Get a free eBook or video every month
- Fully searchable for easy access to vital information
- Copy and paste, print, and bookmark content

At www.packtpub.com, you can also read a collection of free technical articles, sign up for a range of free newsletters, and receive exclusive discounts and offers on Packt books and eBooks.

Other Books You May Enjoy

If you enjoyed this book, you may be interested in these other books by Packt:

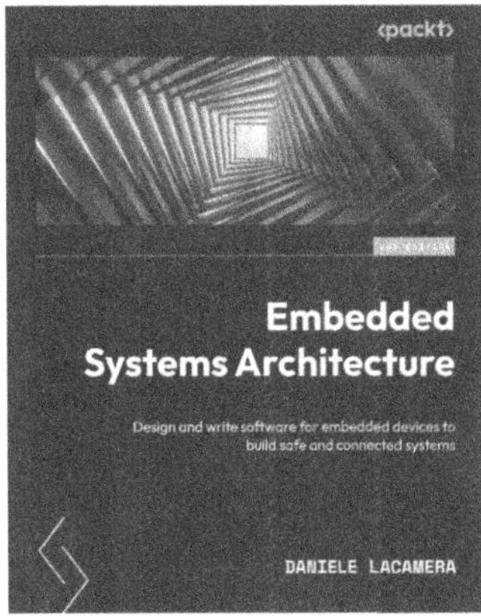

Embedded Systems Architecture, Second Edition

Daniele Lacamera

ISBN: 978-1-80323-954-5

- Participate in the design and definition phase of an embedded product
- Get to grips with writing code for ARM Cortex-M microcontrollers
- Build an embedded development lab and optimize the workflow
- Secure embedded systems with TLS
- Demystify the architecture behind the communication interfaces
- Understand the design and development patterns for connected and distributed devices in the IoT
- Master multitasking parallel execution patterns and real-time operating systems
- Become familiar with Trusted Execution Environment (TEE)

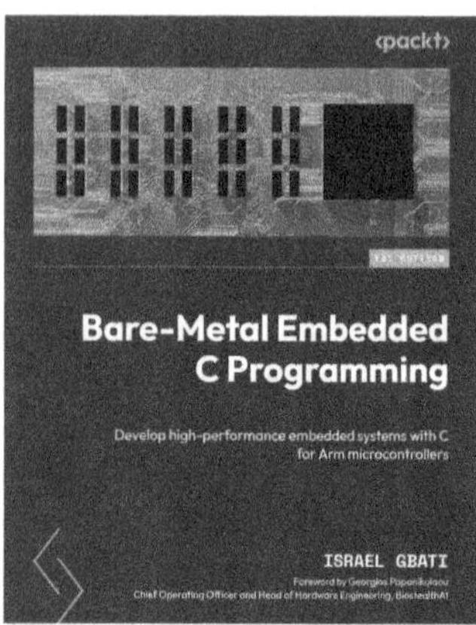

Bare-Metal Embedded C Programming

Israel Gbati

ISBN: 978-1-83546-081-8

- Decode microcontroller datasheets, enabling precise firmware development

- Master register manipulations for optimized Arm-based microcontroller firmware creation

- Discover how to navigate hardware intricacies confidently

- Find out how to write optimized firmware without any assistance

- Work on exercises to create bare-metal drivers for GPIO, timers, ADC, UART, SPI, I2C, DMA, and more

- Design energy-efficient embedded systems with power management techniques

Packt is searching for authors like you

If you're interested in becoming an author for Packt, please visit authors.packtpub.com and apply today. We have worked with thousands of developers and tech professionals, just like you, to help them share their insight with the global tech community. You can make a general application, apply for a specific hot topic that we are recruiting an author for, or submit your own idea.

Share your thoughts

Now you've finished *C++ in Embedded Systems*, we'd love to hear your thoughts! Scan the QR code below to go straight to the Amazon review page for this book and share your feedback or leave a review on the site that you purchased it from.

https://packt.link/r/1835881157

Your review is important to us and the tech community and will help us make sure we're delivering excellent quality content.

Index

www.ingramcontent.com/pod-product-compliance
Lightning Source LLC
Chambersburg PA
CBHW080510030726
47592CB00012B/3312